TO RULE
BRITANNIA

TO RULE BRITANNIA

THE CLAUDIAN INVASION OF BRITAIN AD 43

JOHN WAITE

The History Press

First published 2011

The History Press
The Mill, Brimscombe Port
Stroud, Gloucestershire, GL5 2QG
www.thehistorypress.co.uk

British Library Cataloguing in Publication Data.
A catalogue record for this book is available from the British Library.

ISBN 978 0 7524 5149 7

Typesetting and origination by The History Press
Printed in the EU for The History Press.

CONTENTS

Acknowledgements

I would like to extend my personal thanks to the below listed individuals who, in whatever capacity, have provided their time, advice, encouragement and assistance which in turn has allowed me to produce this work. The list below is quite a select one but it goes without saying that, to everyone else who has contributed in some way to this work, you have my immense gratitude.

Kames Beasley, HM Coastguard.
Gerald Moody, Thanet Archaeology.
John Olden, Photographer, Coventry.
Professor Donald W. Olson, Texas State University.
Dr Frank Panton CBE, Kent Archaeological Society.
John Smith, Archaeologist and Historian, Ludwell, Wiltshire.
Brett Thorn, Keeper of Archaeology, Buckinghamshire County Council.

I would also like to thank Simon Hamlet, my editor at The History Press, for his patience and advice during the writing of this book.

Lastly, I would like to thank my wife, Helen, for the many lost weekends and the numerous evenings when I have come home from work, only to lock myself away in my study for many long hours in order to finish this book. Helen, I can say without hesitation that you are my rock and without your support this book simply would not have been written.

John Waite, December 2010

INTRODUCTION

Although there are still many facts which remain beyond our grasp, if there is one thing that we can say with certainty about the Roman Invasion of Britain in AD 43, it is that the Roman army which came ashore that year was numerous enough and effective enough to be able to quickly establish a strong beachhead on the coast of Britain. We also know that the Romans then quickly capitalised on their opening territorial gains by following up with an effective advance across unfamiliar territory. They then won at least two major engagements against the retreating Britons, before finally achieving their prime objective of the early phases of the invasion by capturing Colchester or, as it was then known, the great tribal capital of Camulodunum.

The net result of that victorious initial campaign was that it swiftly neutralised the chief power base of the only significant source of native British opposition. That is to say: those tribal groups under the direct control of the Catuvellaunian princes, Caratacus and Togodumnus. Moreover, having achieved this the Romans benefited from the fact that that there were also, by then, no hostile tribe still remaining in the south-eastern quarter of Britain that actually stood a chance of mounting any significant degree of resistance to the early stages of the Roman invasion plan.

As well as quickly sweeping initial native resistance aside, this early success consequently left the Romans with a very strong foothold in southern Britain. It also provided them with a large and well-established platform from which to extend their lines of advance further into the country. As for the Britons themselves, any opportunity they may have had to drive the invaders back into the sea had been totally lost by this time. In fact, the available evidence seems to suggest that the only sensible option left open to at least eleven of their rulers was to pledge fealty to their new master; Claudius, fourth emperor of Rome.

Yet the fall of Britain would not be an easy victory for Rome. As soon as the emperor returned home to properly celebrate his Triumph – in more opulent surroundings than could be found in what he doubtless regarded as no more than a backwater tribal capital – those British rulers who were left and who still refused to bend the knee, most notably Caratacus, chose instead to continue the fight against the coming of Rome and the threat of an advancing Roman army. This heralded the start of a new chapter in the story of Roman Britain as, despite the fact that Claudius had claimed his symbolic victory and Camulodunum (Colchester) had fallen, the real fighting for control of the land had yet to begin.

Caratacus and his allies soon threw themselves into prosecuting what would become a lengthy and often guerrilla-style war of opposition. However, although it was a protracted campaign, it really only served to delay the inevitable. Even as the Britons mounted a sustained resistance, Rome responded in kind by flexing its superior military muscle and steadily forcing the frontiers of its occupation in Britain further north and west into the island.

In the period that followed the invasion, which is represented best by those early resistance campaigns, the empire steadily tightened its grip on what would be its newest acquisition until the majority of the island had succumbed; either to irresistible force of arms or to the new and heady inducements of what we would today consider to be civilisation. It would be from this bloody and violent birth that there would finally emerge a new and very different land, and it would be these events which heralded the creation of the brand-new Roman province of Britannia.

As a major event in British history, we need to understand as much as we possibly can about the opening phases of the Roman invasion of AD 43. Our understanding of this period in time is important, not least because it is arguably this one single event which has, in turn, made the greatest overall contribution to the very foundations of what has become modern Britain's distinctive and arguably unique island identity. However, the campaigns which were fought by Rome immediately after the Claudian landings are not something which will be discussed at any length in this work. It is intended instead that the operations conducted against British resistance during the early years of the occupation will be more fully explored in a later volume. That subsequent work will seek to provide a more current appreciation of Caratacus and his world, and his struggle against the invading Romans.

The primary aim of this work is therefore to look closely at the very beginning of Roman dominance in Britain. Nevertheless, in doing so, it seems that there is a good reason why this work should also briefly investigate the very beginnings of the island of Britain. After all, if we are seeking to understand what it is that motivated the Romans to want to conquer Britain, then it must surely be worth telling the story of the island from the very beginning? This then allows us to acquire a basic appreciation of how the land that is Britain actually came to be.

We are presented with the opportunity to do this because, unlike many other modern European countries whose boundaries have principally been defined by warfare and politics, the creation of Britain is far less complicated:

it was shaped exclusively by forces of nature, not human aspirations or territorial greed. The borders of Britain are distinct and obvious, defined wholly by miles of coastline which have been created by the rising of the seas. As such they are not lines drawn on a map, but solid physical boundaries which serve to set Britain firmly apart from its neighbouring countries. Once those natural borders were created, at that distant point in history, Britain's identity first began to emerge.

It consequently seems appropriate that the early section of this work should conduct a brief exploration of the events which occurred during the creation of the island, and follow with a detailed examination of the incursions by Gaius Julius Caesar and Claudius, respectively. It will therefore provide a glimpse of prehistoric Britain: as it was in the millennia before the coming of Rome at a time when the population of the British Isles had first started to forge its cultural identity, separated from the rest of the population of Europe.

At that time, Britain was very much a culture in isolation and clearly different from its neighbours. However, as one might expect, the original Britons would not be able to avoid the attentions of those neighbours forever, and eventually they would be touched by the influences of outsiders as they experienced a steady influx of raiders, migrants and traders, all of whom would come to make their own indelible mark on the island population.

In the period immediately before the coming of Rome (with the exception of those Belgic people who had settled mainly in the southern quarter of the island during the Iron Age) much of the population of Britain who were living beyond the lands adjoining the south coast had, from what we can tell, no significant ancestral connections to the European Celts. Indeed, it appears to be the arrival of those European Celts (a very generic description) and their permanent establishment in Britain which created some form of cultural divide on the island, as the newcomers steadily pushed the indigenous peoples even further back into the interior of the island. The settlers did this whilst at the same time maintaining links to their tribal origins in mainland Europe. And, as we shall discuss, it would be these links with the tribes of mainland Europe, or more particularly ancient Gaul, which would eventually come to contribute to the justification of Rome's plans to invade the island.

It is therefore extremely important that this work should present a basic understanding of the changes which occurred in pre-Roman Britain, and provide a brief overview of the long sequence of events which brought about those great changes to the early cultural map of Britain. This is important because, in the context of the Roman invasions, there is a clear benefit to appreciating why those cultural shifts ultimately served to create a Britain that, for several reasons, would eventually attract the attention of the ancient world's most formidable superpower, the influence of which subsequently laid the foundations for modern Britain's national and cultural identity.

It would clearly be wrong to imply that the arrival of Rome as a civilising influence was a benign process which conferred only benefits on the native Britons. The arrival of Roman culture not only brought war and eroded Britain's cultural identity, but soon came to bleed the country of its many resources on an industrial scale.

Britain has a varied geology which has blessed it with both mineral and agricultural wealth. Therefore, far from the Romans directly intending to share any of the benefits attached to their brand of civilisation with the Britons, a large part of their agenda was obviously to gain control of that which they had previously had to trade for. They would have also wished to absorb the skills of the native population in order to enhance the resources available in their already considerable dominions at that time. It must also be borne in mind that it was not solely for the military and political benefits, which we shall consider later in this work, that the Romans had coveted Britain for so long. Nor was it just the future threat represented by the actions of Togodumnus and Caratacus as they expanded their territories and rattled sabres at Rome which prompted the Romans to mount a successful invasion. There was, in reality, a far bigger picture to consider in which all of the above issues carried a high degree of significance.

As to how the Romans were able to succeed in their plans: well, it would probably be fair to say that, for the majority of ordinary people, one of the most recognisable features of ancient Roman culture would be her vast military capability. In one form or another, the army of ancient Rome has long been a staple of both literary and visual entertainment in modern popular culture. And so too have her legions been admired and emulated by many a great ruler over the centuries since they fought their last battles. But, for all the imitators throughout history who have sought to recreate the martial glory of ancient Rome, Adolf Hitler and Napoleon Bonaparte to name but two, there have been none who have ever been able to fully recreate the awe-inspiring war machine that won one of the greatest and most enduring empires in history.

It is therefore important to acknowledge that, when considering the ancient Romans' cultural legacy to today's world, none of that would have been possible had it not been for the power and brilliance of her army. The Roman army was, after all, an extremely complex and sophisticated organisation, exerting an unsleeping and ever present multilateral power that was essential to the protection and furtherance of the interests initially of the republic, then later the emperor, the senate and the people of Rome.

In the context of ancient warfare, and particularly that of the Roman conquest of Britain, the successes of the early phases of the invasion represent a tremendous military achievement in respect of the planning and execution of such a venture. After all, if we needed an example of the actual level of difficulties the Romans faced then we would do well to keep in mind that even Julius Caesar, one of Rome's most celebrated generals, tried and failed twice to conquer Britain. This fact alone should leave us in little doubt that the task faced by the generals who served Claudius was a very formidable one indeed. Not least because it was a goal which had caused Caesar, one of their most ambitious and driven of leaders, to ultimately abandon his plans for conquest. Yet, in AD 43, the Romans succeeded in their aims, finally prevailing over the obstacles that had so effectively barred Caesar's route to success.

Many of the facts relating to the military campaign that bought about such a swift and decisive opening victory currently remain beyond our grasp. Vital contemporary records have been lost, many no doubt forever, and much of the remaining detail surrounding those early phases has now been heavily obscured by the passage of nearly two millennia. Indeed, as far as written accounts go, much of our understanding of those events is drawn from the single most complete account known to us. However, we must bear in mind that this account was also written retrospectively, well over a century after the events of AD 43 by the historian, Cassius Dio.

Whilst Dio no doubt drew upon more contemporary records to provide us with such a vitally important account of the invasion, it is frustrating to realise that it is those very same accounts which he no doubt referred to which are the ones lost to us. Even more frustratingly, whilst there are other ancient references available to us which mention the Claudian invasion, these are often quite vague and fragmentary in their nature and nowhere near as complete an account as that provided by Dio.

Of the missing accounts, there can be little doubt that the lost writings of Cluvius Rufus, the lost books of Tacitus' *Histories* and perhaps too the missing writings of Fabius Rusticus could have taught us much, given that they were all noted Roman historians writing around the time of the invasion. Given that the re-emergence of these lost volumes is unlikely, however, we are forced to accept that there is now a clear lack of reliable contemporary evidence to refer to. Consequently, there remain aspects of the early months of the invasion that still require answers. That aside, in terms of our actual understanding of the overall picture of the invasion, there is nevertheless much that we should be thankful to Cassius Dio for and also much that we can now be fairly certain of.

Having regard to those supposed certainties, it was for many years an almost universally accepted notion that the Claudian assault force first came ashore on the coast of Kent and that the main beachhead was centred on the area of Richborough which, although landlocked now, was at the time of the invasion a coastal area situated on the western shore of what used to be the southern mouth of the Wantsum Channel. This latter feature was a navigable tidal strait which was something in the order of around 2 miles across in Roman times. This channel was eventually to become completely choked by silt, the deposition of which during the successive centuries following the invasion finally resulted in the loss of that once navigable waterway and the creation instead of an alluvial flood plain which now binds the Isle of Thanet to mainland Kent.

Conversely in more recent years, despite the existence of some persuasive archaeological evidence and the location's obvious strategic appeal, the actual suggestion of a landing on the Kent coast at Richborough has now been roundly challenged both by academics and archaeologists. They have proposed and supported the theory of an alternative landing site located in the area of Chichester, on the Sussex coast.

It has to be said that proposing a plausible alternative as to where Roman forces first landed and the events that followed is nothing new. There is a diverse selection of recorded suggestions available which reflect our growing understanding of the invasion over the years; from the postulations of a number of Victorian antiquarians, right up to the more contemporary popular interpretations by commentators such as Webster, Salway, Peddie and Manley. However, whilst the consideration and interpretation of archaeological and documentary evidence is crucial to aiding our understanding of the landings, it would appear that, so far, much less consideration has been given to the key questions relating to the details of the actual military logistics and the likely use of recognised Roman strategies that would have been needed in order to make it all happen.

John Peddie's work *Conquest – The Roman Invasion of Britain*, first published in 1987, provided a more pragmatic approach to the question of the Roman invasion. Peddie examined more closely the considerable logistical problems that Roman generals would have needed to solve in the planning stages of what was, undoubtedly, a highly complex operation to land and support an estimated 40,000 troops as they made for their prime objective of Camulodunum (Colchester). Peddie's book was really the first comprehensive account to focus on the questions dealing with the raw practicalities of an invasion which, to the Romans at least, probably posed no less a challenge than the task that fell to the host of military planners and strategists that contributed to the success of the D-Day landings in June 1944.

The Romans therefore faced an undertaking arguably at least comparable to their modern counterparts when they first began to consider factors such as the number and types of troops they needed, which theatre of operations those men could be safely drawn from and how to solve the myriad technical and logistical problems that needed to be tackled in order to safely and effectively transport those men. They would then have needed to consider further logistical problems as they established how best to supply and support the armies in the field whilst they followed what must have been a precise campaign plan, all of which was required to be carried out within a limited window of opportunity.

Just as with Operation Overlord in 1944, if the planning for any of these elements was not exacting, then the campaign itself had the potential to fail at any of the crucial stages of its execution. Proper consideration of the actual military planning involved in the invasion is therefore an essential element to the basis of any argument which is intended to support a proposal for the site for the landings.

It is therefore one of the aims of this book to build on Peddie's approach to the invasion by examining more closely the step-by-step considerations faced in the execution of the operational plan and, in doing so, seek to provide clear reasoning as to why a Roman landing on the Kent coast, with particular focus on the importance of Richborough as the main beachhead, would be the most plausible alternative. Its conclusions will consequently be based on discussion of strong practical considerations and will also rely more on examination of the tactical issues that the Roman commanders would have needed to consider in order to stand any chance of success.

There will also be an examination of what seems to be a largely overlooked element of the invasion: the importance of the Classis Britannica, Rome's northern fleet, in bringing about the success of the early part of the invasion. The actual contribution made by the fleet has been widely neglected by writers and commentators over the years, so it will also be the purpose of this book to provide an explanation of how vitally important this part of the invasion force was in ensuring a successful campaign.

Of course, in supporting the argument for Richborough, it is an inevitable consequence that this book will also set out to refute the suggestion that the Roman landings took place in the area of Chichester. It is therefore important that this book should attempt to set out a persuasive argument for just why a landing on the shores of Sussex would be a much less viable option than that of a landing in Kent.

There is no question that our understanding of the events of history is ever changing and constantly evolving with each new discovery and theory, and rightly so. We should never deliberately place ourselves in a position whereby we are content to settle on a particular, established version of history just because we have grown comfortable with it and, as a consequence, have become reluctant to consider other credible alternatives. Yet, in carrying out any reassessment of our current thinking, particularly with regard to the events of nearly 2,000 years ago, we must be able to demonstrate that any reinterpretations we offer have been arrived at as a result of our careful consideration of all of the elements which are critical to forming a well-balanced argument to enhance our understanding of the events. Therefore, it must be reasonable to suggest that in considering a problem as complex as the Claudian landings, there seems to be little value in tabling an argument which is over-reliant on archaeological or historical evidence, whilst at the same time failing to properly explore the many practical considerations and military tactics, the application of which would clearly be so crucial to bringing about the success of the invasion. After all, the fundamentals of the science of military tactics and planning are the same now as they were 2,000 years ago. As one takes the time to consider the many points of view currently on offer, it becomes readily apparent that this would seem to be just the kind of approach favoured by many commentators who have, at one time or another, offered their own view on the landings.

Of course when one holds a strong point of view on a particular subject, it can, on occasion, be extremely difficult to maintain an impartial approach to the issues in question, but that is nevertheless what needs to be done in order to draw any real benefit from the collective opinions which surround a particular debate. This work will therefore also draw upon the various other sources of information that exist which impact upon our deliberations regarding the Claudian landings. It will then attempt to build upon existing knowledge by applying a more belt-and-braces approach to the actual problems associated with the landings, while also seeking to table a newer, more compelling argument which endorses the suggestion of a landing in the area of Richborough.

In taking such an approach, at worst this book may only be regarded as simply attempting to rally fresh support for a dated and obsolete theory. But at best, the hope is that the eventual readers of this work, presumably from various backgrounds and with their own points of view, will also appreciate this book for what it is intended to be: a newer and more practical consideration of a question, the conclusions to which will assist us to better understand the dramatic events that unfolded at the very dawn of recorded British history.

I

A Short History of Pre-Claudian Britain

BRITAIN BEFORE ROME

A Brief Discussion of Prehistoric Britain

Perhaps it may appear odd that, in producing a commentary which is clearly intended to focus on the Claudian invasion of Britain, the account itself would begin with a consideration of a Britain that existed even before man had learned to farm or to fashion tools and weapons from anything other than sticks, bone, flint and stone. However, if we choose to ignore these times we miss the opportunity to make a deeper exploration of how it was that Britain gradually evolved. Consequently we would not understand how it was that Britain slowly turned into something which ultimately prompted Rome to invade. If that opportunity is neglected, then there is an argument that there may yet be something of crucial importance which is missing from the discussion.

It thus seems appropriate that this work should not simply begin by taking what seems to be the conventional approach to an exploration of the Roman invasions. Instead, rather than just beginning with an acknowledgement that there existed a large and well-populated island, lying just off the coast of northern Gaul, which Rome wished to add to its portfolio of conquered territories, we could instead attempt to add a little more value to the discussion. Therefore, this account will begin by conducting a short exploration of just how it was that Britain came into being.

In discussing Rome's designs on Britain, we generally seem content to accept the existence of the prevailing status quo in respect of Britain and Gaul at the time. Therefore, most popular histories which discuss the Roman invasion of Britain tend to start by introducing the island merely as the intended target for Roman ambition, without ever really attempting to offer a broader consideration of how the island and its people actually emerged. If we do not look more closely at the origins of Britain, then we cannot really purport to have a complete understanding of why it was that the likes of Julius Caesar and the Roman emperor, Claudius, actually felt the need to control it. Therefore by exploring the origins of Britain, albeit only briefly, we will at least acquire a basic appreciation of how early British culture evolved on the island. This snapshot will hence provide a perspective of where Britain came from and what the people of the island eventually did in order to create such an attractive target for Rome. Also, at least as far as Caesar was concerned, it will explain how the Britons came to present a threat which was significant enough to prompt him to mount two expeditions to the island.

In addition, such an exploration may also provide some food for thought concerning just how Britain came to be regarded in the way it was by the wider ancient world, with its apparent air of foreboding and mystery. Indeed, to the Romans, this was a land that existed beyond the edge of the known world, even to its near neighbours in Gaul it was on one hand a little-known place but, at the same time, it was also a place which existed at the heart of their culture.

The New Land

It was actually around 8,000 years ago that Britain first began to undergo the changes that would come to provide the setting for the birth of its unique cultural identity; the island nation with which we are now so familiar with today. This is because it was at this period in time that the land mass and accompanying islands which now comprise modern Great Britain actually became separated from the greater land mass which we now regard as continental Europe. Around seven millennia or so prior to this event, our planet had steadily begun to warm up as the Earth began to emerge from the grip of the last great Ice Age. The Pleistocene Glaciations, as it is also referred to, lasted for around 2.58 million years and it finally began to draw to an end around 12–15,000 years ago as global temperatures had steadily begun to rise. This process of gradual warming had caused the great continental ice sheets and glaciers to begin to melt and, as that warming process quickened, sea levels began to rise dramatically.

Before it became an island, Britain as a land mass formed the western extremity of a much greater geographical area which is now referred to as Doggerland. However, our understanding of this vast tract of now submerged land has only very recently begun to advance. This has been due not only to the numerous intensive scientific surveys and studies that have been carried out in recent years, but also as a result of the wealth of finds which are regularly recovered during off-shore industrial operations – most typically commercial trawling within the area of the North Sea. Credit is due then, not only to the efforts of modern science, but also to modern industrial processes, both of which have helped to produce a much clearer picture of the human and animal populations which once lived and roamed across the lost territory of Doggerland.

In very general terms, the area itself seems to have been a large piece of what is now the north-western quarter of Europe. Scientific surveys have revealed that part of its coastline extended across from central Denmark and over to the

Northumbrian coast before continuing north, tracing more or less what is now the current coastline of Scotland.

Although the region was a very large area by any standards, Doggerland would eventually drown as our planet finally emerged from the grip of the Ice Age. The fate of that land was sealed as the vast and ancient fields of ice began to thaw and the resultant meltwater flooded into the oceans, causing their waters to rise. As this process accelerated, both the human and animal population of the region would have subsequently experienced a very swift and dramatic impact on their environment. No doubt those humans and animals that had actually appreciated the nature of the impending threat would have quickly migrated, either back towards the continent or moving west to eventually become the residents of the new island. However, there would also have been those who had remained in the regions to be flooded and, finding themselves no longer able to flee from the advancing threat, they would have been unable to do anything but await the inevitable as their world was altered by a frighteningly swift and visible change, as the rising flood waters quickly covered the land.

Eventually Doggerland was swallowed by the waves, becoming submerged under what is now the North Sea and the English Channel. It was at this point, once these newly created expanses of ocean had separated Britain from Europe, that the scene was set for the formation of Britain's unique island culture. For not only did the completion of this dramatic event culminate in the creation of a large new island, but it also ensured that, for the time being at least, the human population now confined to the island by the rising sea levels would have no choice but to exist separately from their European neighbours. The new Britons would therefore be left in isolation to develop their own culture, evolving free of outside influences until such time as they, or their neighbours, could develop an effective means to regularly cross the sea in significant numbers, thereby restoring contact and a cultural exchange with each other once more.

Ultimately, of course, sustained contact between the people on the opposite sides of the English Channel was restored. But by this time it would seem reasonable to conclude that the people of Britain must actually have become a unique society in their own right, given that contact with their continental neighbours up until this point would have been so negligible as to prevent them from having any real influence on the culture of the early native Britons. Even so, those cultural differences which the people of Britain had developed in isolation would, in time, become diluted by the influences of their neighbours, as links with the wider world continued to become yet more firmly established.

It is tempting, nevertheless, to think that Britain was probably regarded by even their closest neighbours as a land which was still somewhere distant and perilous to reach, and peopled no doubt by a strange race of people of which

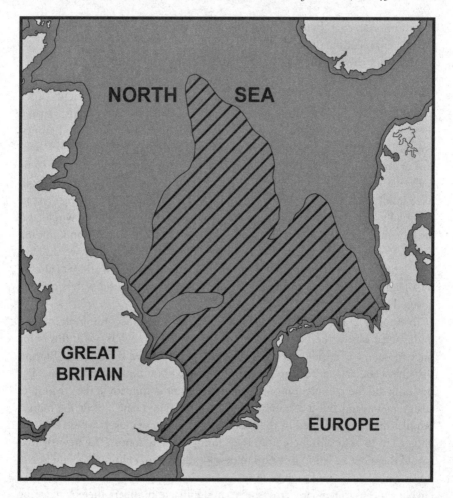

Fig. 1 Conjectural map of the extent of the Doggerland land mass around 10,000 years ago.

only very little was known. Indeed, that mysterious and even foreboding quality which we seem eager to attribute to the earliest eras of Britain is something which is readily apparent in the works of various writers of the classical era, even of those who wrote their accounts after such time as the likes of Caesar had provided an eye on the world of the ancient Briton.

From the Beaker Culture to the Iron Age
The story of the Roman conquest of Britain is as much about the continuation of a cultural journey as it is about war and conquest, and perhaps the

most significant known cultural change in pre-Roman Britain was that which occurred around the middle of the third millennium BC. This was when the Beaker culture spread up into northern Europe from the region of what is now Spain and Portugal.

Named after their very distinctive pottery, the Beaker folk introduced a whole variety of revolutionary changes to the native population of the British Isles, covering matters as diverse as burial practices to new industrial processes. It is not known whether the actual Beaker population themselves migrated in large numbers throughout Europe, or whether their influence was something which had steadily percolated up from their original homelands as a result of cultural exchanges which came about during inter-tribal trading. What is certain is that their influence had a profound and enduring effect on the people of Northern Europe.

The arrival of the Beaker culture in Britain heralded the beginning of the early Bronze Age, as the people of Britain first learned to smelt copper ore and then use that seemingly magical skill to produce the first metal tools and weapons. The acquisition of this knowledge was a revelation to early British society and it heralded an age of great change. What the ancients would have perceived as the almost supernatural ability to produce metal from ore was soon augmented by the development of more advanced metallurgical techniques, as the knowledge required to produce bronze, an alloy of copper and tin, soon followed.

Not only did this new skill revolutionise industry and agriculture in Bronze Age Britain, but it also changed the face of inter-tribal warfare by introducing a new range of more durable and much deadlier weapons to the battlefield. Studies of weapons from around this era have revealed that, far from endorsing the previously held view that these early bronze weapons were somehow inferior to the later iron weapons, they were in fact very resilient and extremely well-designed weapons, many of which were produced to standards which is difficult to replicate even today.

On the other hand, along with the ability to kill more efficiently, these new weapons also provided the owner with a great opportunity to conspicuously display wealth and status, the actual measure of which was dependent on the type and quality of the weapons which they carried. In fact it seems appropriate to suggest that this method of displaying your status by 'wearing' your power and wealth is really an ancient precursor to today's urban and criminal cultures, where overt displays of weaponry and wealth remain crucial to identifying the wearers' status among their own social group or, to use an alternative description, their tribal unit.

However, warfare was only one facet of early British society which had been changed by the advent of metal working, and eventually, by 1600 BC, Britain was experiencing a boom in trade with countries as far away as the

Mediterranean as it helped to feed the growing demand for the raw materials needed to produce ever more quantities of bronze, particularly by exploiting its abundant reserves of tin – a commodity which, among the ancient traders, would become synonymous with Britain. As well as the ability to produce bronze tools and weapons, the people of Bronze Age Britain were mining and working gold by this time, and also clearing large tracts of woodland in order to more efficiently farm crops and livestock.

By 800 BC the Bronze Age had drawn to a close and Britain, with its near neighbours in mainland Europe, was seeing in the dawn of the Iron Age. Not only did this mean yet more advances in industrial processes and agriculture, but it also saw a more pronounced cultural shift as migrations took place across the continent. As the Iron Age progressed the tribes of southern Britain were, from a cultural point of view, beginning to more closely resemble their continental neighbours and eventually they had moved towards becoming a Celtic society, formed by distinct tribal groupings. Yet, for all of the obvious influences that touched Britain from the outside, there seems to have been much left which set Britain and its people apart from everyone else.

Had his writings survived, it would have been a Greek, Pytheas, whose work would be the oldest surviving eye-witness account of Britain. Pytheas was born in the Greek colony of Massilia – now modern Marseille in southern France – in the fourth century BC. He was an explorer and geographer and his works contained the earliest known description of the island of Britain and its inhabitants. Pytheas wrote in detail about Britain, its inhabitants, climate and geography during a journey of exploration around northern Europe. His was a quest which would take him to many little-known lands and which would eventually take him far into the Baltic regions and Scandinavia. Today, only fragments of Pytheas' work survive, with nothing directly surviving of his account of Britain. However, subsequent classical world accounts of Britain, including the work of contemporaries of Pytheas and writers from the first century BC such as Strabo and Diodorus Siculus, seem to have relied on his writings to produce their own descriptions of Britain.

It seems that, as well as geographical descriptions, Pytheas' writings on Britain were a record of his travels across the island, which it is said he completed on foot. Indeed it appears to be Pytheas who, like some ancient tourist, gave the very first account of a visit to Stonehenge, while it still functioned as a major religious site. The loss of his writings on Britain is therefore lamentable, given the obvious importance of the knowledge they contained. Nevertheless it seems fairly certain that they still existed during Caesar's time, and it is difficult to imagine a cultured man such as Caesar not making reference to such writings in order to further his own ambitions.

From the Belgae to Julius Caesar

By the time of Julius Caesar's incursions into Britain in 55 and 54 BC, the indigenous Britons had already experienced a steady dilution of their culture which had arisen, in part at least, from contact with the Belgic tribes and their predecessors who occupied the lands of northern Gaul. The appearance of their cultural footprint came about due to the establishment of permanent trade and commercial links, and also as the result of raiding and the migration of Gallo-Belgic peoples crossing the channel to settle in Britain.

Whether the crossing of these people was something which occurred en masse, or whether this was a gradual process, is something which has yet to be conclusively established. However, in *The Gallic Wars* Caesar hints at the possibility of a time when there could feasibly have been a large influx of people to Britain; when he sets out his understanding of the origins of what he refers to as the Belgic peoples of northern Gaul.[1] According to Caesar, the Belgic tribes originally came from Germany and had crossed the Rhine in order to gain control of the excellent agricultural land in that part of Gaul. This, in turn, forced out the original inhabitants of those parts of Gaul.

If what Caesar says about the origins of the Belgae is accurate, then it is therefore quite plausible to propose the theory that the people who had survived being forcibly driven out of their homelands by the migration of the Germanic tribesfolk may have actually made the decision to cross the short stretch of ocean as an entire population. Those people would be what we today effectively consider to be refugees and, as such, they would have had scant choices open to them once they had been displaced by the invading tribes.

Large-scale migrations of entire tribes were not an uncommon occurrence in the ancient world. Indeed, in *Book I* of *The Gallic Wars* Caesar begins the record of his campaigns with an account of just such an occurrence. The commentary commences with the story of the migration of the Helvetii, a Gallic people whose homelands were located more or less in the area of what is now modern Switzerland, and who were initially persuaded to such an act by Orgetorix, their 'foremost man'.

Caesar recounts that the tribe crossed into Southern Gaul in 58 BC, potentially threatening the existence of the Roman province of Transalpine, Gaul, and thereby provoking Caesar to take immediate military action, both in order to defend his allies and to protect Roman interests in the region. Caesar tells us that Orgetorix died before the Helvetii actually began their migration but, spurred on by his original plan, the tribe had pressed ahead with the venture as they were intent on increasing their lands and breaking free of the formidable natural borders, such as the great rivers and alpine regions, which hemmed them in along much of the extent of their borders.

Eventually, Caesar drove the Helvetii and a number of smaller tribes accompanying them back to their own lands. Still this was not before the migrants had wrought considerable destruction on the towns of the neighbouring tribes, pillaged their goods and supplies and enslaved their people. As a sobering addition to his account of the Helvetian migration, Caesar tells us that his examination of tallies, written by the Helvetii at the start of the migration, recorded that a total of 368,000 people set out on their journey. Yet the census he subsequently conducted of the surviving tribesfolk recorded that only 110,000 of the Helvetii and their companions actually survived what turned out to be a brief and costly incursion into their neighbours' lands.

No doubt, in broadly similar circumstances, the original people of northern Gaul had experienced similar horrors to those which had subsequently accompanied the advance of the Helvetii; they witnessed their homes destroyed and were either murdered, or enslaved, as the ancestors of the Belgae crossed over the Rhine and descended upon their lands. Although the clear difference here was that there was no Caesar to intervene and drive the invaders back, thereby sparing these people from their fate.

As a result, short of standing their ground and fighting a winner-takes-all battle for territory and survival against what Caesar suggests would be a very determined and formidable enemy, it seems logical to assume that the surviving populace would have been compelled to flee in order to survive. It is therefore possible that they could have sailed over to Britain where they settled, either integrating peacefully with the native Britons or forcibly occupying land themselves and dispersing the local people to the interior of the island. If such was the case, then it seems that these early Gallic migrants were destined never to quite manage to rid themselves of the attentions of the Belgae, given that, sooner or later, the Belgae themselves would eventually develop their own interest in settling the very lands they had escaped to.

The arrival of the Belgae in Britain is perhaps effectively typified by the establishment of a branch of the Atrebates tribe in southern Britain. This tribal group is a part of the Belgic peoples and traces its roots directly back to a tribe of the same name that originally hailed from homelands located in the Artois region of what is now northern France. As we shall discuss later, it is the Atrebates who would have a significant involvement in the events surrounding not only Caesar's incursions, but also the later Claudian invasion.

The Atrebates were only one of a number of Belgic peoples to eventually settle in Britain, however, and whether in large numbers or on a more gradual basis, the steady influx of these people and their culture into Britain seems to have been seen most typically around the coastal areas which were closest to their original homelands in the northern regions of Gaul. The possible exception to this would be the Parisii tribe, who occupied the area

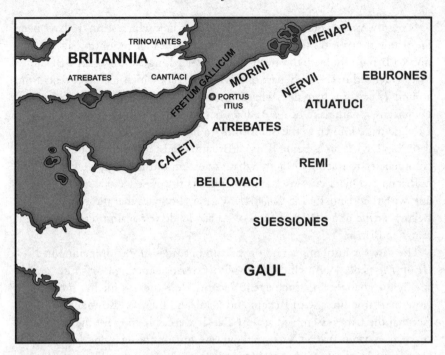

Fig. 2 The distribution of the larger Belgic tribes in northern Gaul and the coastal tribes of the south-east quarter of Britannia.

above the River Humber in what is now the East Ridings of Yorkshire. As their name suggests, they may be connected to a tribe of the same name which lived along the banks of the Seine and gave their name to the modern city of Paris. However, the Gallic Parisii were not Belgic peoples in origin, and lived instead in the region known as Celtica. It is also a matter for debate as to whether the two Parisii tribes were actually linked, or whether archae-ological evidence showing similarities in such matters as burial practices came about as a result of the British Parisii attempting to copy their conti-nental counterparts.[2]

Eventually, it seems Belgic influence spread across the southern half of Britain and there seems to have developed a clear distinction between the tribes settling in these regions and the indigenous tribes of Britain. The latter seem to have then been located more in Wales, the Midlands and the northern and western regions of Britain – with the exception of the Durotriges who still held the coastal areas in Dorset, and the Dumnonii whose lands appear to have occupied the majority of Somerset and all of the Cornish Peninsula. Ultimately, the southern Britons who emerged from all of these centuries of change had now become firmly linked to their neighbours in northern Europe.

It was the very existence of this strong Belgic link which seems to have been the prime motivation for Caesar to seriously consider mounting an expedition to Britain. Indeed, the need to consider taking action against Britain is first evidenced in the early part of *The Gallic Wars*, which records events from around 57 BC.[3] It is here that, whilst discussing the Belgae, Caesar writes of one Diviciacus, a namesake of his Aeduan friend and ally and a previous king of a Belgic tribe known as the Suessiones. In his writings on this matter, Caesar describes Diviciacus as being King of Britain. Whilst it is difficult from Caesar's commentary to quantify exactly what the extent of the kingly power wielded in Britain by Diviciacus was, it at least indicates the presence of a strong political link with the island. In *The Gallic Wars* Caesar also states that those rulers of the Bellovaci tribe, also a Belgic people, who had made war against him, had sought refuge in Britain.[4]

The case for justifying a raid on Britain becomes more compelling in *Book III* of *The Gallic Wars*, which deals with Caesar's campaign of 56 BC against the Belgic coastal tribes such as the Veneti.[5] Here there is further mention of close maritime links with Britain and Gaul, and there is also mention of the fact that the tribes assembled against Caesar were able to enlist the support of 'auxiliaries' from Britain. The strategic case for mounting a raid on Britain is further made out by Caesar in his account of the first expedition to Britain, in 55 BC, when he makes this mention of the problems which the Belgic links to Britain have presented him with: '[Caesar] nevertheless resolved to proceed into Britain, because he discovered that in almost all the wars with the Gauls succours had been furnished to our enemy from that country ...'[6]

Given the above examination of Caesar's writings, it seems apparent that, as far as he was concerned, there was certainly a tactical need to do something about the support that Britain was lending to those in Gaul who were actively hostile to him. After all, until such time as Caesar could prevent the Britons from offering aid to tribes in Gaul, he knew that complete control of the people of Gaul was likely to remain beyond his grasp. However, the need to address a military problem should not be regarded as the only reason why Caesar would cast an eye towards Britain. After all, there is no evidence available to suggest that the 'succour' to which Caesar refers, was something which was limited exclusively to military aid.

In terms of support for his enemies, there was something else about Britain which, putting aside its obvious appeal to him as both a strategic and a commercial target, clearly disturbed and threatened Julius Caesar.

The Druids in Gallic Society

Contained later on within the *The Gallic Wars* Caesar gives us a compelling insight into a further motivation for an attack on Britain, as he provides us with his extensive observations concerning a truly potent influence behind the Gallo-Celtic tribes of northern Europe – that of the order of the Druids.

From what Caesar tells us, it is clear that the Druids, as a sacred and inviolable order, were the cornerstone of Celtic society. As such, whilst it is not the purpose of this book to provide a detailed examination of the Druids and their role in that society, it seems necessary to perhaps provide some insight into how Caesar is likely to have regarded them. This is because it is clear from Caesar's writings that he believed the influence of the Druids, not only upon the tribal nobility but the ordinary people too, may have had a significant effect on his own ability to control the tribes that he had set out to conquer.

In *Book VI* of *The Gallic Wars* Caesar sets out his observations on the Druids. It is a description which, for some modern commentators, is regarded as anachronistic and not really an accurate reflection of the power, influence and status of the Druidic order at the actual time of the Roman conquest of Gaul. However, this view does not seem to fit in with the influence which Caesar indicates the Druids to have held and if, as some modern commentators suggest, the Druids were actually a spent force by this time, then the question which clearly begs an answer is: why then was the order proscribed by Rome and why were concerted attempts made by later generations of Romans to wipe them out?

In his writings on the Druidic order, Caesar is clearly explaining that the Druids had a powerful influence on their people. Indeed, it was an influence which was deeply rooted in the very heart of Celtic society. Caesar tells us that Druids were not only a religious order of priests, but they were also teachers and administrators of the law. They held sufficient power and influence to be able to impose their will on even the tribal nobility and were so revered that they could expect to be welcomed without reservation, even by other tribes living beyond their own land of origin or from people hostile to their own tribe. In effect, it is clear that what Caesar has written about the Druids is not some anecdotal account of an archaic priesthood that had long since fallen out of favour and influence. Instead, his description provides us with a picture of a highly influential section of Celtic society; one who still maintained the potential to pose a real threat to him in terms of encouraging resistance to his plans for the total control of Gaul. It therefore seems reasonable to surmise from Caesar's point of view that, if he could subdue the influence of such an order, then the task of conquering all of Gaul could potentially be made very much easier.

Caesar records his observations of the order of the Druids as follows:

XIII. – Throughout all Gaul there are two orders of those men who are of any rank and dignity: for the commonality is held almost in the condition of slaves, and dares to undertake nothing of itself and is admitted to no deliberation. The greater part, when they are pressed either by debt, or the large amount of their tributes, or the oppression of the more powerful, give themselves up in vassalage to the nobles, who possess over them the same rights without exception as masters over their slaves. But of these two orders, one is that of the Druids, the other that of the knights. The former are engaged in things sacred, conduct the public and the private sacrifices, and interpret all matters of religion. To these a large number of the young men resort for the purpose of instruction, and they [the Druids] are in great honour among them. For they determine respecting almost all controversies, public and private; and if any crime has been perpetrated, if murder has been committed, if there be any dispute about an inheritance, if any about boundaries, these same persons decide it; they decree rewards and punishments if any one, either in a private or public capacity, has not submitted to their decision, they interdict him from the sacrifices. This among them is the most heavy punishment. Those who have been thus interdicted are esteemed in the number of the impious and the criminal: all shun them, and avoid their society and conversation, lest they receive some evil from their contact; nor is justice administered to them when seeking it, nor is any dignity bestowed on them. Over all these Druids one presides, who possesses supreme authority among them. Upon his death, if any individual among the rest is pre-eminent in dignity, he succeeds; but, if there are many equal, the election is made by the suffrages of the Druids; sometimes they even contend for the presidency with arms. These assemble at a fixed period of the year in a consecrated place in the territories of the Carnutes, which is reckoned the central region of the whole of Gaul. Hither all, who have disputes, assemble from every part, and submit to their decrees and determinations. This institution is supposed to have been devised in Britain, and to have been brought over from it into Gaul; and now those who desire to gain a more accurate knowledge of that system generally proceed thither for the purpose of studying it.

XIV. – The Druids do not go to war, nor pay tribute together with the rest; they have an exemption from military service and a dispensation in all matters. Induced by such great advantages, many embrace this profession of their own accord, and [many] are sent to it by their parents and relations. They are said there to learn by heart a great number of verses; accordingly some remain in the course of training twenty years. Nor do they regard it lawful to commit these to writing, though in almost all other matters, in their public and private transactions, they use Greek characters. That practice they seem to me to have adopted for two reasons; because they neither desire their doctrines to be divulged among the mass of the people, nor those who learn, to devote themselves the less to the efforts of memory, relying on writing; since it generally occurs to most men, that, in their dependence on writing, they relax their diligence in learning thoroughly, and their employment of the memory. They wish to inculcate this as one of their leading tenets, that souls do not become extinct, but pass after death from one body to another, and they think that men by this tenet are in a great degree excited to valour, the fear of death being disregarded. They likewise discuss and impart to the youth many things respecting the stars and their motion, respecting the extent of the world and of our earth, respecting the nature of things, respecting the power and the majesty of the immortal gods.

XV. – The other order is that of the knights. These, when there is occasion and any war occurs [which before Caesar's arrival was for the most part wont to happen every year, as either they on their part were inflicting injuries or repelling those which others inflicted on them], are all engaged in war. And those of them most distinguished by birth and resources, have the greatest number of vassals and dependants about them. They acknowledge this sort of influence and power only.

XVI. – The nation of all the Gauls is extremely devoted to superstitious rites; and on that account they who are troubled with unusually severe diseases and they who are engaged in battles and dangers, either sacrifice men as victims, or vow that they will sacrifice them, and employ the Druids as the performers of those sacrifices; because they think that unless the life of a man be offered for the life of a man, the mind of the immortal gods cannot be rendered propitious, and they have sacrifices of that kind ordained for national purposes. Others have figures of vast size, the limbs of which formed of osiers they fill with living men, which being set on fire, the men perish enveloped in the flames. They consider that the oblation of such as have been taken in theft, or in robbery, or any other offence, is more acceptable to the immortal gods; but when a supply of that class is wanting, they have recourse to the oblation of even the innocent.[7]

There are, perhaps, many inferences and explanations which can be drawn from the description which Caesar has provided us with. However, what seems inescapable is the fact that Caesar has effectively identified the order as a very real threat to his own designs. The Druids were, at least as far as Caesar was concerned, the one binding influence that was common to all of Gaul. They were at the very heart of all matters religious, political, legal and cultural and, as such, were capable of causing real problems for him as they were the only group of people who had the potential to bring together all of the tribes of Gaul, in opposition to his plans for total conquest. In providing us with his description of the Druids, Caesar has therefore set out a clear motive as to why he would need to stifle the influence of this order and to take steps to emasculate its power and influence, or preferably to stamp it out entirely.

If such was the case that Caesar did intend to mount a specific offensive against the order, then what better way to advance his aims than to carry the fight to Britain? After all, it is the very place which he describes as being both the origin of the Druidic order and the place to go for those who wished to train to become Druids themselves. It is therefore possible that, as far as Caesar was concerned, Britain at that time represented what we today might regard as a terrorist training camp; where anti-Roman beliefs and practices were passed down to new generations of activists who were capable of radicalising the populace and encouraging them to rebel.

Lastly, for all that the influence that Britain and its people and culture had on Caesars designs in Gaul, there were also other, more alluring things about Britain which would have attracted the attentions of a man like Caesar; a man who craved wealth and power, and who was relentlessly in pursuit of both. What he saw in Britain was an island, pregnant with the promise of great personal wealth and presenting an opportunity to earn the kind of fame and power that could only come about as the result of completing what would then be regarded as an almost impossible feat of arms. Britain possessed an enviable catalogue of tradable commodities such as industrial and precious metals, cereal crops and slaves. While he continued the fight in Gaul, Britain was lying just tantalisingly out of the reach of Caesar and his legions, and to a man like him, the pull of Britain would have been irresistible.

Subsequently, since it appears from the above analysis that Caesar actually had three compelling reasons to invade Britain, it is not difficult to see exactly why the scene was eventually set for Caesar to make his plans to conquer the island.

Notes

1 Julius Caesar, *The Gallic Wars – Book II*, Chapter IV
2 Cunliffe (1974)
3 Julius Caesar, *The Gallic Wars – Book II*, Chapter IV
4 Ibid., Chapter XIV
5 Ibid., *Book III*, Chapters VIII–IX
6 Ibid., *Book IV*, Chapter XX
7 Ibid., *Book VI*, Chapters XIII–XVI

CAESAR'S INVASION OF BRITAIN – 55 BC

The Prelude to Caesar's British Raids

Since 58 BC, Julius Caesar had been waging war in Gaul and the territories that lay to its north. In that first year he had begun his campaigning by driving back the migrating Helvetii tribe and then ejecting the German king, Ariovistus, from the territory of the Sequani. By 57 BC he had defeated the Belgic tribes and had also experienced a rebellion on the Swiss side of Gaul by the Nantuates, Veragri and Seduni, as the 12th Legion under Salvius Galba bore the brunt of a tribal uprising, forcing the legion to engage in a desperate battle for survival from its winter quarters in an isolated Alpine fortress.

The campaigning season of 56 BC saw Caesar's armies engaged in fighting with a large collection of Gallic tribes, initially with those who lived along the Atlantic coast of Gaul such as the Veneti. He then carried his campaign back into the region of Aquitania, where the Romans inflicted a heavy defeat on the Aquitani and Cantabri. Finally in that year, Caesar also bought war upon the Menapii and Morini, the latter of whom were the Belgic tribe which occupied that part of the coast of northern Gaul which lay closest to the island of Britain.

The next year, 55 BC, Caesar turned his attentions to Britain itself, but not before he had slaughtered a further two migrating tribes, the Usipetes and the Tenctheri, who were Germanic peoples who had crossed the Rhine into northern Gaul. In the aftermath of his brutally efficient response to these intrusions, he had then crossed the mighty River Rhine by executing what is widely regarded as a stunning feat of military engineering; ordering the construction of a fixed, timber-frame bridge. What is remarkable about this project is that the completion of the entire building project was, according to Caesar, achieved in only ten days. He then concluded this show of Roman force by mounting a brief but very destructive foray into the territory of the German tribes, before withdrawing back into Gaul and destroying his remarkable bridge behind him.

Finally, after three years of fighting which took him across hundreds of miles of territory and left a body count behind him which, even by that stage of the Gallic campaigns, had easily reached genocidal levels, Caesar was ready to take on Britain.

In the excerpt from *The Gallic Wars* which is reproduced a little later in this work, Caesar seems to suggest that his reasoning for staging a raid into Britain was to at least find out more information about the people who he believed were actively supporting his enemies in Gaul; apparently by providing them with reinforcements. He also wished to learn more about the island, by conducting what would amount to a tactical appraisal of its natural features such as harbours and landing spots.

However much effort Caesar may have put into explaining the conduct and apparent justification for his military campaigns and what they actually achieved for Rome, it is clear that there were other, more personal motivations which drove him on to achieve what he did. Amidst all of the obvious self-publicity that Caesar had ultimately created in writing his accounts of the Gallic campaigns, it is abundantly clear from these accounts that he was also driven by other considerations. In fact it is clear that he was very much spurred on by a desire to increase both the measure of authority which he wielded and considerably boost his personal wealth.

It therefore seems certain to have been this very part of his character which ultimately spurred him on to mount not one but two expeditions to Britain, both of which posed obvious and grave risks and which could well have ended far more disastrously than they actually did. Consequently, even though Caesar in his record of the two raids has done his best to convince his readership that both missions were a success, it is clear that this was not actually the case. In reality Caesar not only failed to neutralise Britain militarily, he also missed out on the desired outcome of greatly expanding his already considerable personal wealth and of basking in the substantial fortune and glory that such a breathtaking conquest would have bestowed upon him.

Caesar Looks to the Western Horizon

In his account of the campaigns which he fought in Gaul, it is Julius Caesar who provides us with the first ever personal report to actually describe the people of Britain and the island they inhabit. In other words his record of what he found is, to our knowledge, the oldest surviving complete eyewitness account of the island of Britain. It is therefore appropriate that we should recognise Caesar's commentaries on the island, and its inhabitants, as the very beginning of recorded British history. It also seems appropriate for that reason that this chapter should commence by allowing Caesar himself to provide us with his own initial observations on the subject, delivered in *The Gallic Wars* in the context of the build-up to his first expedition, in 55 BC:

XX. – During the short part of summer which remained, Caesar, although in these countries, as all Gaul lies towards the north, the winters are early, nevertheless resolved to proceed into Britain, because he discovered that in almost all the wars with the Gauls succours had been furnished to our enemy from that country; and even if the time of year should be insufficient for carrying on the war, yet he thought it would be of great service to him if he only entered the island, and saw into the character of the people, and got knowledge of their localities, harbours, and landing-places, all which were for the most part unknown to the Gauls. For neither does any one except merchants generally go thither, nor even to them was any portion of it known, except the sea-coast and those parts which are opposite to Gaul. Therefore, after having called up to him the merchants from all parts, he could learn neither what was the size of the island, nor what or how numerous were the nations which inhabited it, nor what system of war they followed, nor what customs they used, nor what harbours were convenient for a great number of large ships.[1]

It is interesting to note that, in the very first words used to introduce his account of Britain, Caesar is telling us that, on the one hand, he was perfectly aware of the fact that the Britons had provided support to his enemies during his campaigns against the Gauls. Yet, on the other hand, Caesar is also suggesting that not even the Gauls themselves knew that much about the island, or its inhabitants. Furthermore, the details of the island which he requires appear to be largely unknown even to merchants, whom he describes in the main as the only outside visitors to the islands. This much is apparent in his reference to his fruitless efforts to extract intelligence about Britain from the merchants he had gathered from all over, specifically in order to interrogate them about what to expect in Britain.

We know that Caesar did make a further effort to gather some intelligence for his first raid. This is because he also mentions in his description of the prelude to the raid that he despatched a warship, under the command of one of his tribunes, Gaius Volusenus, to conduct a reconnaissance of the closest part of the British coast. However, it does not appear that Volusenus returned with intelligence of any great import as he seems to have failed to properly identify any areas along the coast where a landing in force would be most likely to succeed. In fact, Caesar goes on to say that Volusenus so feared falling into the clutches of the Britons that he spent the entire five-day expedition aboard ship, not once caring to set foot on the island and instead preferring to conduct his reconnaissance of Britain exclusively from the deck of his warship.

Moreover, it was not until Caesar had taken the decision to make the channel crossing and find out for himself about Britain that he finally became all too aware of the real nature of the island and its inhabitants. As we shall shortly discuss, it was that seemingly incautious and poorly briefed initial approach which almost cost Caesar dear. It was also one which could have dramatically changed the course of world history, had he not been fortunate enough to sail away from the islands with his life. However, in what was his usual style, Caesar comes across as being quite matter of fact in delivering his description of his time in Britain and of acknowledging the misfortune and the very real danger which he and his men had been forced to confront. What is more, at times he seems almost to be actively understating the perils which existed.

Regardless of Caesar's attitude to the risks, perhaps it may even have been this view of the island as a land swathed in mystery – which he speaks of so early on and which persists in later historical accounts by others – that could almost have brought disaster upon the Emperor Claudius' plans for invasion. After all, if we are to accept Cassius Dio's account of events, then immediately prior to the sailing of the Claudian invasion force the army which had been gathered for the task had initially refused to sail. In setting out to explain this, Dio provides us with the suggestion that this was because the troops assembled by Claudius in AD 43 were reluctant to fight a campaign beyond the boundaries of the known world.

In military tradition, the past deeds of units are passed down to successive generations of soldiers, contributing to their own *esprit de corps*. It would have no doubt been via this medium that many of the Claudian troops would have become aware, to a greater or lesser degree, of the expeditions by Caesar. They must surely have taken in all of the stories passed down by their predecessors; no doubt many of them being made up of soldiers' fireside tales which were very probably embellished by successive generations of narrators in the ninety-seven years which had passed since the last of Caesar's raids. In fact, the large-scale circulation of the right kind of rumours, or sinister tales, could easily have had a very destabilising effect on the morale of Claudius' army.

To our modern sensibilities, this may seem like a slightly odd reason for bringing about a near mutiny. Especially when the body of men in question is a 40,000 strong Roman assault force which, certainly for its time, would represent a very formidable and powerful invasion force. However, it is important that we should bear in mind that, despite its devastating potential as a professional army in the field, the Claudian invasion force was made up of men whose lives were, like any other person from that time, dominated by religious practices and beliefs which, in turn, were founded on deeply rooted superstitions.

Religion in the Roman world was not conducted on a par with the practices and observances associated with more modern, monotheistic systems of faith. It was more about maintaining equilibrium with a large number of both divine and supernatural powers. It was also about making sure that due respect was regularly paid to the myriad spirits and forces of nature that controlled the world around them. In fact the Romans needed to keep favour with a plethora of guardian spirits which, on a sliding scale of importance, presided over such things as people, places, objects and occasions.

It was observance of the festivals and rituals relative to these spirits which was also combined with the routine worship of both minor and major deities. These last were gods and goddesses who controlled anything from good luck to the afterlife. Simply put, the average Roman of this period would have no real concept of how the 'one size fits all' doctrines of today's most dominant world religions could work. Therefore, to a Roman soldier, setting out on a mission of this kind was not simply a question of unconsciously stepping off a boat onto the far-flung shore of Britain; it was more about stepping completely out of a world which you knew exactly how to deal with and appease and into one which you, nor the men next to you, knew anything about. Carrying out Claudius' order to conquer Britain was not just about the soldiers having conviction in their own ability to wage war; it was also about them overcoming the fear of placing themselves in an environment where the normal rules may not apply.

As he prepared to make his first foray into Britain in 55 BC, Caesar saw that reluctance amongst his men to disembark from their ships, too. Yet he attributed the unwillingness of his own men to leave the safety of the ships chiefly to the depth of water that the heavily armoured troops were to jump in to. Despite the obvious physical risks it is easy to imagine that these soldiers were, to a degree at least, also held back by their fear of the unknown. This is particularly understandable in the case of Caesar's men, given the fact that at that time Britain and its inhabitants would have probably been seen as even more mysterious and foreboding than it was in Claudius' time. Especially if we recognise that, for Caesar's troops, there would have been no second- or third-hand accounts of the island and its people to refer back to, just the unsettling knowledge that as soon as they set foot on the shores of Britain they were all going to be operating beyond the edge of the known world.

Caesar's Expedition of 55 BC

There seems little doubt that the landings of 55 BC were, as previously suggested, poorly planned, hastily executed and dogged with misfortune. In addition it is clear from Caesar's writings that the situation in Gaul at this time was still far from stable. Consequently, in mounting a raid on Britain so late in the year, he was probably dangerously overstretching his resources. He was also clearly risking the lives of both himself and his men by embarking on a mission from which there was a very real possibility that they may not return. Nevertheless, as risky as the first mission was, it seems that the apparent meddling of the Britons in his campaigns against the Gauls had ultimately caused Caesar to take the view that swift action needed to be taken in order to deny the Gallic tribes any further support from Britain.

Caesar records that, even before he had set sail for the island, the Britons had received word of his intentions and had sent diplomatic envoys across to Gaul. These envoys had approached Caesar and offered both hostages and their allegiance. Caesar goes on to record that he then sent them back home, accompanied by a tribal leader called Commius 'The Gaul', king of the Gallic Atrebates. It would be this man, Commius, who would be tasked by Caesar with persuading the British tribes to become protectorates of Rome. Caesar had meanwhile sent the tribune Gaius Volusenus on a reconnaissance mission to the island, while he had assembled his invasion fleet in Portus Itius (Boulogne) and concluded his affairs with the recently defeated Morini tribe.

Notwithstanding a lack of reliable or detailed intelligence relating to Britain, Caesar and his expeditionary force eventually crossed the channel in a night sailing in what appears to be little more than 100 ships of varying types. He arrived off the coast of Britain next morning with a force of two legions at his disposal, but without his cavalry support. Apparently, the cavalry transports had set sail later than the main contingent and from a different location. Caesar records that his cavalry were being carried in eighteen ships, but these had been delayed as they had missed the opportunity to sail with the tide and had subsequently been carried back towards the coast of Gaul.

Almost instantly upon his arrival off the coast of Britain, Caesar was faced with a reception committee of Britons whose substantial numbers and clear willingness for a fight had effectively made a Roman landing on the coast impossible. Caesar was therefore forced to find another landing spot for his troops and, even when he had managed this, he was met with a fearsome response by the Britons as they mounted attacks upon his men with cavalry and chariots; thwarting initial attempts and at the same time discouraging later attempts by the Roman troops to land and engage.

It is almost tempting to think that this stand-off may well have resulted in the end of the mission, had it not been for one man. This was the un-named aquilifer of the 10th Legion who, seeing that his comrades needed some further encouragement to master their fears and summon up the pluck to force their way ashore, took matters into his own hands to save the day. Caesar tells us that this un-named hero, having no doubt offered a quick prayer to the gods, shouted out: 'Jump down, comrades, unless you want to surrender our eagle to the enemy. I, at any rate, mean to do my duty to my country and my general.' With that, Caesar says, he leapt from the ship into the waves and, carrying the sacred standard of the legion's eagle aloft, struck out for the beach.

This, of course, was just what the Roman troops had needed to galvanise them into action and, unwilling to submit to the terrible shame of losing their sacred eagle, they jumped into the surf from their ships all at once and waded ashore after their valiant eagle bearer, engaging the enemy in a ferocious battle to gain a foothold on the beach. In due course, after a hard-fought action with absolutely no cavalry support, the Roman infantry managed to shove back the defending Britons, driving them off and consolidating their position.

Based on the description given by Caesar, it has been largely agreed by antiquarians and modern historians that the first landing occurred around the area of Deal in Kent, on either 26 or 27 August 55 BC.[2] Indeed, a team headed by Dr Donald W. Olson, Professor of Physics at Texas State University, conducted research into tidal patterns along the Kent coast, the results of which underpin the view that the coast around Deal was Caesar's landing site. However, the results of their research also provided a compelling argument to suggest that the landings were actually more likely to have occurred on either 22 or 23 of August of that year.[3]

Olson and his team identified that the tidal conditions which had been experienced by Caesar along the Kent coast in 55 BC would next be duplicated in August 2007. There was therefore a rare opportunity to investigate tidal patterns around the time of Caesar's landings, as similar conditions had not been seen since 1901 and would not be duplicated again until 2140. They therefore conducted experiments in the area in order to conclusively establish the direction of the tidal patterns which had been experienced by Caesar.

The findings of their experiments were read in conjunction with classical descriptions of tidal activity at the time of the landings, and also took into account the possibility of a transcription error as to the number of days it took for the ships carrying Caesar's cavalry to arrive off the coast of Britain. In that regard, it has previously been accepted that this was four days after the landings. However, Dr Olson and his team were taking an observation into account which was made by the British historian Robin G. Collingwood, who proposed that a transcription error had occurred from the original Latin manuscript and that the actual number of days it took for the cavalry to arrive was seven or eight.[4]

Subsequently, on the basis of the scientific data which they had obtained from their own research, combined with both the suggested date revisions by Collingwood and the various classical descriptions of tidal conditions, Olson and his team were able to say that Caesar probably did come ashore somewhere in the area of Deal beach, given that their eventual findings indicated that the tides on the newly calculated date would have been flowing up the coast of Kent and would therefore have carried Caesar's vessels along on a northerly course.

Having successfully forced his way ashore, Caesar was again sought out by tribal envoys. The Britons were, it seems, somewhat taken aback by the fighting superiority and bravery of the legionaries and decided that discretion was perhaps the better part of valour on this occasion. The Britons therefore apologised for their actions and sought peace; they promised Caesar obedience and offered the customary handing over of hostages. They even returned his envoy, Commius, who it transpires had been taken prisoner pretty much as soon as he had landed in Britain.

However, Caesar's opportunity to enjoy his success was short indeed. Soon after his arrival his fleet of eighteen cavalry transports had arrived off the coast, only to be ravaged by stormy seas which scattered the formation and forced them to return to Gaul. As if to add insult to injury, the same storm also wrought havoc amongst the rest of Caesar's fleet as it either lay beached or at anchor, incurring catastrophic losses and serious damage.

Now, without a sufficient number of serviceable ships to carry them, Caesar and his troops were effectively stranded in Britain and without the supplies necessary to allow them to sit the approaching winter out in Britain. Haste, it seems, had prompted Caesar to make fundamental errors by sailing late in the year and neglecting to make proper contingency plans. In addition, the intelligence-gathering interviews he had conducted prior to his mission, with those who were allegedly familiar with the coast of Britain, had failed to alert him to the fact that Atlantic tides run particularly high during the time of a full moon. Clearly, the absence of this piece of information had proven to be a potentially disastrous gap in his knowledge.

The situation could hardly have been bleaker, but matters were about to take an even worse turn as, once more, the Britons experienced another change of heart and seeing that the Romans were now at a distinct disadvantage, they decided the time was right to renew hostilities with their unwelcome visitors.

In such a dire situation it was fortunate for the Roman troops indeed that their commander was able to think on his feet. Anticipating that an attack by the Britons was imminent, Caesar had ordered the gathering of as much food as his men could lay their hands on. He had also ordered immediate repair work to his storm-battered fleet, which was effective enough to have seen all but twelve of the original vessels restored to seaworthiness.

Caesar tells us that hostilities were actually resumed when the 7th Legion were on a foraging mission to gather corn. The Britons, knowing the Romans' intentions and identifying the most probable place that the Romans would choose to raid the crops, had taken up position overnight and waited in ambush. Once the legionaries had lain down their arms and were hard at work harvesting the corn, the Britons sprung their trap and launched their attack with cavalry and chariots. The use of the latter Caesar describes in some detail, thereby rendering a unique account of an aspect of the British way of war, which we are told had long previously died out on the continent.

Caesar was subsequently able to mount a hastily gathered rescue mission and the Romans eventually managed to fight off their attackers. However, he decided that it was too risky to pursue the fleeing Britons and instead returned to camp. Here a prolonged spell of bad weather forced the Romans to remain until a large force of Britons re-appeared and descended on the camp, intent on wiping out the much smaller Roman force. By now, however, Caesar's force had been augmented by the addition of around thirty horsemen who had accompanied Commius, and the Romans were able to defeat the Britons once more and force them to flee.

It seems that, by this time, Caesar himself had also made the decision that discretion may be the better part of valour after all and, after receiving yet another deputation from the fickle Britons, he took the available hostages he had been promised and set sail for Gaul.

Caesar Back in Gaul

When considering Caesar's incursions into Britain, it is extremely important that the raids are looked at in a wider context. It is therefore essential that some consideration is given to the events that form a background to them. Only by considering those events can we develop a fuller understanding of what was going on in Caesar's world and of the issues he was juggling with, on top of managing his ambitions for Britain. It is therefore appropriate that some consideration should be given to the events which occurred between the raids on Britain.

As far as the first incursion goes, it certainly would seem that it was more a case of profound good luck than good judgement that Caesar and his men had managed to sail away from the shores of Britain. Yet even as Caesar had accomplished the sea-crossing back to Gaul, further troubles were to beset him as soon as he set his feet on the continent once more. Whilst the majority of Caesar's fleet had managed to put safely into port, two of his transports had been carried further south and subsequently found themselves making land fall in the territory of the Morini. The Morini quickly decided that this unexpected opportunity for sack and plunder was too good to be passed up and, seizing upon their considerable numerical advantage, around 6,000 of them eventually set about the hapless Roman soldiers, numbering around 300 in all, as they set out on a march to rejoin the main body of the army.

As far as Caesar was concerned, relations with the Morini were peaceful at that time, as they had been since he had set out for the shores of Britain. However, it seems that the peace which existed with the Belgic peoples at this time was very precariously balanced and it only took this incident to shatter that peace and cause an explosion of extreme violence as Caesar reacted to the threat.

Having quickly received word of the treacherous attack by the Morini, Caesar despatched all of the cavalry then at his disposal to assist the troops at the mercy of the tribe. Having held out for more than four hours, the beleaguered Roman column was at last bolstered up by arrival of the column of cavalry who, Caesar says, killed a large number of the Morini as they fled from the scene of the previously unequal contest. There followed swift and very effective punitive action against the Morini as the tribune Labienus was despatched at the head of the legions which had fought in Britain, to deal with the subsequent uprising by the tribe. Troops under the command of Quintus Titurius Sabinus and Lucius Arunculeius Cotta also carried out brutally effective operations against the Menapii, whose lands lay to the north of the Morini. As their homes were torched and their crops plundered by the Roman forces, the Menapii fled their settlements, hiding out in dense woodland in an effort to avoid Caesar's terrible retribution.

As Caesar set down the record of his successful suppression of the tribal revolt, he noted somewhat wryly that, having quartered his men in Belgica for the winter, he becomes aware that only two British kingdoms actually sent the hostages they had agreed to deliver up to him. The rest, it seems, were conspicuous by their absence. It would therefore seem reasonable to conclude that, for all of the time, effort and losses involved in the first raid on Britain, there was actually no great value to it all. Caesar was unable to gain any real military advantage from the raid. Furthermore, he suffered the loss of men, ships and stores, and came away from the islands having created absolutely no political advantages at all. While he concludes his account of the first raid on Britain in his usual matter-of-fact style, it seems obvious that the whole affair would have left Caesar with a very bad taste in his mouth.

However, for all the negatives that can be identified within the context of the first expedition to Britain, Caesar would still have gained at least some benefit from his experiences. He would certainly have gained some sort of measure of the Britons, both as a society and from the perspective of their military abilities. He would also have gained valuable intelligence about the land, simply by putting aside the negative results of the raid and instead treating the incursion as an extended reconnaissance in force. Therefore, although he had come away from Britain with little physical evidence to show for his efforts, he at least had plenty of food for thought to see him through another winter away from Rome.

Events Prior to the Second Expedition

If Caesar thought that his immediate troubles were over with the suppression of the Menapii and the Morini, then the events which occurred during the winter between the British raids were to prove him utterly wrong.

It is clear from the outset of *Book V* of *The Gallic Wars* that Caesar was firmly resolved to return to Britain. It is also clear that his intention was to prosecute a much larger campaign which would finally serve to cast aside any residual pretence there may have been about mere fact-finding missions. Indeed, he now came to refer directly to his coming plans for a second invasion as a 'war' against the Britons. However, the winter of 55–54 BC would ultimately provide him with more to think about than just quartering his troops for the winter, or drawing up his plans for waging a war against the Britons in the following campaigning season.

Prior to leaving for Italy for the winter, Caesar left orders with his commanders that they should construct as many ships as they possibly could, in preparation for a second invasion of Britain the next year. Caesar provides us with a detailed account of his requirements, outlining the bespoke designs for the ships which he intended to use to transport large amounts of cavalry and infantry.[5] He also bids his commanders to make arrangements to gather supplies in from Spain for fitting-out and equipping the vessels, which were either to be built from scratch or refurbished in preparation for the landings.

Yet even with the preparations for the invasion well under way, Caesar was about to experience a troubled winter. No sooner had he left the annual assizes of Gaul than he found it necessary to deal with the Pirustae, an Illyrian tribe who had been launching attacks over their frontiers against neighbouring territories. Upon arrival in Illyricum, situated on what is now the eastern coast of the Adriatic, Caesar levied troops and assembled them to move against the Pirustae. These actions made it abundantly clear to the Pirustae just what Caesar intended and the tribe were instantly subdued by the clearly perceived threat of immediate war. Consequently, they agreed to offer up hostages and assured Caesar that reparations would be made to the injured parties. This seems to have satisfied Caesar, who subsequently appointed arbitrators to deal with the finer points of the peace agreement while he crossed back into Gaul.

Caesar's affairs in Illyricum appear to have taken up much of the winter, and he was therefore reliant on his commanders in Gaul to carry out the instructions he had left regarding the coming invasion of Britain. Having arrived back in Gaul, Caesar conducted a tour of his winter camps which revealed that 600 transport vessels and twenty-eight warships had been built. Furthermore, the vast majority of the ships were fully fitted-out and ready to sail. Caesar therefore ordered that all of the ships should be assembled at Portus Itius (Boulogne), in order to make final preparations for the crossing to Britain.

However, it appears that Caesar had little time to admire the fruits of his men's efforts, or actively contribute much further to the invasion preparations in port, as further trouble was brewing which needed to be dealt with. This time it was with the Treveri; the tribe would not accept Caesar's authority and were instead seeking to form an alliance with German tribes. Caesar responded to this by taking four legions and 800 cavalry into the land of the Treveri, which was situated in northern Gaul and bordered the Rhine.

The Treveri were at this time experiencing an internal struggle for power between two of their chieftains, Indutiomarus and Cingetorix. Of the two men, it was Indutiomarus who was hostile to Caesar. Caesar was conscious of the need for a swift return to Portus Itius to complete his plans for the invasion of Britain. He therefore seems to have allowed this to sway his decision making and decided against military action. Consequently, after some political manoeuvring with the tribe, he withdrew after urging the Treveran chiefs to support Cingetorix. This was to prove to be a somewhat hasty decision and a critical error of judgement on Caesar's part, as he had now left a bitter and resentful enemy at his back in the form of Indutiomarus. It would be this oversight which, as we shall discuss later, would ultimately cost Caesar dear in the winter that immediately followed his final return from Britain in 54 BC.

It is at this point in *The Gallic Wars* that one really has to question just what it was that motivated Caesar. Why was he so clearly determined to mount another invasion of Britain? Particularly when his first mission was not that far short of an unqualified disaster and, additionally, that he had spent most of the intervening winter dealing with threats and problems both near and far. The very fact that Caesar was intent on pressing ahead with a second raid on Britain at this time, setting aside his possible motivations, must at least raise questions as to his actual proficiency as a military strategist. After all, even though it seems Caesar was well aware of the threat level in Gaul at this time, he nevertheless seems to have drawn the conclusion by then that the reward for success still far outweighed the consequences that would befall him and his men if his gamble failed.

It is very clear from his description of the events of that winter that Caesar's military and political position in Gaul could be described, at best, as unsafe. The very existence of circumstances, such as those prevailing in Gaul at the time, should therefore have indicated to any good commander in the same situation that they were not yet in sufficient control and that their current position needed to be stabilised. Therefore, if Caesar had wanted to reduce the risks, common logic seems to suggest that he should have at least taken further steps to consolidate his position in Gaul before giving any further consideration to dividing and thereby weakening his forces.

Caesar was clearly still at a point whereby the prevailing conditions were still compelling him to conduct many more reactive than proactive operations. This should therefore have indicated to him that his position was not yet strong enough and that he could not really afford to over-reach himself. However, despite the apparent instability of his position and the clear need to remedy this, Caesar was determined to press on with his plans for Britain.

By the end of the winter he had committed five legions and 2,000 cavalry to the task. By diverting a significantly large amount of troops to another theatre of war, Caesar certainly seems to give the impression of a reckless and impetuous man, rather than a good, solid commander who has fully reconciled himself to taking what he considers to be an acceptable risk. Ultimately, Caesar's decision to press on with his plans for a second raid on Britain not only hugely depleted his military strength in Gaul, but it also created a potential situation whereby neither the British or Gallic contingents of his army could easily send reinforcements to each other, if the other army needed to be supported. What also seems to be astonishing is that Caesar actually acknowledged the political fragility of the situation in Gaul prior to the second raid on Britain, given that his writings confirm that he had assembled most of the tribal leaders of Gaul in Portus Itius, with the intention of taking them with him to Britain. Caesar is quite clear in explaining his reasoning for this, given that he tells us that he simply does not trust them not to plot and scheme in his absence.

History has ultimately provided us with a testimonial of Caesar as a man who, from his early beginnings, was clearly a habitual risk taker. Although it is not the purpose of this work to make an assessment of the conduct of Caesar's campaigns in Gaul, it is nevertheless difficult to avoid asking oneself another question about Caesar: was he consciously playing a game of incredible brinksmanship in committing the greater part of his army to another raid on Britain? Or was he, in reality, a careless commander whose successes in Gaul are actually more attributable to the outstanding quality of his soldiers, subordinate commanders and extreme good luck, rather than any real tactical brilliance on his part?

In posing such a question, one is of course calling into question the professional reputation of a man who is widely acknowledged as one of the most celebrated military commanders in history. However, whilst it is certainly tempting to continue by entering into a deeper discussion of this point, it is nevertheless a matter which, due to the complexities involved in these issues, is best left for examination in a work more closely dedicated to the subject.

Notes

1 Julius Caesar, *The Gallic Wars – Book IV*, Chapter XX
2 Ibid., Chapter III
3 Donald W. Olson, Doescher, Beicker & Gregory (2008)
4 Robin G. Collingwood, *Roman Britain & the English Settlements* (1937)
5 Julius Caesar, *The Gallic Wars – Book V*, Chapter I

THE SECOND EXPEDITION – 54 BC

The Return to Cantium

With preparations complete for sailing, Caesar was beset by further delay as adverse north-westerly winds prevented the fleet from putting to sea for another four weeks. At the end of this delay Caesar was also forced to send troops to pursue and kill one of the assembled tribal leaders, Dumnorix of the Aedui, after he had fled the camp on the eve of sailing. Dumnorix's subsequent capture and killing at the hands of Caesar's men probably did nothing to ease the nerves of the tribal chiefs, especially considering that Dumnorix had previously stirred the assembled chiefs up with rumours that Caesar would slaughter them all upon their arrival in Britain, in order to finally rid himself of those he considered to be trouble makers.

Caesar must have felt greatly relieved as he finally set sail, leaving Labienus to manage affairs in Gaul with a total of three legions and 2,000 cavalry. Although it appears that even the second crossing was not without mishap, as the fleet was driven off course by strong tides before it finally managed to make an unopposed landing on the same beaches Caesar had located the previous year. Caesar details that, although a large army had massed to oppose the Roman landings, they quickly withdrew at the appearance of so many ships. As it transpired, the avoidance of large, set piece battles with the Romans would be a tactic that the Britons would employ consistently throughout the remainder of Caesar's time in Britain.

Once ashore with his men, Caesar's opening action was to immediately pursue the Britons with the greater part of his army, leaving his ships under the care of one of his commanders, Quintus Atrius, 300 cavalry and ten cohorts of troops. The opening engagement saw the Britons make use of their cavalry and chariots, and also making small skirmishing forays from what appears to be an established, defended stronghold located in woodland. The Britons' use of such places would be a further feature of the British way of fighting which Caesar would have cause to mention on a number of occasions. Although Caesar acknowledges the defensive strength of the position, it does not seem to have overly troubled the men of the 7th Legion who managed to overrun the fortifications by advancing in *testudos* and filling the ditches with earth, before scaling the perimeter defences. As soon as this was accomplished the defending force of Britons fled.

It was when Caesar was preparing to pursue the Britons who had taken flight from his advance of the previous day, that the misfortune of the previous year's raid came back to haunt him once more. A messenger from Atrius brought him the news that, just as had happened the previous year, a great storm had risen up and battered his fleet, with the result that many of his ships were now damaged or beached. Caesar was therefore forced to postpone his advance and return to the anchorage to survey the damage which his ships had sustained.

It is not possible to say for certain whether, having learned a lesson from the previous raid, Caesar had already recognised the need for a contingency plan to deal with such issues. We cannot therefore say with any confidence whether or not Caesar had previously instructed Atrius to build defences and to haul his fleet onto the beach. Although this is ultimately what Caesar did, scarcely two days had passed since he had landed and even if he had issued such an order, his men would never have been able to accomplish the task in the time available; Caesar subsequently explains that it eventually took ten days of continuous toil to complete this. Caesar's account of the incident does however suggest that the order to do these things was probably given retrospectively, clearly to prevent a possible reoccurrence and further damage being caused to the fleet. Therefore, this provides us with a further indication that Caesar may not have taken the time to plan properly, or that he had learned lessons from the last raid.

By this point in *The Gallic Wars*, Caesar has provided us with much of the information needed in order to attempt to identify his landing area. Caesar confirms in his account of the second raid that the actual landing spot is the same as he used in both expeditions. It is therefore very important we correctly identify this spot, not only in order to develop a fuller understanding of his British raids, but also to identify what coastline he was most familiar with. In doing so, we may therefore gain some idea as to what possible intelligence he and his officers may have come to hand down to the planners of the later Claudian invasion.

The historical clues which exist in Caesar's accounts regarding both of his raids are as follows:

These matters being arranged, finding the weather favourable for his voyage, he set sail about the third watch, and ordered the horse to march forward to the farther port, and there embark and follow him. As this was performed rather tardily by them, he himself reached Britain with the first squadron of ships, about the fourth hour of the day, and there saw the forces of the enemy drawn up in arms on all the hills. The nature of the place was this: the sea was confined by cliffs so close to it that a dart could be thrown from their summit upon the shore. Considering this by no means a fit place for disembarking, he remained at anchor till the ninth hour, for the other ships to arrive there. Having in the meantime assembled the lieutenants and military tribunes, he told them both what he had learnt from Volusenus, and what he wished to be done; and enjoined them (as the principle of military matters, and especially as maritime affairs, which have a precipitate and uncertain action, required) that all things should be performed by them at a nod and at the instant. Having dismissed them, meeting both with wind and tide favourable at the same time, the signal being given and the anchor weighed, he advanced about seven miles from that place, and stationed his fleet over against an open and level shore.[1]

From this excerpt relating to his first raid, we are able to ascertain that Caesar arrived off a part of the British coast which was overlooked by high cliffs with a very narrow beach. Deeming this unsuitable for a landing, Caesar then sails a further 7 miles, to 'an open and level shore'.

Our next clues as to the location of the landing site are provided in *Book V*, when Caesar supplies us with his account of the following years' landings:

When these things were done Caesar left Labienus on the continent with three legions and 2000 horse, to defend the harbours and provide corn, and discover what was going on in Gaul, and take measures according to the occasion and according to the circumstance; he himself, with five legions and a number of horse, equal to that which he was leaving on the continent, set sail at sunset and was for a time borne forward by a gentle south-west wind, he did not maintain his course, in consequence of the wind dying away about midnight, and being carried on too far by the tide, when the sun rose, espied Britain passed on his left. Then, again, following the change of tide, he urged on with the oars that he might make that harbour of the island in which he had discovered the preceding summer that there was the best landing-place, and in this affair the spirit of our soldiers was very much to be extolled; for they with the transports and heavy ships, the labour of their rowing not being for a moment discontinued, equalled the speed of the ships of war. All the ships reached Britain nearly at mid-day; nor was there seen a single enemy in that place. Caesar afterwards found from some prisoners that, though large bodies of troops had assembled there, they were alarmed by the great number of our ships, more than eight hundred of which, including the ships of the preceding year, and those private vessels which each had built for his own convenience, had appeared at one time, and they had quitted the coast and concealed themselves among the higher points.[2]

Caesar then adds to this, in the following chapter, with a description of the landing beach itself, along with some vitally important clues as to its location:

> Caesar, having disembarked his army and chosen a convenient place for the camp, when he discovered from the prisoners in what part the forces of the enemy had lodged themselves, having left ten cohorts and 300 horse at the sea, to be a guard to the ships, hastens to the enemy, at the third watch, fearing the less for the ships for this reason, because he was leaving them fastened at anchor upon an open shore of soft sand; and he placed Quintus Atrius over the guard of the ships. He himself, having advanced by night about twelve miles, espied the forces of the enemy. They, advancing to the river with their cavalry and chariots from the higher ground, began to annoy our men and give battle. Being repulsed by our cavalry, they concealed themselves in woods, as they had secured a place admirably fortified by nature and by art, which, as it seemed, they had before prepared on account of a civil war; for all entrances to it were shut up by a great number of felled trees. They themselves rushed out of the woods to fight here and there, and prevented our soldiers from entering their fortifications. But the soldiers of the seventh legion, having formed a Testudo and thrown up a rampart against the fortification, took the place and drove them out of the woods, receiving only a few wounds. But Caesar forbade his men to pursue the fleeing Britons for any great distance; both because he was ignorant of the nature of the ground, and because, as a great part of the day was spent, he wished time to be left for the fortification of the camp.[3]

In terms of the actual direction which the fleet sailed in, there is a useful indication in the penultimate extract from *The Gallic Wars*. It suggests that Caesar had most likely sailed on a general northerly course in order to reach the landing beach, given that he says he saw the coast of Britain passing on his left. In addition, the research by Dr Donald W. Olson and his team, which was discussed in the last chapter, would seem to be compelling enough to allow us to conclude that Caesar's fleet did sail up the coast of Kent, rather than around to the south coast. Therefore, with good evidence for the fleet's direction of travel now in place, we are in a very favourable position to pinpoint the actual location of the landings by using the clues available.

It is important that we build our appraisal by starting with an examination of what is currently regarded as the most likely location, namely Walmer or Deal. With regard to these locations, perhaps the most important element of this presumption is that the cliffs which Caesar refers to regarding his first sight of Britain are those in the area of what is now the port of Dover. However, if we make a closer examination of the information available, it would seem that the cliffs referred to in Caesar's account may not be those

in the immediate area of the port, which are so favoured by previous commentators. As Olson points out, there have been many notable academics
and historians in the past who have all drawn the conclusion that Deal or
Walmer were where Caesar came ashore. All base their conclusion on the
notion that Dover was the location of the high cliffs mentioned by Caesar.
Yet, if we look at this theory more closely, it does not appear to stand up to
scrutiny that well.

The first problem with this view is that the location of Dover has been
arrived at by using a reference by the Greek historian, Cassius Dio, describing
the first raid by Caesar as follows:

> To this land, then, Caesar desired to cross, now that he had won over the
> Morini and the rest of Gaul was quiet. He made the passage with the infantry
> by the most desirable course, but did not select the best landing-place; for the
> Britons, apprised beforehand of his voyage, had secured all the landings on the
> coast facing the mainland. Accordingly, he sailed around a certain projecting
> headland, coasted along on the other side of it, and disembarking there in the
> shoals, conquered those who joined battle with him and gained a footing on
> dry land before more numerous assistance could come, afterwards he repulsed
> this attack also.[4]

The key reference in this text is the mention of 'a certain projecting headland', which those who favour Dover have taken to be a reference to the
headland at South Foreland, just to the north of Dover. Yet Caesar does not
mention this feature in his own description of the coast. Moreover, Cassius
Dio wrote his account of the events somewhere in excess of 250 years after
they actually happened. There is then sufficient reason to be suspicious of the
reliability of such a detail, particularly as Caesar never mentions it, although
still writes in enough detail to record other natural features and measures of
distance. It is therefore difficult to accept that Caesar would neglect to have
recorded such an obvious feature.

The overall description given by Caesar himself as to the actual coastal
topography is somewhat limited and he mentions only tall cliffs, fronted by
a narrow beach which was totally unsuitable for a landing. Therefore, if we
discount South Foreland from our deliberations, we are left with a considerable
stretch of Kentish coastline matching that description, which stretches along
from Dover and travels north to a short distance past St Margaret's Bay.

Nevertheless, further useful clues are contained in his references to the
landing beach itself, which Caesar refers to as an open shore of soft sand
which lies 12 miles from a fortified settlement, close to a river. If we work on
the fact that Caesar sailed a further 7 miles up the coast from Dover then we

would indeed reach Deal. However, as we attempt to triangulate a position for the landing beach, we need to keep in mind that the miles we are referring to are Roman miles, and not the modern mile. The difference being:

1 Roman Mile = 1.48km = 1,620yds (or 142yds less than a modern mile)

The first problem we encounter with Deal is the beach itself. Deal beach is steep and comprised entirely of shingle deposits. It does not therefore meet the criteria set out in Caesar's description of needing to be flat and sandy. Because it slopes, it would also prove to be hugely difficult to drag large ships on to. In addition, there is no known large Iron Age settlement, or a river which is about 12 Roman miles distant from Deal. These factors would also eliminate Walmer, which lies a short distance south of Deal.

However, if we accept the possibility that Caesar's fleet could have appeared off the coast further north of Dover, then we are still able to match alternative locations which would fit with Caesar's descriptions of looming cliffs and a narrow beach. It is therefore possible that the alternative location could be the aforementioned St Margaret's Bay. If Caesar then sailed around 7 miles up the coast from this location, he would be landing in the area of what is now modern Sandwich.

What is persuasive about the argument for this location being the true landing site is that the steep shingle beaches running up from Deal gradually begin to level off, until the beach in the area of Sandwich becomes the only large stretch of flat and sandy beach along this part of the Kent coast. The last compelling piece of evidence is gained by following a course inland and on a westerly heading. At a distance of around 12 Roman miles you would then encounter the River Stour as it flows by Canterbury, the ancient tribal settlement of Durovernum Cantiacorum. Even more compelling is the fact that to the west of Canterbury lies Bigbury Hill Fort, a location which is a fortified position that was in use at the time of Caesar's raids and located close to the River Stour. This would therefore tally exactly with Caesar's description of the opening events of the second raid as it gives us a defended settlement, close to a river.

Consequently, with so many elements of the description matched, it is extremely difficult to ignore the proposal that Caesar's landings were actually in the area of Sandwich.

Cassivellaunus

Having taken action to resolve the problems with his fleet, Caesar turned his attentions once more to the campaign against the Britons and set off back to the location of his last encounter with them. It is at this point in Caesar's account that the name of a British chieftain first emerges. He was the first ever Briton to be mentioned by name and was the man who not only lead British resistance against Caesar, but whose successors would ultimately come to contribute to the reasons for Claudius to invade. He was Cassivellaunus.

In reality, there is very little that we know about Cassivellaunus. His tribal origins are uncertain, as Caesar does not actually name the tribe which he belongs to and it is not entirely clear where his stronghold was located at the time of the second raid. As to his origins, there is a theory that his name is made up of various elements of the Celtic language and that a possible translation may be 'Vellaunos of the Cassi', which is one of the tribes Caesar names as seeking his protection against the aggressive actions of Cassivellaunus. The possible inference is that, having experienced an acrimonious parting of the ways with his own tribe, Cassivellaunus established his own tribal group. Although, this is of course entirely speculative.

As to the location of Cassivellaunus' stronghold, it is generally held that Cassivellaunus established a settlement at Wheathampstead, in modern-day Hertfordshire, just a short distance north-east of Verulamium (St Albans). This is the earliest identifiable settlement that it is possible to link to Cassivellaunus. However, whilst Caesar's writings have been useful in plotting a location for his landing beach, there is less accuracy available to us when it actually comes to describing the location of Cassivellaunus' main stronghold. Nevertheless, his writings do seem to indicate that Wheathampstead would be a very likely possibility.

Caesar tells us that the location of Cassivellaunus' territory was actually on the north side of the Thames and 75 miles from the sea.[5] Although it does need to be borne in mind at this point that Caesar is referring only to the location of Cassivellaunus' 'territory' and not to the location of any settlement. Therefore, if we follow a straight, approximately westerly course from Sandwich, this would place us close to the area of what is now central London. It would also place us close to the fording point where it is believed that Caesar's army later used to cross the Thames.

This description could therefore lead us to conclude that this part of the Thames acted as a natural frontier marker for the southern extent of Cassivellaunus' territory. Subsequently, had Cassivellaunus withdrawn to Wheathampstead after the ensuing battle on the Thames, then Caesar would have needed to march a total distance more in the order of 98 Roman miles. However, given the description of the seemingly lengthy march to contact which Caesar describes after he had crossed the Thames, this does seem to have taken some time to complete and would therefore help to make Wheathampstead a definite possibility.

Previously, we have discussed what Britain was like prior to the incursions of Caesar. However, Caesar's account makes it clear that, before his arrival, south-eastern Britain was, by then, already paying the price for the ambitions of Cassivellaunus. Caesar tells us that Cassivellaunus was constantly at war with the other tribes. This makes it clear that Cassivellaunus was already employing the expansionist polices which would later increase the power and influence of the Catuvellauni, a tribe which would be Cassivellaunus' legacy to Britain and one which would eventually come to feel the full might of Rome's military power.

With the arrival of Caesar's legions in Britain once more, the Britons appear to have set aside their internecine feuding and instead appointed their most recent enemy, Cassivellaunus, to lead the resistance against the threat of Caesar. This is clearly an endorsement of the military power that he was wielding at the time, as it would seem pointless to nominate any but the most powerful and militarily adept of tribal rulers to take control, and respond to what would have been considered such a dire emergency and universal threat.

The Fight against Cassivellaunus

Caesar explains that, once he had dealt with the problems with his ships, he returned to the defended settlement where he found Cassivellaunus had assembled many more men to face him. It then seems that a running battle erupted between the protagonists, which started with an engagement between a Roman cavalry column on the march and British horses and chariots. Having repulsed this attack the Romans were then assailed by a surprise attack from the surrounding woodland, which resulted in a raging infantry battle in front of the defended settlement which, as previously discussed, could have been at Bigbury.

It was at this point that Caesar became acquainted once more with the British tactic of rushing in to engage his troops and then quickly withdrawing; hoping to goad the heavily armoured legionaries into giving chase, in order to separate parties of them from the main body of the army. Clearly, the Britons had identified that it was pointless to try and engage large numbers of Roman troops in more conventional warfare. The Britons knew that the Roman infantry formations were at their most lethal when they were given the opportunity to use disciplined formation tactics to carve up large numbers of opponents who had elected to fight a head-on engagement with them. The Britons therefore decided to play to their strengths and utilise the advantage of their great speed and mobility in an attempt to reduce their foe in a more piecemeal fashion.

Caesar also refers to the fact that the Britons fought in open order and kept a good supply of reserves, rotating their warriors throughout the engagement so that the tiring legionaries were always forced to fight fresh opponents. However, in what seems to have been a punishing error of judgement on the part of Cassivellaunus, the Britons descended on a force comprised of three legions and a cavalry contingent who had been sent out on a foraging mission. The Britons fared very badly in this engagement and suffered many losses, forcing them to flee the field or be cut down by the superior Roman force. Caesar comments that, after this engagement, the Britons never again elected to face him in a more conventional mass battle.

Caesar then advanced to the Thames and made preparation to ford the river, most commonly believed to be at Brentford, in order to enter Cassivellaunus' territory. The point on the river where the Thames is joined by the Brent is relatively shallow with a bed of gravel; hence the name 'Brent' 'ford'. However, as we shall examine in more detail later in this work, the idea that Caesar's army forded the Thames at Brentford is by no means a foregone conclusion. Indeed, there is a second alternative, proposed by Thornhill, which we will discuss in the context of the crossing of the Thames made by the Claudian army.[6] The proposal being that Caesar actually crossed the Thames at another ancient fording point, close to the Thames Estuary.

Nevertheless, it seems that Cassivellaunus was equally resolved to preventing the crossing of the Thames and had deployed a large force to check the Roman advance. As Caesar tells us, the Britons had also taken care to fortify the area with sharpened stakes which had been both dug into the bank and also submerged in the river itself. For all the men and defensive measures which Cassivellaunus had put in place to prevent the crossing, the advancing Romans exhibited incredible courage in the face of both determined defenders and deadly obstacles. Caesar recounts that his legionaries forded the river, wading up to their necks in the waters of the Thames, but with such speed that they emerged on the far bank at the same moment as the Roman cavalry and immediately routed the defending Britons.

Cassivellaunus must have realised by this time that the enemy he faced was unlike any other foe that he had ever ventured to take on before. It must have become clear to him at this point that he was going to have considerable difficulty in mounting a credible response to the threat which Caesar and his army posed. Ultimately, his response was to disband his infantry and instead retain a contingent of around 4,000 chariots, which he would use to harass the advancing Roman column while at the same time dispersing the local population and their cattle ahead of the Roman advance. To Cassivellaunus' credit, Caesar himself acknowledges that it was the employment of this strategy which ultimately prevented his men from laying waste to as much of the local populace and territory than he had intended.[7]

At this point, Caesar was met by a deputation from the Trinovantes, a large and powerful tribe whose capital was located at Camulodunum (Colchester, in Essex). Geographically speaking, this fits very well with the location of the fording point suggested by Thornhill, as it is much closer to Trinovantean territory. Caesar tells us that he had previously received a prince of this tribe, Mandubriacus, while still in Gaul. Mandubriacus had placed himself under Caesar's protection after his father, the king of the Trinovantes, had been killed by Cassivellaunus. Caesar consequently returned Mandubriacus to the tribe and assured them all that the young prince would be protected. However, this was to be done on condition that the tribe should furnish him with forty hostages and a supply of grain, which the Trinovantes duly produced. In his discussion of the location of the ford, Thornhill makes the entirely logical point that if Caesar had in fact forded the Thames closer to its estuary, then he would have crossed directly into Trinovantean territory. This would have enabled the Trinovantes to supply grain and hostages to Caesar much more easily as they would not need to travel into Catuvellaunian territory to do so. However, we shall more closely explore the merits of this crossing point later in the work.

A perhaps understandable result of this decision was that Caesar was soon approached by ambassadors from a collection of other tribes, who were also willing to offer their surrender to Caesar on condition that he protected them too against the aggression of Cassivellaunus. Caesar names these tribes as the Cenimagni, Segontiaci, Ancalites, Bibroci and the Cassi. From these tribes, he subsequently learned that Cassivellaunus' stronghold was not far from his current location, and he was then able to advance on the stronghold and deliver a brief but decisive attack on the fortifications and totally overpower the defenders. Given what we have already discussed as to the actual location of Cassivellaunus' tribal seat, it seems that this location is most likely to have been Wheathampstead.

However, whilst we have good evidence to suggest that Wheathampstead was most likely to have been Cassivellaunus' capital, it is interesting to note the potential scale of co-operation which he was afforded by those who had previously been in conflict with him. This is best demonstrated by the fact that Cassivellaunus seems to have taken control of what appears to be Bigbury in the opening phases of Caesar's push inland. If this was the case then it seems that the other tribal leaders had also placed their strongholds at his disposal, as well as handing over command of their warriors.

By the time Wheathampstead had fallen, Cassivellaunus was acting from a position of desperation; he then issued orders to four Kentish Kings, Cingetorix, Carvilius, Taximagulus and Segovax, to launch an all-out surprise attack on the landing site where Caesar had beached his ships. This also proved to be ineffectual however, and again the Britons suffered badly in losses, with one of their nobles, Lugotorix, being captured. It seems that Cassivellaunus had come to realise that the situation was now hopeless. With the odds continually stacking up against him, he sought terms from Caesar, using Commius 'the Gaul' as a go-between.

Proceedings potentially now became somewhat rushed, as Caesar explains that he had decided it was necessary to return to Gaul for the winter. Summer was nearly at an end and Caesar judged that Cassivellaunus would at least be able to hold out until the weather prevented his return to Gaul, cutting him and his men off without supplies. Caesar states he was also worried about the situation in Gaul, endorsing the previously explored view that the second mission was ill-considered and that he had not adequately planned for a prolonged campaign.

As far as we know, Caesar never came face to face with Cassivellaunus. He seems instead to have been content to let Commius tidy up affairs, while he made preparations for the voyage back to Gaul. It nevertheless seems astonishing at this point to note that, just when it seemed that Caesar had got Cassivellaunus on the back foot, he declined to make one last push to defeat him totally and instead decided to withdraw from Britain. For Caesar it seems that time had simply run out. Though, in view of the events that would follow, it actually proved to be the right choice to make.

With the decision confirmed, hostages were demanded from the Britons and an agreement was reached which required Cassivellaunus to pay an annual tribute to Rome and to discontinue any further aggressive acts against Prince Mandubriacus or the Trinovantes. Once the hostages were delivered, Caesar marched his army back to his ships and prepared to leave. It was here that he experienced one final piece of bad luck, so emblematic of his time in Britain.

Due to the fact that he had suffered shipping losses, which meant that he could not embark his men in one trip, Caesar decided to make the journey back to Gaul in two trips; intending for some of the first wave of ships to return to Britain once they had landed their passengers in Gaul. This was not to be, however, as the number of ships he required from Gaul did not arrive in time. Therefore, in order to avoid the tidal changes caused by the autumn equinox, Caesar crammed his men aboard the vessels which were then at his disposal in Britain and sailed back to Gaul.

How odd it must have seemed to any Britons observing his departure that, after all the bloodshed, after wreaking such devastation and defeat on the tribes, Caesar would come to make such a hurried and almost humiliating exit from their land. Particularly after securing what would ultimately prove to be such a worthless arrangement with Cassivellaunus.

Notes

1 Julius Caesar, *The Gallic Wars – Book IV*, Chapter XXIII
2 Ibid., *Book V*, Chapter VIII
3 Ibid., *Book V*, Chapter IX
4 Cassius Dio, *Roman Histories – Book XXXIX*, Chapter LI
5 Julius Caesar, *The Gallic Wars – Book V*, Chapter XI
6 P. Thornhill (1976), pp. 119–28
7 Julius Caesar, *The Gallic Wars – Book V*, Chapter XIX

BRITAIN BETWEEN THE INVASIONS

By the Sword Divided

To Caesar, Britain must have been nothing but a distant collection of memories as yet another winter in Gaul descended. Trouble had been on the horizon since he had failed to deal effectively with Indutiomarus, the Treveran chieftain whose intense resentment of Caesar had been fomenting since he had left for Britain. Indeed, it was Indutiomarus who was instrumental in starting a mass tribal revolt in the winter after Caesar had returned from Gaul. The uprising itself began with the slaughter of an entire army under his two commanders Cotta and Sabinus, both of whom perished in the ambush which followed on from the opening attack on their winter quarters.

As the flames of rebellion rose across Gaul, Caesar and his troops became embroiled in a hectic battle to regain control of the land and, after this most desperate of winters, Caesar seems never to have cast a covetous eye to the western horizon again.

With the threat of Caesar now removed, Cassivellaunus was once more free to renew hostilities with the neighbouring tribes. However, whilst it is clear that Cassivellaunus wielded considerable strength and influence at this time, it is not so clear what his actual position was in the established British tribal hierarchy. As we have discussed, we know from Caesar that the other British tribal leaders placed him in overall command of opposition to the Roman landings. We know too that Caesar placed his territory as north of the Thames and that, prior to the arrival of the Romans, Cassivellaunus was already actively waging war against his neighbours. He had already killed the king of the Trinovantes tribe, forcing his son, Prince Mandubriacus, to flee to Gaul and seek protection from Caesar. Yet Caesar never once names the tribe to which Cassivellaunus belonged. Nor for that matter does he mention by name the tribe which we now know as the Catuvellauni, whom Cassivellaunus is widely believed to have founded. It would therefore be reasonable to form the view that, at the time of Caesar's raids, the tribe itself had probably not yet been properly established. Instead, it seems distinctly possible that Cassivellaunus was a local warlord whose power was ever more rapidly in its ascendancy.

It may have been the case that, having broken away from his ancestral tribe, Cassivellaunus formed his own group of followers and embarked upon a campaign to secure his own kingdom. Eventually he became powerful enough to form his own tribe and the Catuvellauni subsequently appeared on the tribal map of late Iron Age Britain. Indeed, Cunliffe refers to this possibility in his reference to power shifts emerging as a result of unaffiliated war bands displacing the established aristocracy.[1] It would certainly seem, in the years immediately preceding Caesar's raids, Cassivellaunus and his followers were not the only group operating independently of the established tribes. Although, from what we now know, it seems reasonable to take the view that Cassivellaunus and his followers ultimately proved to be the most successful.

The key to when the Catuvellauni first emerged doubtless lies locked up in the period immediately after Caesar had departed for Gaul for the last time. Although entirely speculation, it would nevertheless make sense to assume that a man as seemingly ambitious as Cassivellaunus would have eventually realised that, with all of the problems the Romans faced in Gaul, Caesar was unlikely to return and scupper his plans further. It could have been at that point that Cassivellaunus decided it would be a good time to dissolve any residual alliances with his neighbours, which would then leave him free to resume the push for yet more power and allow him to concentrate on the establishment of his own tribal unit. After all, any agreements reached with other tribal leaders were likely to have held good only while the threat of Caesar remained, requiring the tribes to maintain a united front under one overlord. For Cassivellaunus, once he was sure that Caesar was clearly out of the way, it was therefore going to be business as usual.

At this point it seems appropriate to also consider the question of what actually happened to those tribes which Caesar mentions as sending ambassadors to place themselves under his protection, specifically because of the threat Cassivellaunus posed to them. In *The Gallic Wars*, the Cenimagni, Segontiaci, Ancalites, Bibroci and Cassi tribes all sent envoys to Caesar, specifically because Caesar had pledged his protection to the Trinovantes and subsequently installed the rightful heir, Mandubriacus, as their king.[2] As a result of this, the aforementioned tribes must have then felt confident enough to attempt to shake off the looming threat of Cassivellaunus and make an approach to Caesar, hoping to elicit the same degree of protection which had been offered to the Trinovantes.

It has been suggested that the Cenimagni which Caesar refers to are actually the Iceni tribe, and an early error in transcription created the name 'Cenimagni' when a reference to the 'Great Iceni', or 'Iceni Magni', was most probably incorrectly translated from the original Latin manuscripts. However, even if this explanation might serve to provide a more familiar identity for one of the tribes mentioned, this still does not explain what happened to the other four.

Given the relationship which Caesar suggests these tribes had with Cassivellaunus at this time, there is a clear possibility that, with Caesar and his legions out of the way, Cassivellaunus decided to take his revenge on these peoples for effectively selling out to Rome. After all, if Cassivellaunus had ever been in a position whereby he needed to cloak his own ambitions with some form of justification, what better argument could he present to his neighbours than to point out that he was exacting retribution on traitors who had willingly allied themselves with a common enemy? When considering the credibility of this suggestion we do need to keep sight of the fact that Caesar had posed a direct threat to the interests and freedom of every tribal group in south-east Britain. Consequently, it seems hard to imagine that anyone would have sprung to the defence of the tribes that had tried to forge an alliance with Caesar as Cassivellaunus turned his military power against them. What is more, even if they actually disagreed with any punitive action taken by Cassivellaunus, they may have lacked sufficient military strength to back-up any open expression of their displeasure.

Once those tribes who had sought the protection of Caesar had been subjugated and their tribal hierarchy had been toppled, Cassivellaunus would have been in a position to have taken control of their lands, placing himself in overall control of the people. Such a move would, as suggested, no doubt have allowed Cassivellaunus to take the moral high ground with his neighbours. Moreover, it would also have given him increased land, power and wealth, effectively creating the foundations for increased expansion. In addition it would explain why, if these people were effectively subsumed into Cassivellaunus' territory, they were never heard of again after Caesar first mentioned their names.

The Rise of the Catuvellauni

Although we are still unable to say for certain just when it was that the Catuvellauni tribe came into being, it does seem very likely that the tribe was born out of the constant power struggles that had been going on for some time before Caesar's arrival in Britain. Indeed, these internal conflicts would continue until they were finally curtailed by the arrival of the Claudian invasion force.

Of all the tribes located in the south-eastern quarter of Britain, it was clearly the Catuvellauni who had emerged as the dominant tribal power and it would be their relentless push for expansion and the subjugation of their neighbours which would ultimately provide Rome with a reason to invade once more.

It is widely believed that the tribe's first *oppidum* was based at Cassivellaunus' early stronghold at Wheathampstead, a short distance to the north east of Verulamium (St Albans). As we have mentioned, this is the location where we believe Cassivellaunus made his final efforts to resist Caesar's advance. However, excavations at the site of the Wheathampstead *oppidum* would suggest that occupation of the site ended around the start of the last decade of the first century BC. After this time, the site had fallen out of use and occupation then shifted around 5 miles to the south-west, to the site of the *oppidum* at

Verulamium. Occupation of this site then seems to have continued to around the time of the Claudian invasion of Britain.

Although occupation of Verulamium continues into the first century AD, its importance as a tribal capital for the Catuvellauni was diminished in the early years of the new century when the capital was transferred from Verulamium to Camulodunum (Colchester). Cunliffe suggests that this shift is evidenced by the extent of the defensive earthworks at the Verulamium site.[3]

What remains of Verulamium's defence works are now best represented by the existence of Beech Bottom Dyke and Devils Dyke, which are the remnants of large bank and ditch defences which appear to have formed part of the outer defensive perimeter for the *oppidum* and its environs. Although the defences found at Verulamium are large, they are not as large and complex as those located at Camulodunum. They may only therefore serve to represent the early stages of development of the defences, which required no further enlargement once the Catuvellaunian seat of power had shifted to Camulodunum and the political importance of the site had diminished.

Britain after Cassivellaunus

It is not possible to say for certain when Cassivellaunus died, or who his actual heir was. However, by the time of his death it would seem that he had achieved his ultimate goal of founding his own dynasty, and that the Catuvellauni were by then intent on continuing with the territorial aspirations of their old king.

The next Catuvellaunian leader we can identify is Tasciovanus. However, we are unable to say for certain whether he was the son of Cassivellaunus, or whether he was perhaps his grandson. Coin evidence indicates that Tasciovanus ruled predominantly from Verulamium, as this is where he minted his coins, from around 20 BC onwards. Although there is also coin evidence to show that, some time after 20 BC, Tasciovanus was issuing coinage with the Camulodunum mint mark. Presumably he had managed to briefly take control of the Trinovantean capital, possibly seizing control from Addedomaros, the next known Trinovantean ruler after Mandubriacus. This is therefore clear evidence that, whilst the Catuvellauni were not yet powerful enough to permanently seize control of neighbouring territory, they were, as previously suggested, actively engaged in attempting to expand their borders by this time. Consequently, it seems as far as the Catuvellauni were concerned at this juncture, the undertaking which Cassivellaunus had given to Caesar, not to molest the Trinovantes, was clearly defunct.

Tasciovanus did not maintain control of Camulodunum for long however, and it would ultimately be his son, Cunobelin, who finally took control of the capital and the kingdom from the next Trinovantean king, Dumnovellaunus, sometime before AD 7. Indeed, evidence of the aftermath of Catuvellaunian aggression to their neighbours even appears in the official records of Rome and in a reference written by no less than Augustus himself.

The funerary inscription of Augustus, the *Res Gestae Divi Augusti*, or *The Deeds of the Divine Augustus*, was set out in his will and circulated by senatorial decree after his death in AD 14.[4] Copies of the inscription were set up on public monuments throughout the Roman Empire, although the original version was inscribed into a pair of bronze tablets which were located outside his great mausoleum in Rome. The well-preserved remains of the mausoleum still stand today and are located near to the Ara Pacis Augustae, or Altar of Augustan Peace, on the northern part of the Campus Martius and close to the River Tiber. Although the greater part of the structure of the mausoleum remains, the vast majority of the decorated façade, including the original inscriptions in Bronze, have not survived.

Essentially, the inscription itself was a record of Augustus' public life and records such things as his military victories, political appointments and achievements and matters such as public benefactions. The most complete version of the inscription survives from the Monumentum Ancyranum, which was a temple set up to the Divine Augustus in what is now modern Ankara in Turkey. It is in the later part of the inscription, where Augustus makes mention of a list of foreign rulers who he describes as 'suppliants', that we find evidence of the power struggles going on in Britain. Augustus alludes to them thus:

Fig. 3 The remains of Augustus' Mausoleum in Rome. (Author's photograph)

'Kings of the Parthians, Tiridates, and later Phrates, the son of King Phrates, took refuge with me as suppliants; of the Medes, Artavasdes; of the Adiabeni, Artaxares; of the Britons, Dumnobellaunus [sic] and Tim...'[5]

Here then is direct evidence of the expansion of the Catuvellauni. Augustus describes the Trinovantean Dumnovellaunus' arrival at his court specifically to take refuge, being received, as previously mentioned, as a 'suppliant.' This excerpt can refer only to the driving out of Dumnovellaunus by the Catuvellaunian Cunobelin. Yet it also mentions one other British king, whose name only partially survives as 'Tim...'. If, as most believe, this name is actually that of the Atrebatean king Tincommius, then it is also good evidence to demonstrate that around the time Cunobelin was ousting Dumnovellaunus from power, the Atrebates were also experiencing power struggles on an internal level.

It is still debatable whether Tincommius was the son or even grandson of Commius 'the Gaul', the one-time ally of Caesar who fled to Britain around 52 BC after eventually siding against Caesar with his Gaulish nemesis, Vercingetorix. The reason for the doubt is that it has not yet been conclusively established whether Commius the Gaul was succeeded directly by Tincommius, or whether Tincommius inherited the throne from another Commius who first succeeded the original.

There is some coin evidence to suggest that the original Commius was succeeded by a son of the same name, 'Commius the Younger', as Atrebatean coins from that period can be found stamped with '*COM COMMIUS*', which can be translated as 'Commius, son of Commius'. Nevertheless, what is fairly certain is that Tincommius did succeed a king named Commius to the Atrebatean throne and ruled from Calleva Atrebatum (Silchester), situated in the northern half of the tribal lands. Meanwhile his brother, Eppillus, gained control of the southern half of the kingdom, ruling from Noviomagus (Chichester). It would be this part of the Atrebatean peoples which would subsequently come to be called the Regnenses, after the time of the Claudian invasion. It is widely believed that, during the internecine power struggles, Eppillus then drove Tincommius from power around AD 5, forcing him to seek refuge in Rome with Augustus, while Eppillus assumed overall control of the Atrebates.

To return to Augustus' *Res Gestae*, there seems to be no reason to doubt the reliability of the translation of the inscription and it is therefore interesting to note the specific use of the word 'suppliant' to describe the actions of the kings listed. This indicates that, although the various kings Augustus mentioned were appealing to him for assistance, it does not necessarily follow that they were already vassals of the emperor by the time they had arrived in Rome.

This view is supported by an interesting excerpt from Suetonius' account of the life of Augustus, from *The Twelve Caesars*:

But he never made war on any nation without just and due cause, and he was so far from desiring to increase his dominion or his military glory at any cost, that he forced the chiefs of certain barbarians to take oath in the temple of Mars the Avenger that they would faithfully keep the peace for which they asked; in some cases, indeed, he tried exacting a new kind of hostages, namely women, realizing that the barbarians disregarded pledges secured by males; but all were given the privilege of reclaiming their hostages whenever they wished.[6]

This part of the account of Augustus' life seems to make it clear that Augustus harboured no aspirations with regard to extending the physical boundaries of the empire and it must therefore follow that he had no real designs on following up on his adoptive father's plans regarding the acquisition of Britain. However, it is interesting to note how Suetonius describes Augustus' approach to those who 'wished to keep the peace for which they asked'. It seems that as well as extracting an oath from foreign rulers in this regard, Augustus may also have required them to levy some sort of tribute, alongside offering hostages, in order to ensure that the peace was maintained. It is possible to find evidence of this in the writings of Strabo, when he offers his description of Britain.

Strabo's description of Britain itself differs very little, in essence, from that given by Caesar.[7] Strabo has clearly taken the time to embellish the original account with some research of his own. Still, it is reproduced here in its entirety (Strabo's reference to Ireland is not included) to demonstrate that between the relatively few years which divide the writing of the two accounts, the wider world had learnt little more about Britain than was originally reported by Caesar:

Britain is triangular in shape; and its longest side stretches parallel to Celtica, neither exceeding nor falling short of the length of Celtica; for each of the two lengths is about four thousand three hundred – or four hundred – stadia: the Celtic length that extends from the outlets of the Rhenus as far as those northern ends of the Pyrenees that are near Aquitania, as also the length that extends from Cantium (which is directly opposite the outlets of the Rhenus), the most easterly point of Britain, as far as that westerly end of the island which lies opposite the Aquitanian Pyrenees. This, of course, is the shortest distance from the Pyrenees to the Rhenus, since, as I have already said, the greatest distance is as much as five thousand stadia; yet it is reasonable to suppose that there is a convergence from the parallel position which the river and the mountains occupy with reference to each other, since at the ends where they approach the ocean there is a curve in both of them.

There are only four passages which are habitually used in crossing from the mainland to the island, those which begin at the mouths of the rivers — the Rhenus, the Sequana, the Liger, and the Garumna. However, the people who put to sea from the regions that are near the Rhenus make the voyage, not from the mouths themselves, but from the coast of those Morini who have a common boundary with the Menapii.(On their coast, also, is *Itium*, which the Deified Caesar used as a naval station when he set sail for the island. He put to sea by night and landed on the following day about the fourth hour, thus having completed three hundred and twenty stadia in his voyage across; and he found the grain still in the fields.) Most of the island is flat and overgrown with forests, although many of its districts are hilly. It bears grain, cattle, gold, silver, and iron. These things, accordingly, are exported from the island, as also hides, and slaves, and dogs that are by nature suited to the purposes of the chase; the Celti, however, use both these and the native dogs for the purposes of war too. The men of Britain are taller than the Celti, and not so yellow-haired, although their bodies are of looser build. The following is an indication of their size: I myself, in Rome, saw mere lads towering as much as half a foot above the tallest people in the city, although they were bandy-legged and presented no fair lines anywhere else in their figure. Their habits are in part like those of the Celti, but in part more simple and barbaric – so much so that, on account of their inexperience, some of them, although well supplied with milk, make no cheese; and they have no experience in gardening or other agricultural pursuits. And they have powerful chieftains in their country. For the purposes of war they use chariots for the most part, just as some of the Celti do. The forests are their cities; for they fence in a spacious circular enclosure with trees which they have felled, and in that enclosure make huts for themselves and also pen up their cattle – not, however, with the purpose of staying a long time. Their weather is more rainy than snowy; and on the days of clear sky fog prevails so long a time that throughout a whole day the sun is to be seen for only three or four hours round about midday. And this is the case also among the Morini and the Menapii and all the neighbours of the latter.

The Deified Caesar crossed over to the island twice, although he came back in haste, without accomplishing anything great or proceeding far into the island, not only on account of the quarrels that took place in the land of the Celti, among the barbarians and his own soldiers as well, but also on account of the fact that many of his ships had been lost at the time of the full moon, since the ebb-tides and the flood-tides got their increase at that time. However, he won two or three victories over the Britons, albeit he carried along only two legions of his army; and he brought back hostages, slaves, and quantities of the rest of the booty. At present, however, some of the chieftains there, after procuring the friendship of Caesar Augustus by sending embassies and by paying court to him, have not only dedicated offerings in the Capitol, but have also managed to make the whole of the island virtually Roman property. Further, they submit so easily to heavy duties, both on the exports from there to Celtica and on the imports from Celtica (these latter are ivory chains and necklaces, and amber-gems and glass vessels and other petty wares of that sort), that there is no need of garrisoning the island; for one legion, at the least, and some cavalry would be required in order to carry off tribute from them, and the expense of the army would offset the tribute-money; in fact, the duties must necessarily be lessened if tribute is imposed, and, at the same time, dangers be encountered, if force is applied.[8]

Britain in the Early First Century AD

Whilst the passage by Strabo provides us with a very interesting and illuminating account of Britain and its natives, it also provides us with clear indications as to the nature of the relationship which prevailed at that time between Rome and the British ruling classes. What makes the account more valuable is the fact that it is a rare contemporary comment on the situation in Britain which existed between the invasions of Caesar and Claudius. We should therefore seek to afford it a little more credibility than accounts written by later classical commentators, such as Suetonius or Cassius Dio.

Strabo clearly states that, by the time he penned his account of Britain, Rome was attracting considerable revenues from Britain by way of the imposition of import/export duties on trade goods which were being exchanged between Britain and the continent. He also tells us that the sight of a Briton in Rome by that time does not seem to be particularly uncommon and that diplomacy was by then well established between Britain and Rome. Certainly it would seem that Augustus had come to take a more pragmatic approach to the question of Britain, rather than seeking to subdue the island by force at this time. However, despite the fact that Suetonius tells us that Augustus had no plans to expand the borders of the empire, this does not mean that he never considered the idea of an invasion of Britain.

In his *Roman Histories*, Cassius Dio explains that around 34 BC Augustus, or Octavian as he was then known, was seeking to secure a prestigious victory, primarily in order to emulate his adoptive father, Caesar.[9] However, after advancing into Gaul Augustus was forced to abandon his plans in order to deal with uprisings in Pannonia and Dalmatia. Dio further explains that, in 27 BC, Augustus returned to Gaul with the intention of mounting an invasion of Britain.[10] Yet he was again deterred from launching the operation by unrest, this time amongst the Gauls. Dio also mentions that the Britons were indicating that they may have been willing to come to terms with him at this point.

The following year, Dio continues, Augustus was back in Gaul and once more preparing to invade Britain; it would appear that the Britons had failed to come to terms, as previously expected.[11] Nonetheless Augustus was again forced to abandon his plans as a further revolt had diverted him, this time by the Salassi, a tribe located principally in what is now the Italian Alps. It therefore seems that, from this point on, Augustus set aside his plans to invade and may well have eventually secured the terms he had been seeking from the Britons via diplomatic channels.

From what Strabo tells us of this time, it is clear that Rome eventually began to generate a healthy income from her associations with Britain. It would thus seem to make no sense at all to invest huge amounts of treasury money on another attempt to seize control of the island, even if, as Strabo rather optimistically suggests, control of Britain could be achieved by the deployment of a single legion and a force of cavalry. The truth of the matter seems to be that Augustus was clearly much better off by continuing to receive the revenue generated from the trade agreements he had forged with the islands, rather than taking the enormous risk of mounting another invasion. After all, even if we were to disregard the fiscal cost represented by the various wars that Augustus had needed to commit troops to, particularly against the German tribes, we must bear in mind that, by AD 9, he had suffered a huge depletion of military strength in Germany.

In this year Augustus lost an entire army, comprised of three legions and their attendant column under the command of Publius Quinctilius Varus, when the Cheruscan noble, Arminius, lured them into an ambush and slaughtered them almost to a man in the Teutoberger Forest. The disaster so traumatised Augustus that, in his account of Augustus' life, Suetonius begins by explaining that Varus nearly 'wrecked the empire'.[12] Suetonius continues by explaining that the defeat prompted Augustus to impose a number of emergency measures, including mounting night patrols of Rome to deter uprisings. Suetonius goes on to tell us that Augustus left his hair and beard untrimmed for months and took to beating his head off the doors around his palace while calling out: 'Quinctilius Varus, give me back my legions!' Varus by this time was beyond any capacity to obey his emperor, given that he had fallen on his own sword during the later stages of the battle. Apparently, his corpse was later burned and dismembered by the Germans who are then said to have sent his head to Rome where, arguably being afforded more honour than it was due, Varus' head was subsequently interred in the family vault.[13]

The accounts written by various classical historians indicate that, given the ongoing problems that Rome had with Germany during the early half of the first century AD, any further thoughts of another invasion of Britain would have been ill-advised. Augustus, Tiberius and Gaius (Caligula) all had their problems with Germany and it would only be the wildly unstable mind of Caligula which, as we shall discuss shortly, ever gave the idea any further serious thought.

Thus it was that the Catuvellauni were able to expand virtually unchecked, eventually coming to control a vast area which would seize control of the entire Trinovantean kingdom and then spread south across the Thames to take in much of the territory of Cantium (Kent). They would also seize the northern

Atrebatean seat of Calleva Atrebatum (Silchester). This last event appears to have taken place around AD 25, when Cunobelin's brother, Epaticcus, pushed south, taking the town of Calleva and then holding control of the northern part of the Atrebates' kingdom for around ten years. Then, upon the death of Epaticcus, control passed to Cunobelin's son, Caratacus.

The prelude to the Claudian invasion is best typified by the flight to Rome of a further two British rulers, Verica and Adminius. The first of these, Verica, ruled over that part of the territory of the Atrebates which had not initially fallen under the control of the Catuvellauni. His rule is thought to have begun by around AD 15, when he ousted his brother, Eppillus, to seize overall power over the tribe. However, his control of the Atrebates was soon to be continually eroded by the advance of the Catuvellauni into Atrebatean territory, first by Epaticcus and then by Caratacus. It would seem that it was the threat posed by the latter of the two which finally forced him to flee to Rome and approach Claudius for his support, shortly after he became emperor.

As far as we can gather from the available records, Verica's hurried departure to Rome is the last recorded instance of a British leader appealing directly to a Roman emperor for military support. However, it is the circumstances surrounding the departure of the ruler before him, Adminius, which is most interesting.

Adminius first appears in classical records in Suetonius' *The Twelve Caesars* and is described as being the son of Cunobelin, a king of Britain.[14] Adminius is believed to have controlled the kingdom of Cantium (Kent) and to have succeeded Eppillus (who had been installed as a tribal leader in Cantium after Verica had ousted him from his rulership over the Atrebates). It is unclear whether Eppillus exercised control over the entire tribal region of Cantium, ruling from Durobrivae (Rochester), or whether he was merely responsible for a specific region. In fact, putting aside the problem of Eppillus, attempting to follow the royal lines of succession for Cantium before this time becomes very problematic.

Whilst it is fairly certain is that Eppillus succeeded a king named Vosenios, prior to this very little is known. The only name we have of a tribal ruler reigning before Vosenios, and after the four kings of Cantium mentioned by Caesar, is Dumnovellaunus. However, this name is no longer thought to be linked to his Trinovantean namesake, and is now more widely regarded as a separate Cantiacan noble who may have been in power towards, or just after the end of, the first century BC. What is interesting about the Cantiaci is the fact that Caesar specifically names four kings of Cantium, namely: Cingetorix, Carvilius, Taximagulus and Segovax.[15] This may therefore indicate that the kingdom itself was split into sub-regions and ruled by local chieftains, who were possibly accountable to a supreme tribal council and ruler, rather like the system of government which was thought to have been employed by the Coritani, a tribe located in central Britain.

With regard to events just prior to the Claudian invasion, it is believed that Cunobelin appointed his son Adminius to take charge of Cantium, around AD 30. Moreover, distribution of coin finds issued by Cunobelin throughout the region indicate a strong likelihood that the old king was already exercising some form of control over Cantium, some time before he appointed what is thought to be his eldest son as an administrator.

Adminius has been connected to the name '*Amminus*', which is stamped on locally issued coin finds which are thought to have been minted at Durovernum Cantiacorum (Canterbury).[16] If we accept the connection of the two names we can therefore regard this as good evidence to demonstrate that he was, for a time at least, a well-established ruler, given that he was minting and issuing his own coinage. However, at some stage it would seem that Adminius incurred the displeasure of his father, Cunobelin, as we know that he was subsequently driven out of Britain by Cunobelin and that he then fled to the continent with a small band of loyal followers. Adminius then sought out the emperor, Caligula, who, in his characteristically eccentric and wildly unstable manner, promptly wrote a letter to the senate to inform them that he had in fact secured the surrender of the entire island.

As far as the available classical records are concerned, there are no further mentions of Adminius and we therefore have no way of saying conclusively what happened to him. It is possible that Tacitus' *Annals* for the years AD 37–47 may have clarified this for us, but these writings are lost to history and, for now at least, we are only able to speculate on what happened to him.

As for Caligula, his subsequent bizarre approach to his version of an invasion of Britain seemed more to be a spontaneous act and one which was prompted by the appearance of Adminius. It also seems to have been intended to humiliate and chide his troops for what Caligula perceived to be their past misdemeanours, rather than pose any serious threat to the Britons on the other side of the channel. Suetonius tells us that, having arrayed his artillery on the shoreline, Caligula ordered his troops to collect sea shells, which he described as the spoils of victory over the sea. He then commissioned the construction of a tall lighthouse to mark the occasion and awarded each of his troops four gold pieces. Having by then possibly alienated the greater part of his northern army, he turned his attentions to planning his Triumph which, if Suetonius' description is accurate, seems likely to have required the participation of Adminius and his entourage.

Salway suggests, and Manley agrees, that Caligula's attempt at an invasion of Britain may actually have been pre-planned, and that the failure of the operation may well have been due to the refusal of Caligula's troops to sail.[17] Because of this, Claudius may subsequently have been able to avail himself of the invasion plans which Caligula's staff had previously drawn up, thereby greatly assisting his own preparations. However, Suetonius' account of the episode seems more to imply that the expedition was prompted by the sudden appearance of Adminius in Caligula's camp, rather than there being any real intention on Caligula's part to mount a full-blown invasion of Britain.

If such were the case then it seems extremely doubtful that Claudius could have learned anything particularly valuable by way of consulting the records of Caligula's advanced preparations, as there seems to have been so little time available to facilitate the formulation of plans. Plans which would have needed to be extremely detailed, and which must have mostly been compiled by Caligula's generals as they made their way to the assembly point at Portus Itius (Boulogne) on the coast of the Fretum Gallicum (Straits of Dover). It is therefore doubtful that such detailed records ever existed. Certainly, a more spontaneous and wildly expensive act of folly on the part of Caligula seems to tie in better with what we know of his dangerously changeable character by this period in his life. Ultimately, it would be his unpredictable and often extremely cruel behaviour which would come to cost Caligula his life; he was assassinated just a few short months after his faux invasion of Britain.

If Caligula's attempt at invasion was nothing more than a flamboyant exercise of an abuse of power, however, the next attempt at a Roman invasion of Britain would see success finally secured by a man whose ascent to power was no less than remarkable.

Claudius – Conqueror of Britain

That Claudius ever became emperor of Rome at all is extraordinary, to say the least.

He was born on 1 August 10 BC to Drusus, son of the empress Livia, and Antonia, daughter to Mark Anthony. He was also brother to Livilla and Germanicus, the much loved hero of the Rhine campaigns. However, even from his earliest years it seems that Claudius was a source of acute embarrassment to his illustrious family, by virtue of the various infirmities he was beset with since birth. From the descriptions which have been provided by such classical historians as Suetonius, we know that Claudius was born with a club foot and may possibly have suffered from cerebral palsy, ultimately giving rise to the now familiar modern theatrical portrayals of a man who was burdened by impaired speech, a shuffling gait and involuntary twitches and spasms.[18]

For much of his life, Claudius was widely regarded by his family as being somewhat dull witted. Conversely, he is recorded as being a keen scholar who is credited with publishing various academic titles and an autobiography, none of which have survived the passage of time. Nevertheless, this clear demonstration of his intellectual capability does not seem to have stopped his family from constantly agonising as to whether or not Claudius should have been allowed to undertake any public duties, or be given any public offices. So low was his own mother's view of Claudius that she is reported to have referred to him as 'a monster of a man, not finished but merely begun by Dame Nature'.[19]

Antonia's view may have been shared by many others in her family, despite this Claudius seems to have won a limited degree of support from Augustus who, while clearly reluctant to place Claudius in any position which may cause both him and the Imperial family any public embarrassment, recognised Claudius' intellectual qualities. This seems to be well qualified by the account given of Claudius' early life by Suetonius, as he quotes the letters sent by Augustus to Claudius' grandmother, Livia, posing the question of what to do about him.

Certainly the view which was expressed by Augustus – that Claudius would be subjected to ridicule – proved to be a justifiable concern: as he grew older he was constantly abused and ridiculed by both family members and court servants alike. On the other hand, even though such behaviour appears to have been common in court circles, Claudius seems to have been widely held in some high regard by both individuals and civic bodies outside of the palace. Therefore, given the regard in which Claudius was actually held by the city populace overall, this may perhaps indicate that the concerns expressed by Augustus were not as justified as they were originally perceived to be.

Claudius was in fact given his first taste of a major public office under the reign of his nephew Caligula. This would prove to be a strange and dangerous time for Claudius, given that the newfound power and responsibility that he had acquired under Caligula, including a term in the consulship, could have been curtailed instantly if the notoriously unstable Caligula had decided, for whatever reason, that Claudius needed to die. It is no small wonder then that Claudius is widely held to have played up to the common perception that he was a harmless fool who posed no threat, which was a tactic he appears to have employed simply in order to stay alive.

On 24 January AD 41, after the assassination of Caligula by a tribune of the Praetorian Guard, Claudius is said to have fled in terror for his life; hiding behind a curtain in the palace where he was later discovered by a palace guard. He then seems to have spent the next twenty-four hours or so within the camp of the Praetorian Guards, while the issue of whether to revert back to the Republican system of rule was considered by the senate. Eventually, the public and the troops got their way and Claudius, by then 50 years old, was declared emperor.

Though it appears that Claudius was ultimately a popular emperor, it also seems apparent that the first years of his reign were unremarkable and, as such, Claudius needed an achievement of note in order to endear himself further and secure his reign. That opportunity arose in AD 43 when Suetonius records that

Britain was 'in a state of rebellion because of the refusal to return certain desert-ers'.[20] Whilst the details are not clear, this could be held to mean that Caratacus and Togodumnus were pressing Rome to return their brother Adminius and perhaps also the other exile, Verica of the Atrebates. Certainly, the remark also suggests that both of the exiles were alive and perhaps resident in Rome at the time the demand was made.

It seems unlikely, however, that such demands by what would clearly be seen as upstart barbarians would be taken seriously, unless they were being backed up by an effective threat. After all, Britain could never have been regarded as posing a serious military threat to Rome. It does not therefore require a great stretch of the imagination to arrive at the conclusion that the Britons could instead have backed up their demands by threatening to withdraw from trading agreements, thereby posing a far more worrying threat to the substantial revenues which Rome was receiving via their trade links with Britain. Consequently, as well as having a clear political agenda for invading Britain, Claudius may well have had a valid strategic reason to act, by virtue of the fact that the Britons were threatening to shut down a vital source of income for the Imperial treasury and also to halt the supply of essential trade and industrial goods, such as metals and cereal crops, until such time as their demands were met.

Faced with such an option, Claudius would have needed to take urgent action. So, as the Roman generals drew up their plans for invasion, Britain awaited its fate in ignorance of what was to come.

Notes
1 B. Cunliffe (1974), p. 61
2 Julius Caesar, *The Gallic Wars – Book V*, Chapter XXI
3 B. Cunliffe (1974), p. 83
4 Caesar Augustus, *Res Gestae Divi Augusti*, or *The Deeds of the Divine Augustus*
5 Ibid., Part VI, Chapter XXXII
6 Suetonius, *The Twelve Caesars – The Life of Augustus*, Chapter XXI
7 Julius Caesar, *The Gallic Wars – Book V*, Chapter XIII
8 Strabo, *Geography – Book IV*, Chapter V
9 Cassius Dio, *Roman Histories – Book 49*, Chap 38
10 Ibid., *Book 53*, Chap 22
11 Ibid., *Book 53*, Chap 25
12 Suetonius, *The Twelve Caesars – Life of Augustus*, Chapter XXIII
13 Velleius Paterculus, *The Roman History – Book II*, Chapters CXVII–CXIX
14 Suetonius, *The Twelve Caesars – Gaius (Caligula)*, Chapter XXXXIV
15 Julius Caesar, *The Gallic Wars – Book V*, Chapter XXII
16 D.F. Allen (1976)
17 Salway (1981), p. 61; Manley (2002), p. 82
18 Potter (2007), p. 64
19 Suetonius, *The Twelve Caesars – The Life of Claudius*, Chapter III
20 Ibid., Chapter XVII

II

The Claudian Invasion –
A Perspective

5

ARMIES & GENERALS

To Raise an Invasion Army

By taking the decision to invade Britain, Claudius and his advisors would have been embarking on a course of action which would not have been undertaken lightly. It therefore also seems a certainty that they would have harboured no doubts about the complexities of just what they were setting out to achieve. They would have been fully aware that this would be an objective which could not be accomplished by employing the same rash and spontaneous efforts made by Caligula. Furthermore, had they studied the various surviving records of Caesar's ill-fated raids, which they must surely have done in great detail, they would also have realised that even the ability to land a Roman army on British soil was, on it's own, still no guarantee of success. Particularly if that capability was not supported by effective forward planning.

It must have been clear to the architects of the Claudian invasion plan that if the preparations to invade were deficient in just one of several key elements, then the enterprise was likely to fail. In addition, given that one of the objectives of the invasion was to provide Claudius with what would effectively be a major public-ity coup, then the knock-on effect of such a failure on Claudius' reign could have been disastrous. As a result, any such failure was not an option.

Although no historical records survive to offer us a definitive idea of exactly when this planning started, the sheer scale of the preparation required must at least provide us with a compelling argument to say that work must have begun very early on in Claudius' reign. After all, we need only look at the failure of Julius Caesar to subdue the south-east corner of Britain over two campaigning seasons. This, coupled with the evidence of his consistent failure to plan in more detail and learn from his previous mistakes, makes it obvious a more meticulous approach to the preparation was required in order to make the venture a success.

The argument for a long planning phase is also supported by the fact that, plans set down on paper aside, the sheer task of assembling sufficient numbers of troops, shipping and supplies in one place is not something which could have been achieved very quickly. As we will examine later in this work, the amount of grain which would be needed to feed the men and animals of the invasion force alone could not have been procured and then distributed without first undertaking lengthy preparations for its collection and storage. The sheer magnitude of what was being proposed meant that, if they were to produce a viable invasion plan, the Claudian planners would also need to give careful consideration to many other different questions and problems, none of which were likely to have 'quick fix' solutions.

First of all, they would need to list the objectives they wished to achieve, both in the early phases of the invasion and then onwards to the prime objective, whilst at the same time determining the overall time they needed to allow in order to achieve all of their objectives. There could be no repeats of Caesar's poor planning: sailing too late in the year and then running out of campaigning time as the change of seasonal sailing conditions called an effective halt to any further campaigning and forced a withdrawal. However, the Claudian planners also needed to be mindful of the fact that by sailing too early in the year, they again ran the increased risk of encountering powerful storms which could bring about the destruction of the invasion force at sea, before it even got the chance to drop anchor off the shores of Britain.

In addition, whilst setting out those objectives the planners would have needed to carefully consider what size of army would be required for the task. They would then need to determine where they should sail from and land; how many ships it would take to transport such an army; and how that army would then be provisioned. Furthermore, once the army had landed and engaged the enemy, the planners would have to decide how best that army could receive ongoing logistical support, in order to sustain its advance throughout the early phases and then on towards its final objective.

Before any army could be shipped out to assault Britain, all of these questions would need to have been given detailed consideration. However, what would also have been equally important to the success of the plan would be to choose the right army. The Roman army was made up of both legions, which were effectively heavy infantry regiments, and a wealth of auxiliary units, which provided anything from heavy cavalry capabilities to lightly armed skirmishing troops. Combined together, the legions and auxiliaries were capable of forming large and versatile battle groups. This therefore meant not only deciding on the numerical strength of the army, but also what specialisms and operational experience would be advantageous within the various units in order for them to be the most effective choices. It would then need to be identified where the various units could be drawn from. However, this would need to be done without compromising Roman interests or destabilising control of the local populace within the region where they were stationed. Any suggestion that either or both may happen may then have required the planners to arrange for their immediate replacement by a new unit, which only added to the myriad practical problems which would have to be overcome.

Once the decision had been made on which units would make up the invasion force, the Claudian planners would then need to calculate how long it would take to assemble these men at the port of embarkation. Finally, once all of these decisions had been made, perhaps the most crucial aspect to all of this planning would be the choices as to who would be the invasion commanders. These would be the men with proven campaigning ability and loyalty to their emperor, who were perceived as being the most trusted to physically assemble and then lead such a large army. These men would also be those deemed to be most capable of effectively implementing the invasion plans. They would not only need to be capable of working effectively within the parameters of the overall plan, but would also need to be capable of implementing the ongoing adaptation of the overall campaign strategy, as local conditions dictated.

Later chapters of this book will examine the various questions posed by the invasion plan itself. Given their obvious importance to the successful outcome of the campaign, we will also discuss the various Roman army units which we can say were involved in the invasion. Closer examination of those units will be dealt with later in this chapter. However, it seems more appropriate at this point to first continue with a consideration of the various commanders we can still identify, who were responsible for both overall control of the invasion force and of a number of its elements.

Claudius' General – Aulus Plautius

Very little is known about the early years of the man who would come to lead Claudius' great army across the sea to Britain. Therefore, whilst it is possible to discuss Plautius' family connections with some degree of confidence, the ability to give a definitive account of his early life has now effectively been denied by the passage of time. Yet the capability to reconstruct a brief and speculative timeline for his very early career is possible, given what we do know of his later career and the structure of the *cursus honorum*, or 'course of honours.' This is the list of the sequence of offices through which a Roman political candidate must rise to achieve high office.

Each office carried its own set of responsibilities and had a minimum age at which appointment to that particular office could be achieved. However, it should be borne in mind that the minimum ages for progress through the offices differed between the Republican period and the Imperial period, given that the minimum ages in the Republic were older than those set out in the Imperial period. (See Appendix E.)

The branch of the Plautii to which Aulus Plautius belonged is believed to have hailed from Trebula Suffenas. This was a Sabine town, the modern location of which is unclear, although there are several suggestions for this. It seems likely that he was descended from an influential Plebeian family that boasted not only of strong connections to powerful families within the elite of Roman society, but also held the favour and support of the Imperial family. In fact, those Imperial connections seem already to have been firmly established by the time Augustus had founded the first Imperial line, the Julio–Claudian dynasty.

Birley suggests that Plautius was probably born in the year 5 BC.[1] The suggestion is based on a reliance of the supposition that Plautius is the 'Aulus, the Quaestor of Tiberius', who is credited with writing down the text of the '*Senatus Consultum de Cn. Pisone patre*'. The work itself is precisely dateable as it records a date given for the creation of the document by the emperor Tiberius as being 'on the fourth day before the Ides of December in the consulship of [Marcus Aurelius] Cotta [Maximus Messalinus] and [Marcus Valerius] Messalla [Barbatus Messalinus]'. This therefore provides us with a modern calendar date of 10 December AD 20. Consequently, if we subtract the minimum age for an Imperial quaestor from this date, we arrive at the suggested year of birth: 5 BC. The suggestion of this date does seem to stand further scrutiny, given that it is known that Plautius served as a praetor in AD 26 and later became a suffect consul in AD 29, succeeding Caius Fufius Geminus as first consul in July of that year. Had Plautius indeed been born in 5 BC he would, at the time he was appointed, have been eligible for both posts. This was by virtue of the fact that he had by then only just attained the minimum age required to allow his nomination and subsequent election to the office in question.

Working forward from this birth date, we are therefore also able to surmise that Plautius would have become eligible for the first appointment on the list, that of vigintivir, a minor magistrate, by around AD 13–14. He would then have become eligible to hold the office of military tribune by AD 15 which, in very broad terms, equated to a junior staff officer within a legion. There were six tribune posts to each legion, each of which varied in seniority (see Appendix F). Birley suggests that, because of the probable dates associated with Plautius' progress through the *cursus honorum*, this could mean that he saw service as a military tribune under Germanicus in Germany around that time, or with his wife's uncle, Lucius Pomponius Flaccus, in Moesia.

If Plautius had attained the respective posts at the ages suggested, then it is clear that Plautius was a very capable and ambitious young man who was able to advance through the posts of the *cursus honorum* at the earliest opportunities available to him. It would also indicate that he was well favoured and well connected. After all, attaining the minimum age for election to a particular position was not, on its own, any guarantee that the candidate would succeed to the post. His appointment also depended on the support of others, from all political levels.

In 2 BC Marcus Plautius Silvanus, first cousin to Plautius' father, shared the consulship with Augustus. He also boasted an impressive military record, including winning the *ornamenta triumphalia*; granting him the right to wear

Triumphal regalia whilst being allowed the high honour of a public parade, or Triumph, through Rome. These honours were granted to an individual to celebrate an important military victory under his command.[2] His mother, Urgulania, was also a close friend to a woman who is widely regarded as one of the most powerful and formidable women in Roman history, the empress Livia, wife to Augustus. However the connections of this branch of the Plautii to the Imperial family were not entirely without their darker moments. Urgulania's daughter, Plautia Urgulanilla, became the first wife of the future emperor, Claudius.[3] However, the marriage ended in divorce when she was suspected of murder and accused of adultery.[4] This had been preceded in about AD 24 by a scandal which culminated in the assisted suicide of her brother, Silvanus.

Tacitus explains that Silvanus murdered his wife, Apronia, by hurling her out of a window.[5] He then claimed ignorance of the act, explaining that it must have been a suicide which happened while he was sleeping. The emperor Tiberius personally investigated the matter and discovered obvious signs of a struggle in the bed chamber at the couple's home. He then committed the matter to the senate for trial. Whilst awaiting trial, the hapless Silvanus was sent a dagger by Urgulania, his grandmother. However, Tacitus explains that Silvanus' own attempts to end his life were to prove unsuccessful and rather than go against what appear to be the wishes of the Imperial family, we are told that he: 'had his veins opened.'

Shortly after this unfortunate episode, Silvanus' first wife, Numantina, was acquitted of driving her husband mad by the use of witchcraft, or as Tacitus describes it: 'by incantations and philtres.' Nevertheless, these unfortunate episodes did not prove harmful to the family's relationship with the Imperial family and court in the long term and Aulus Plautius subsequently married Pomponia Graecina, whose uncle, the aforementioned Lucius Pomponius Flaccus, was a favourite of Tiberius'. Pomponia also counted Tiberius' granddaughter, Julia, as a personal friend.

After his term as suffect consul in AD 29, Aulus Plautius eventually rose to become a provincial governor, shortly after Claudius became emperor. The available evidence strongly suggests that the province in question was Pannonia.[6] This placed him in precisely the right location to win the gratitude and trust of the new emperor when, in AD 42, he was involved in putting down a revolt aimed at toppling Claudius which was led by Lucius Arruntius Camillus Scribonianus, who was a former second consul (AD 32) and who was at that time of the revolt the governor of the neighbouring province, Dalmatia. Such a demonstration of loyalty and military prowess, along with his previous campaign record and the heavyweight family connections that he could boast of, would have no doubt have had a tremendous influence in leading Claudius to decide to appoint Aulus Plautius as the general who would head the command team which would lead the invasion army to Britain.

However, Claudius would need to support Plautius with the right men to form that team and it is they who we shall look at next.

Gnaeus Sentius Saturninus – Some Brief Notes

In the context of the Claudian invasion of Britain there is only one known historical text which links Gnaeus Sentius Saturninus to the event. The intriguing reference is made in the *Breviarium Historiae Romanae* by the fourth century Roman historian Eutropius, and is set down thus: Claudius waged war on the Britons (a country) where no Romans had set foot since the days of C. Caesar and when it had been vanquished by Cn. Sentius and A. Plautius, distinguished members of noble families he held a magnificent triumph.'[7] The name 'Cn. Sentius' refers only to the *praenomen* and *nomen* of the individual – his given name and his *gens* – which identified his tribal origin. However, for the purpose of this work we will refer to him by his *cognomen* – a form of nickname – Saturninus.

Eutropius' mention of Saturninus' involvement in the invasion clearly does not accord with what Dio has to say concerning the key Roman figures in the invasion, indeed he is not even mentioned by Dio as being involved. Nevertheless, this single mention has produced a number of papers over past years which seek to suggest what role, if any, Saturninus played in the invasion.

Saturninus was himself the son of an earlier Gnaeus Sentius Saturninus, who was second consul in AD 4 serving alongside Sextus Aelius Catus. Saturninus also held the governorship of the province of Syria in AD 19. Black suggests that the younger Saturninus' role in the invasion was a significant one.[8] However, this view was very quickly refuted in a paper by Professor Michael Fulford and Dr Sheppard Frere, who offered the alternative argument that Saturninus was actually responsible for the reorganisation of the Atrebates tribe after the invasion.

Black commenced his argument by referring to the discovery of a *vadimonium*, or contract, from Pompeii. This document was inscribed on a wax tablet and attested that it had been drawn up: 'In the Forum of Augustus, in front of the triumphal statue of Cn Sentius Saturninus.' Black then made reference to Dio's comments concerning Claudius' granting of *ornamenta triumphalia* to the senators who took part in the campaign in Britain, suggesting that this, combined with the reference by Eutropius, confirmed Saturninus' involvement in the campaign.[9]

Yet within the quoted excerpt, Dio also mentions that the honour was not only reserved for ex-consuls 'but the rest as well'. One therefore surely has to take into consideration the point that, with others being granted such honours, is this evidence sufficient to compel us to conclude that Saturninus did in fact hold a key position in the hierarchy of the invasion staff? Could it not therefore also be argued that Saturninus had held a lesser role and had in fact been honoured for merely being part of the larger staff entourage to Plautius? Although we have taken the opportunity to briefly consider the question of Saturninus' role in the invasion, it is not a question which this work purports to provide a definitive answer to – given that the wider aim of this work is to focus more on the mechanics of the operation.

Before dispensing with this subject, it is perhaps worthy of one final thought. In AD 41, at the time Caligula was assassinated, Saturninus held the position of consul. At the end of *Book LIX* of *The Roman Histories*, Chapter XXX, Cassius Dio mentions that after Caligula was killed, the senate and consuls furiously debated what would happen next in terms of how the empire would be governed. Dio tells us:

> All those who in any way acknowledged the authority of the senate, were true to their oaths and became quiet. While the scenes just described were being enacted around Gaius, the consuls, Sentius and Secundus, immediately transferred the funds from the treasuries to the Capitol. They stationed most of the senators and plenty of soldiers as guards over it to prevent any plundering from being done by the populace. So these men together with the prefects and the followers of Sabinus and Chaerea were deliberating what should be done.

The account then becomes more interesting at the beginning of *Book LX* when Dio adds the following commentary:

> Claudius became emperor on this wise. After the murder of Gaius the consuls despatched guards to every part of the city and convened the senate on the Capitol, where many and diverse opinions were expressed; for some favoured a democracy, some a monarchy, and some were for choosing one man, and some another. In consequence they spent the rest of the day and the whole night without accomplishing anything. Meanwhile some soldiers who had entered the palace for the purpose of plundering found Claudius hidden away in a dark corner somewhere. He had been with Gaius when he came out of the theatre, and now, fearing the tumult, was crouching down out of the way. At first the soldiers, supposing that he was some one else or perhaps had something worth taking, dragged him forth; and then, on recognizing him, they hailed him emperor and conducted him to the camp. Afterwards they together with their comrades entrusted to him the supreme power, inasmuch as he was of the imperial family and was regarded as suitable.
>
> In vain he drew back and remonstrated; for the more he attempted to avoid the honour and to resist, the more strongly did the soldiers in their turn insist upon not accepting an emperor appointed by others but upon giving one themselves to the whole world. Hence he yielded, albeit with apparent reluctance.
>
> The consuls for a time sent tribunes and others forbidding him to do anything of the sort, but to submit to the authority of the people and of the senate and of the laws; when, however, the soldiers who were with them deserted them, then at last they, too, yielded and voted him all the remaining prerogatives pertaining to the sovereignty.[10]

What becomes abundantly clear from this commentary is that, whilst the military were certain that Claudius should succeed as emperor, the senate and consuls

were engaged in a heated debate over whether there should be another individual allowed to succeed to power, or even whether Rome would be better
off becoming a republic once more. There can be no doubt from Dio's account
that Saturninus and his fellow consul were not over-enamoured with the idea of
replacing one emperor with another, and they were both seemingly very active in
trying to prevent Claudius' accession.

On that basis, it is perhaps therefore worth asking the question: why should
Claudius want to place a man, who had clearly been so active in attempting to
deny him power, in a key role within a venture which was crucial to his future
survival as emperor?

Vespasian – An Emperor in Waiting

Of those who are known to have taken part in the Claudian invasion of Britain,
it is the story of the life of Vespasian which is perhaps the most fascinating. Rising
from more humble beginnings, Titus Flavius Vespasianus would first forge a reputation as a formidable military commander before going on to become emperor,
founding the Flavian dynasty and ruling for ten years until his death in June AD 79.
However, much as it is tempting to provide a brief retelling of Vespasian's life in
full, this work will only concern itself with providing a short account of his early
years, up to his role in the Claudian invasion of Britain.

In his account of Vespasian's life in *The Twelve Caesars*, Suetonius makes an
early reference to Vespasian's background by remarking thus of his family origins: '…They [the Flavians] were admittedly an obscure family, none of whose
members ever enjoyed high office …' Vespasian was born in Falacrina, near the
town of Reate in the Sabine region of Italy, on 17 November AD 9. He was
the son of Flavius Sabinus, a tax collector, and Vespasia Polla, who was sister to
a senator. Vespasian had one elder brother, Sabinus, whom we shall hear more
of later. Suetonius records that Vespasian's grandfather, Titus Flavius Petro, was
a centurion or volunteer reservist who fought in the army of Gnaeus Pompey
at the battle of Pharsalus. Petro survived the battle and returned home with
an honourable discharge and a free pardon. He subsequently set himself up
in business as a tax collector, which then appears to have become the family's
chief occupation.

Despite what one would think of as being a somewhat unpopular nature
of business, Suetonius records that Vespasian's father was actually honoured via
the erection of statues in various cities in the province of Asia where he had
operated. It is said that they were inscribed as being dedicated 'to an honest
tax gatherer'. Perhaps this token of open public esteem is a good indication
that, despite the nature of the work involved, Sabinus was in fact an honourable
and respectable man and one who had not felt tempted by the opportunity

to indulge in the corruption that was so evident in the Roman establishment, either by petty official or by those who held higher office.

After retiring from this role, Sabinus became a money lender to the Helvetii tribe, which would be his last position before he died, leaving Vespasia Polla to bring up their two sons. However, the boys' mother was from a good family in Nursia and her father, Vespasius Pollio, had a solid military background – previously holding three colonelcies and the position of Praefectus Castrorum, or camp prefect. It therefore seems feasible to assume that the grandfather's influence, along with the successful political career of their uncle, had a defining effect on the upbringing of the two boys.

Vespasian himself was brought up on the estate of his paternal grandmother, Tertulla. However, it would be some time before the young Vespasian harboured any ambitions to follow his older brother Sabinus into the senate. A move which only eventually came to pass after he was driven to it by his mother, who goaded him into becoming a candidate by effectively playing on sibling rivalries and regularly referring to Vespasian as 'your brother's footman'.

Having commenced the ascent of the *cursus honorum* with a posting as a military tribune in Thrace, there then followed a posting to Crete and Cyrenaica as a quaestor. After struggling to win an aedileship, Vespasian subsequently achieved a praetorship at the first attempt, probably in either 39 or AD 40. However, the posting which would eventually ensure his involvement in the invasion of Britain came upon Claudius' accession in AD 41, when the new emperor's secretary of state, Narcissus, favoured Vespasian by securing him the command of Legio II Augusta. By this time the legion were operating in the upper Rhine region. Vespasian remained in command of the legion when it was subsequently despatched to take part in the invasion of Britain.

Vespasian's career as a legion commander, or legate, has the distinction of being recorded by more sources than any other legion legate to serve in Britain.[11] It would be Vespasian's service in Britain to which the likes of Dio, Josephus and Tacitus would make the most favourable of references, given that he was at some point hailed by them all as a mighty conqueror and one who owed his reputation chiefly to his actions on campaign in Britain. Of those accounts, it is the short reference provided by Josephus which perhaps goes beyond the boundaries of credibility and instead steps into those of outright flattery, given that he effectively credits the conquest of Britain to Vespasian himself. Josephus tells us: 'By force of arms he had added Britain, till then unknown, to the empire, so enabling Nero's father Claudius, who had not lifted a finger himself, to celebrate a triumph.'[12]

Without doubt, as we shall discuss later, Vespasian did wage a very effective campaign along the south coast which contributed greatly to the overall success of the opening phases of the invasion. But to attribute the entire conquest of Britain to him by force of arms is evidently over-generous. Although for modern readers to expect Josephus to write from an objective point of view about the achievements of Vespasian is also perhaps a little unrealistic on our part. After all, it was Vespasian to whom Josephus owed his very life and his subsequent comfortable existence in Rome. Prior to his association with the future emperor, Josephus was in fact an enemy of Rome and was active as a regional commander during the Jewish revolt in Judea. In AD 67 he was eventually captured by Vespasian at the 47-day-long siege of Jotapata, which is now the town of Yodfat, located in Lower Galilee, Israel. His release and subsequent grant of Roman citizenship arose directly from his personal prediction to Vespasian that he would soon become emperor. The fascinated, if perhaps a little perplexed, Vespasian subsequently kept this unlikely prophet under comfortable arrest conditions for the next two years until, as predicted, he was proclaimed emperor in AD 69.

However, particularly in the accounts of his later life and career, Vespasian always seems to come across as a very human and personable kind of man. This sits admirably with his tough, no-nonsense physical image, a strong sense of which has been preserved in his surviving sculptures. Vespasian's facial features are instantly recognisable and it seems fitting perhaps to complete this account of the man with one last reference, again by Suetonius, which refers both to his physical appearance and the more genial aspect of his persona, even after becoming the emperor of Rome: 'Vespasian was square bodied, with strong, well-proportioned limbs, but always wore a strained look on his face; so that once, when he asked a well known wit: "Why not make a joke about me?" The answer came: "I will, when you have finished relieving yourself".'[13]

Other Known Legates of the Invasion Army

Whilst it is possible to say with certainty that Vespasian was the legate of II Augusta, no such certainty can be credited to the actual role of his brother, Sabinus, in the Claudian invasion. Though we are not able to place him in command of a particular legion, it is however possible to establish from the description of the invasion which Cassius Dio has handed down to us that Sabinus was more than likely a legate with command of one of the invading legions.

Other than that which we have already mentioned concerning the early lives of the two Flavian brothers, there is not a great deal more that can usefully be added concerning Sabinus' career prior to becoming involved in the invasion. Nevertheless, what little we can add does provide us with some faint shadow of what manner of man he used to be.

Sabinus was born in AD 6 and was murdered in Rome in December AD 69 by soldiers supporting the then emperor, Vitellius. Whilst he was in Rome acting as Vespasian's representative in negotiations to persuade Vitellius to abdicate, Sabinus had been seized after a siege on the Capitoline Hill. Having captured

Sabinus, the soldiers publicly hacked him to death and decapitated him whilst Vitellius looked on. However, in describing the act of his murder and then providing an obituary for Sabinus, it is Tacitus who gives us some sense of the life and qualities of Sabinus:

> Thus died a man who was far from being despicable. He had served the state for thirty-five years, winning distinction in both civil and military life. His upright char-acter and justice were above criticism; but he talked too easily. This was the only thing that mischievous gossip could say against him in the seven years during which he governed Moesia or in the twelve years while he was prefect of the city. At the end of his life some thought that he lacked energy, many believed him moderate and desirous of sparing the blood of his fellow-citizens. In any case all agree that up to the time that Vespasian became emperor the reputation of the house depended on Sabinus.[14]

Gnaeus Hosidius Geta is also one of the positively identifiable legates mentioned in the classical texts recording the invasion. His career prior to this point is not well attested, although overall the quantity of information that is available is more or less comparable to that which is available for Sabinus.

It is clear that Geta held the position of praetor sometime prior to AD 42. In addition, he does appear in the historical record for that year when Cassius Dio makes mention of his involvement in operations in Mauretania, which had been commenced by his predecessor, Gaius Suetonius Paulinus, the man who later, as governor of Britain in AD 61, put down the revolt by Queen Boudica of the Iceni. Dio tells us that:

> The next year the same Moors again made war and were subdued. Suetonius Paulinus, one of the ex-praetors, overran their country in turn as far as Mount Atlas, and after him Gnaeus Hosidius Geta, a man of the same rank, made a campaign, marching at once against their general Salabus and defeating him on two different occasions.[15]

The next significant mention for Geta then appears in Dio's account of the inva-sion of Britain, the detail of which will be dealt with later on in this work.

Birley mentions that the Hosidii clan were likely to be of the Patrician class and that their home town was Histonium, which is now the small town of Vasto, located on the Adriatic coast of central Italy.[16] Unfortunately, as with Sabinus, it is not possible to conclusively link Geta with any of the legions which participated in the invasion. Therefore, when discussing the legions involved in the invasion, any connections which may subsequently be made concerning Sabinus and Geta to a particular legion would be purely speculative.

The last of those nobles which we can positively link to the invasion army is perhaps the most obscure and most often overlooked of all. In the direct context of the invasion he appears only in the account provided by Suetonius, within his commentary on the life of Claudius.[17] Marcus Licinius Crassus Frugi is described by Suetonius as one of the campaign generals who, having won Triumphal regalia in Britain, marched behind the Empress Messalina's carriage in Claudius' British Triumph. Frugi, we are told, did not wear a purple-trimmed toga as did the other generals because he had previously earned the same honour. He therefore wore 'a palm embroidered tunic and rode a caparisoned charger'. There is little else we can say about Frugi's life. As his name suggests, he was the adoptive great-grandson of the triumvir Marcus Licinius Crassus. Having served as a praetor, Frugi became consul in AD 27 alongside Lucius Calpurnius Piso, during the reign of Tiberius.

In the part of his work which discusses Pagan cemeteries, Lanciani tells us that Frugi was also a governor of Mauretania and was married to Scribonia, with whom he had three sons.[18] However, despite having so distinguished a background, Lanciani laments the fortunes of the family and quotes Seneca as saying that Frugi was 'stupid enough to be made emperor'. This appears to be a passing reference to Frugi's unwise decision to name his eldest son Pompeius Magnus, after his maternal grandfather. This was a move which first excited the resentment of Caligula who subsequently had the overtly pretentious name changed in return for the boy's, and probably Frugi's, life. However, his standing with Claudius was high and, as a wedding present, Claudius restored the boy's name upon his marriage to his daughter, Antonia. The high regard in which Claudius held Pompeius again attracted the attentions and then ultimately the deadly jealousy of Empress Messalina, which culminated in her persuading Claudius to execute not only the hapless Pompeius in the spring of AD 47, but also his father and mother. Lanciani concludes his account of the family with a list of further misfortunes which led, perhaps with some inevitability, to the execution of the remaining two sons.

Legio II Augusta

As previously mentioned in the section dealing with Vespasian, it is well attested that Legio II Augusta was based in Germania Superior (upper Germany) immediately prior to the invasion. At that time, the legion was based on a major crossing point of the Rhine at Argentoratum (Strasbourg, France). Prior to this, during the early years of Augustus' reign, the legion was based further north, again on the Rhine and close to Mogontiacum (Mainz, Germany).

The history of the legion prior to their reconstitution under Augustus is not so clear, however. It is possible that the original formation was raised around 43 BC by Augustus, or Octavian as he was then known, and Gaius Vibius Pansa. The legion was believed to have been referred to as II Sabina, in recognition of the region from which the troops were originally recruited. It is known that this legion took part in battles against the forces of Mark Anthony and later, when Anthony had formed the second triumvirate with Octavian and Marcus Aemilius Lepidus, it took part in the decisive action at Philippi in eastern Macedonia in 42 BC. Here, two of Caesar's assassins, Marcus Junius Brutus and Gaius Cassius Longinus, were defeated. Beyond this period it has been suggested that the unit was known as II Gallica; if this is correct then this would place it as operating in Gaul, prior to AD 30. The Triumphal Arch of Augustas, which stands in the Roman town of Arausio (now modern Orange in France), records that veterans of the legion were given land and settled there.

In 27 BC Augustus was granted powers by the senate which, amongst other things, allowed him to carry out sweeping military reforms. Augustus subsequently reconstituted the legions and arising from this reorganisation of the army were three newly formed legions, II, III and VIII, all of which carried the title 'Augusta' and whose emblem was the Capricorn, Augustus' birth sign. Legio II Augusta also later used a Pegasus and the figure of the god Mars as unit emblems. However, it is uncertain when these additional emblems were adopted.

At the time Augustus had reorganised the structure of the army, the legion was based in the province of Hispania Tarraconensis, which is now roughly the area of northern Spain and Portugal. They subsequently campaigned in Augustus' war against the Cantabrians, which was a major campaign that saw the involvement of several other legions and which lasted for around twelve years, between 25–13 BC. The legion then remained in the region until they were redeployed to Germania Superior.

It is likely that the legion were sent to Mogontiacum directly in response to the loss of the three legions under Varus in AD 9. They then took part in Germanicus' campaigns against the German tribes, between the years AD 14–16, before moving to their new home at Argentoratum. It is from there that the legion marched to the invasion point of embarkation at Portus Itius, on the coast of Northern Gaul.

Legio IX Hispana

As one of the oldest legions in the Roman army, IX Hispana was already stationed in Gaul at the time Julius Caesar became governor in 58 BC. Caesar first mentions the legion directly in his descriptions of his early campaigns against the Gauls in 57 BC. In this part of his account, Caesar describes the legion's part in the rout of the Gaulish contingent of the Atrebates tribe, whilst supported by Legio X.[19] Caesar again mentions the legion in his account of the campaigns against the Bellovaci and other allied tribes in 52 BC.[20] Caesar's initial description of the units he was to use in the action related to the VII, VIII and IX legions, which he refers to as: 'Three veteran legions of exceptional valour …'

In 49 BC, after the legion had been posted to Hispania, Caesar again called on their services and they took part in the battle of Ilerda, against the forces of Caesar's great rival and one time fellow triumvir, Gnaeus Pompey (Magnus). The legion was subsequently posted to Dyrrhachium in Macedonia around 48 BC where they suffered heavy losses in engagements around the besieged town with Pompey's forces. What was left of the legion then formed up with the VIII legion and took part in the battle of Pharsalus in August of that year. This was the battle which finally saw the defeat of Pompey, prompting him to flee to Egypt and meet with his ignominious end at the hands of the young pharaoh, Ptolemy XIII.

The IX Hispana then took part in Caesar's African campaigns, and those members of the legion who had survived these campaigns were subsequently sent back to Italy, settled and provided with pensions. However, the disbandment was not to last long and the legion was reformed in 41 BC by Octavian, who used them to break Sextus Pompeius' occupation of Sicily. The legion remained under Octavian's control and eventually saw action against the forces of Mark Anthony at the battle of Actium, which took place on the Ionian Sea near the Greek town of the same name on 2 September 31 BC. Subsequently, the legion returned to Spain and was also one of the units engaged in the aforementioned war against the Cantabrians. It was during this phase of their service in Spain that it is believed they acquired the honorific title of 'Hispana', possibly in recognition of their distinguished service in respect of that campaign.

Some four years after Augustus' war with the Cantabrians had ended, in 20 BC, the IX Hispana were redeployed to Germania. Very little is known of their service during the period up until their next redeployment, to the province of Pannonia, around AD 9. The decision to redeploy the legion is thought to have been due to the need to withdraw from the eastern Rhine region, after the Varus disaster.

Pannonia was the last province the legion was to be based in prior to leaving for Britain. It is bordered both to the north and east by the River Danube and the area today takes in many of the modern Balkan and central European states, such as Slovakia, Croatia, Serbia, Slovenia and Bosnia. The presence of the legion is well attested in the region around this time and, other than possibly being required to send detachments of troops for operations in Africa, the main body of the legion remained at its base in the town of Siscia. This town is now modern Sisak in central Croatia and during Roman times the location of the legionary base would have proved strategically vital, given that it was, and still is, a major river port sitting at the confluence of three large rivers, the Sava, Kupa and Odra.

Although it is not known what emblem the legion actually used it is possible that, because the legion was one raised by Caesar, they may have displayed a bull.

Legio XIIII Gemina

The 'Gemina' element of the legion's name is thought to imply that the unit itself had been formed from two separate units, or twinned. Formation of the legion is attributable to Caesar, prior to the commencement of his campaigns in Gaul. In *The Gallic Wars* Caesar confirms that the legion was one of three which had been levied in Italy, around 55 BC.[21] However, during that year the legion suffered heavy losses whilst on operations in the territory of the Eburones. Caesar had placed the legion under the command of Quintus Tullius Cicero, brother to the famous orator, Marcus Tullius Cicero. The legion had been tasked with guarding Caesar's baggage train, which was located at the fortress of Atuatuca, in the middle of Eburonian territory.

German tribes had been raiding across the Rhine that year, directly into Eburonian lands, and upon learning that Caesar's baggage train was nearby and only lightly defended, a large cavalry force from the Germanic Sugambri tribe fell on the fortress, intent on securing a considerable amount of Roman booty. Despite a heroic defence by the legionaries, the Germanic raiders managed to wipe out two of the legion's cohorts before the garrison was relieved by the main body of the army in the region. However, due to the stout defence put up by the legion, the German raiders failed in their objective of plundering the baggage train.

It has been widely suggested that the XIIII Gemina was the legion which was destroyed in the previous year, 54 BC, when the Eburones revolted and destroyed the army of Cotta and Sabinus in its winter quarters at the fortress at Atuatuca. However, this may not be a credible claim because, although Caesar confirms that the legion which was destroyed in that attack was one of the three legions which had been raised north of the Po the previous year, Caesar also specifically mentions that Cicero took a legion to make its winter camp in the territory of the Nervii at that time.[22] It therefore also seems plausible to suggest that, based on the assumption that Cicero retained command of that legion, this was the same legion which was attacked at Atuatuca the following year.

Nevertheless, if the above assertion is correct, then the XIIII Gemina did not spend the winter of 54–53 BC without incident as, once they had made camp in Nerviian territory, they were subsequently besieged by the Nervii and had to be relieved by Caesar. From Caesar's description of the attack it would appear that, although the situation had been extremely grave at times, the legion suffered far less losses than they would later sustain in the attack on Atuatuca the following year.

Given the size of the army needed to perform such an operation it is likely that the XIIII Gemina took part in the siege of Alesia in 52 BC when Caesar completely surrounded the hilltop fortified town, which was occupied by the Gaulish chieftain, Vercingetorix. Like the IX Hispana, the XIII legion also took part in the battle of Ilerda in 49 BC against the forces of Pompey. Both legions then seemed to follow a common destiny for a time, participating in the battle of Pharsalus, then being sent home to Italy and disbanded before being reformed for use in Caesar's campaigns in Africa. Legio XIIII fell under the command of Octavian too, and was used to suppress the rebellion by Sextus Pompeius.

It is thought that after the war between Octavian and Mark Anthony, when Octavian became the emperor Augustus and reconstituted the legions, the XIIII acquired it's Gemina title, after it was brought up to strength by the use of veterans from Anthony's disbanded legions. It would then have also acquired the Capricorn as its unit emblem, marking it out as one of Augustus' legions. The legion is often referred to by its additional honorific titles: Martia and Victrix (Legion XIIII Gemina Martia Victrix). However, these titles were not acquired until after AD 61 when it is believed the legion earned the additional *cognomens* of 'martial and victorious' for the part they played in suppressing the Boudican revolt. Those other titles will not therefore be used in this work, given that to do so they would clearly be quoted out of context.

Having been posted to Illyricum, the legion then moved to take part in the suppression of a large-scale uprising in Pannonia, which started around AD 6 and took three years to put down. The legion was then moved to a new base on the Rhine at Mogontiacum (Mainz, Germany), in response to the Varus disaster in AD 9. The legion remained at its new base throughout the first half of the first century AD and contributed to various operations within the region, including Caligula's campaigns in Germany, before it was eventually despatched to the shores of Britain.

Legio XX Valeria

Like the XIIII Gemina, the XX is perhaps best known by its full title, Legio XX Valeria Victrix. However, the 'Victrix' *cognomen* was, as with the case of the later *cognomens* of legion XIIII Gemina, almost certainly awarded as a result of the role played by the legion in suppressing the Boudican revolt. In this work therefore, the 'Valeria' *cognomen* will be the only honorific title referred to, given that it seems more likely that this last title was awarded prior to the legion's involvement in the invasion of Britain. The possible origins of the 'Valeria' *cognomen* will be discussed shortly.

The actual details concerning how and where the legion was raised from are uncertain, although it is generally held that the XX were a brand new legion which was raised by Augustus sometime after 31 BC, seeing as the legion is only mentioned in historical records after Augustus took power. However, there is an interesting reference in Cassius Dio's *Roman Histories* concerning the standing legions and their titles, which Dio relates whilst describing the disaffection amongst the legions around 3 BC, and where they were garrisoned at the time of writing his account in the second century AD:

> The soldiers were sorely displeased at the paltry character of the rewards given them for the wars which had been waged at this time and none of them consented to bear arms for longer than the regular period of his service. It was therefore voted that twenty

thousand sesterces should be given to members of the pretorian guard when they had served sixteen years, and twelve thousand to the other soldiers when they had served twenty years. Twenty-three, or, as others say, twenty-five, legions of citizen soldiers were being supported at this time. At present only nineteen of them still exist, as follows: the Second (Augusta), with its winter quarters in Upper Britain; the three Thirds – the Gallica in Phoenicia, the Cyrenaica in Arabia, and the Augusta in Numidia; the Fourth (Scythica) in Syria; the Fifth (Macedonica) in Dacia; the two Sixths, of which the one (Victrix) is stationed in Lower Britain, the other (Ferrata) in Judaea; the Seventh (generally called Claudia) in Upper Moesia; the Eighth (Augusta) in Upper Germany; the two Tenths in upper Pannonia (Gemina) and in Judaea; the Eleventh (Claudia) in Lower Moesia (for two legions were thus named after Claudius because they had not fought against him in the rebellion of Camillus); the Twelfth (Fulminata) in Cappadocia; the Thirteenth (Gemina) in Dacia; the Fourteenth (Gemina) in Upper Pannonia; the Fifteenth (Apollinaris) in Cappadocia; the Twentieth (called both Valeria and Victrix) in upper Britain. These latter, I believe, were the troops which Augustus took over and retained, along with those called the Twenty-second who are quartered in Germany – and this in spite of the fact that they were by no means called Valerians by all and do not use that name any longer. These are the legions that still remain out of those of Augustus; of the rest, some were disbanded altogether, and others were merged with various legions by Augustus himself and by other emperors, in consequence of which such legions have come to bear the name Gemina.[23]

The use of the honorific title of Valeria clearly has uncertain origins. Suggestions vary from links to their former commander in Illyricum and governor of the province, Marcus Valerius Messalla Messallinus, and also the town of Valeria in Illyricum where they were once stationed. There is also a very doubtful link to Claudius' third wife, the adulterous Valeria Messalina. As previously mentioned, it is also suggested that the name was awarded alongside the 'Victrix' title for the legion's part in crushing the Boudican rebels in Britain.

The legion's first real taste of battle came in 25 BC when it was sent to Hispania Tarraconensis to take part in Augustus' war against the Cantabrians. However, it seems that the XX were not caught up in this war for its entire twelve year duration as it is believed they were subsequently posted to the Balkans, possibly around 20 BC. It was intended that, whilst still in Illyricum in AD 6, the legion would become part of a massive army which would be used to carry out a campaign planned by the future emperor, Tiberius, against King Maroboduus of the Marcomanni. These people were a Germanic tribe who had previously been defeated by Germanicus and were afterwards located in what is now modern Bohemia. However, Tiberius' plan never bore fruit as the Pannonian uprising of the same year meant that many of the legions allocated to the operation had to be diverted to the task of subduing the revolt. The plan was therefore abandoned at an early stage.

From there the legion was moved to Germania Inferior, following the Varus massacre in AD 9 where they were garrisoned at Oppidum Ubiorum (Cologne, Germany). Soon after the accession of Tiberius the legion moved to Novaesium, which is now the modern German town of Neuss, located on the confluence of the rivers Rhine and Erft. This base is believed to be the oldest Roman military base in the region and the legion remained here until it was called upon to take part in Claudius' plan to invade Britain. The emblem of the XX Valeria was a charging wild bore.

The Auxiliary Contingent

If we are content to accept the widely held view that the Claudian invasion force was around 40,000 strong, then this would indicate that the auxiliary forces accompanying the legions were of an almost equivalent numerical strength. It has been speculated that the invasion force could have numbered as many as 45,000. However, for the purposes of this work, the assumption will be that legion strength was fairly well matched by auxiliary numbers. Therefore, as we are clear that four legions participated in the early phase of the invasion, 40,000 would be a sensible estimate to work with.

Keppie states that the strength of an early Imperial legion was between 5,000 and 6,000.[24] However, if we wish to obtain a more specific figure for the maximum fighting strength of an early Imperial legion then it is possible to calculate this from its various components (see Appendix F), thus providing us with a total combat strength for each legion of just over 5,300. Therefore, the combat strength of all four legions combined could have amounted to a figure exceeding 21,200. If we are to assume that all four legions were at full strength at the time they landed in Britain, albeit that this would be improbable due to the likelihood of some previous routine operational wastage, it would then require a supporting auxiliary contingent of around 19,000 troops to achieve the figure suggested.

Each of these auxiliary units would have its own specialist role to play. Unlike the legions, individual auxiliary units were mainly support arms made up of a single cohort which could be either quingenary, 500 in strength, or milliary, 1,000 in strength. Until fairly recently, the auxiliary cohorts of the Roman army were often regarded almost as the ancient-world equivalent of 'cannon fodder'; sent into battle first in order to weaken the enemy in preparation for the main assault by the legions. However, this dated view is much too simplistic and quite far removed from the actual truth of the matter. Whilst it is true that the Roman army in battle could deploy auxiliary infantry and cavalry to make early forays to harass enemy forces, destabilise formations and probe for weaknesses, the capabilities of the various auxiliary units extended far beyond these roles. In fact, what is of vital importance when trying to understand the role of the auxiliary forces within the Roman army is the need to consider the sheer diversity of specialisms on offer.

By the mid-first century AD the Romans had conquered much of the world as they knew it and had acquired an empire which stretched westwards from Arabia and Asia Minor, encircled the entire Mediterranean and extended deep into eastern, central and northern Europe. The native warriors whom the Roman army encountered and subsequently defeated as they expanded the frontiers of their empire, would afterwards come to provide the state with an incredible array of specialist fighters. These were the warriors which would so effectively compliment the irresistible hitting power of the legions, leaving them free to concentrate on more conventional heavy infantry roles without the need to diversify into more specialised combat roles.

There is of course nothing to suggest that the Romans were incapable of producing more specialised fighting units and it is well known that legionaries did receive training in specialisms such as riding, archery and slinging. But, with so many conquered peoples able to provide a wealth of fully trained specialists, the Romans had no need to train their own units and would, in the main, probably not have been able to produce soldiers of an equivalent quality to their foreign counterparts. This is largely due to the fact that many of these auxiliary contingents, particularly archers and horsemen, were trained from a very early age. Very often their particular specialisms were also a deeply rooted cultural characteristic, the effects of which could never be duplicated by simply selecting random individuals to train in a particular discipline.

For instance: cohorts of highly skilled Hamian archers, originally from the hot dry lands of the Levant, were used by the Romans to provide deadly fire support in battle. Trained almost from an age when they could first pick up one of the composite bows which were native to the region, such men would have been able to direct highly accurate, concentrated fire on a given target or, if required, lay a hail of arrows down on a given area. As with many auxiliary units, these particular warriors would continue to serve in Britain long after the Claudian invasion and their presence in such places as Hadrian's Wall is well attested via a wealth of monumental inscriptions.

Used at closer ranges than those of the archers, slingers from places such as the Balearic Islands could provide similar support by either bringing aimed individual shots to bear on the enemy, or by unleashing a hail of sling stones or cast-lead shot down upon their targets. Although extremely simple, the sling was a highly effective weapon in the right hands and various classical accounts verify the ability of well-trained slingers to inflict terrible injuries as well as fatal shots upon their opponents. There are even surviving ancient descriptions of the medical procedure needed for the removal of sling shots which have become lodged in the bodies of soldiers.

As well as archers and slingers, the Romans could also put many specialist cavalry units on to the field, such as light and heavy cavalry, lancers, horse archers or scout units. Nevertheless, within the context of the Claudian invasion it is virtually impossible to say for certain exactly which auxiliary units came ashore in the initial landings. For the most part, any suggestions as to the identity of those units would be speculation. In addition, if we are unable to name the majority of the units confidently then we are subsequently unable to say whether the units were either quingenary or milliary and we are therefore unable to even offer more informed speculation as to how many auxiliary units took part – hence the preference to use a notional but plausible figure in this work. Although not reproduced here, Peddie has provided a speculative list of possibilities which is in part supported by the existence of inscriptional evidence which attests to the presence of the particular unit in Britain at around the time of the invasion.[25]

Speculation aside, there is one auxiliary unit which we can confidently identify from the account of the invasion which Dio has provided. Although the particular group referred to just happens to be considered one of the most remarkable irregular fighting forces under Roman control. They were the Batavians, and the identification of their clear involvement in the opening phases of the invasion arises principally from the following excerpt of Dio's account:

> The barbarians thought that Romans would not be able to cross it [the River] without a bridge, and consequently camped in rather careless fashion on the opposite bank; but he [Plautius] sent across a detachment of Germans, who were accustomed to swim easily in full armour across the most turbulent streams.[26]

Such a description could really only relate to the Batavii, a Germanic tribe which inhabited the marshes and swamps of what is now Holland, close to the modern city of Nijmegen. Perhaps the first reference to these warriors is given by Caesar in *The Gallic Wars*, describing the location of their homeland as follows: 'The Meuse rises from mount Le Vosge, which is in the territories of the Lingones; and, having received a branch of the Rhine, which is called the Waal, forms the island of the Batavians …'[27] The swampy and inhospitable nature of their lands meant that the Batavians were required to develop very specialised warfare techniques to defend their lands, making them an ideal choice to support water-borne operations or to fight in less conventional battle conditions, such as marshland. What is perhaps surprising about these warriors is that as well as their ability to deploy infantry in such conditions, they were also strong equestrians with the ability to field cavalry units, either separate from the infantry or as a part-mounted cohort, or *cohors equitata*. This was often a milliary cohort made up of equal numbers of infantry and cavalry. This ability clearly made them a formidable and versatile fighting force and one which was much prized by the Romans, as evidenced in Tacitus' description of these warriors:

1 The cliffs at St Margaret's Bay, Kent are a precise match for the shoreline which Caesar describes as being unsuitable for landing his army. Due to the high cliffs and narrow beach, any attempt to land his men would have left them dangerously exposed to missiles being hurled from above by the waiting Britons as they tracked his ships sailing along the coast. (Author's photograph)

2 Deal beach looking north, clearly showing the high shingle ridge which, had Caesar used the location as a landing site, would have posed serious difficulties for beaching his heavy timber transport vessels and warships. (Author's photograph)

3 An alternative view of Deal beach in Kent – including the town pier. The pier structure and, in particular, the person standing close to its base give a clear idea of the size of the gravel shelf and the steep gradient of the shingle above the high tide line which Caesar's men would have needed to overcome in order to beach their ships. (Author's photograph)

4 Sandwich beach, Kent as it stretches north towards the present coastline of Thanet. Note the much flatter beach surface compared to Deal and the broad sandy foreshore which more closely fits Caesar's description of the landing beach. This would have been much more suitable for landing large numbers of troops in the shallows off the beach, prior to pulling the fleet ashore. (Author's photograph)

5 Chichester Harbour, Sussex as seen from Hayling Island, Hampshire. This vast sheltered anchorage would have been easily capable of accommodating the entire Claudian invasion fleet. However, the major tactical and logistical problems associated with launching an attack on Colchester from here mean that it is very unlikely to have been a suitable venue for the landings of AD 43. (Author's photograph)

6 A view looking out across Richborough fort. At centre-left are the massive outer perimeter walls of the later Saxon Shore fort. At the centre of the photo is the base for the great monumental stone arch which once stood here. In the far distance can be seen Pegwell Bay and the coastline of Thanet around the area of Ramsgate. (Photograph by John Olden, reproduced by kind permission. With additional thanks to English Heritage, Richborough)

7 The photograph shows part of the exposed section of the earliest phase of Roman military occupation at the Richborough fort site. Although the ditches are now somewhat overgrown, the orientation of the original double ditch defences which once fronted the Claudian turf and timber rampart are clearly visible. (Author's photograph. With additional thanks to English Heritage, Richborough)

8 A view of the River Medway, looking back toward the modern settlement of Burham. Note the ridge of hills in the background of the photo, which overlook the fording point. (Photograph by John Olden, reproduced by kind permission)

9 The fordable section of the River Medway at low tide. Note the ripples in the water which indicate that the water is flowing just above the gravelly river bed; the surface flow being disrupted as it breaks over submerged objects on the bed. (Photograph by John Olden, reproduced by kind permission)

10 Modern reconstructions of a *gladius* and a *pugio. See* Appendix J.

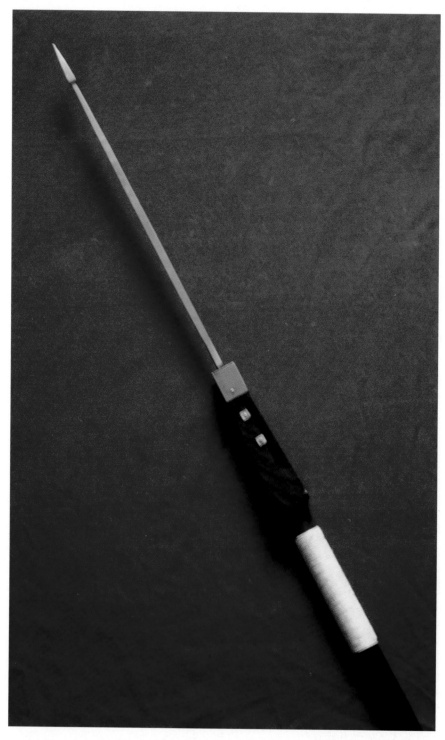

11 Modern reconstruction of a Roman legionary *pilum*. *See* Appendix J.

12 Modern reconstruction of a Roman legionary helmet. *See* Appendix J.

13 Monumental statue of Claudius. *See* Appendix J.

14 Modern reconstruction of a legionary *scutum*. *See* Appendix J.

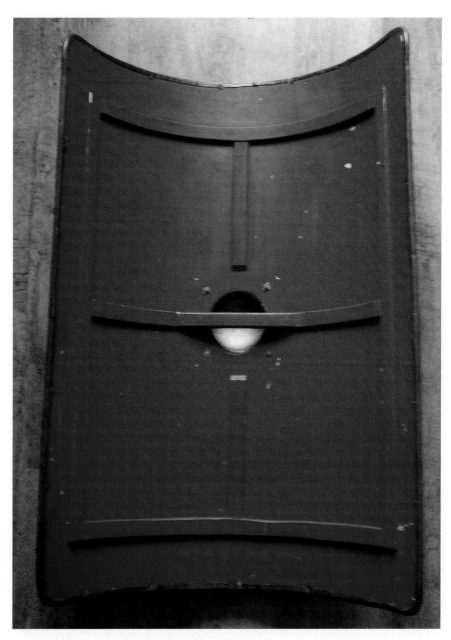

15 Rear of *scutum*. *See* Appendix J.

16 A Caesarian legionary. *See* Appendix J.

17 A Claudian legionary in
marching order. *See* Appendix J.

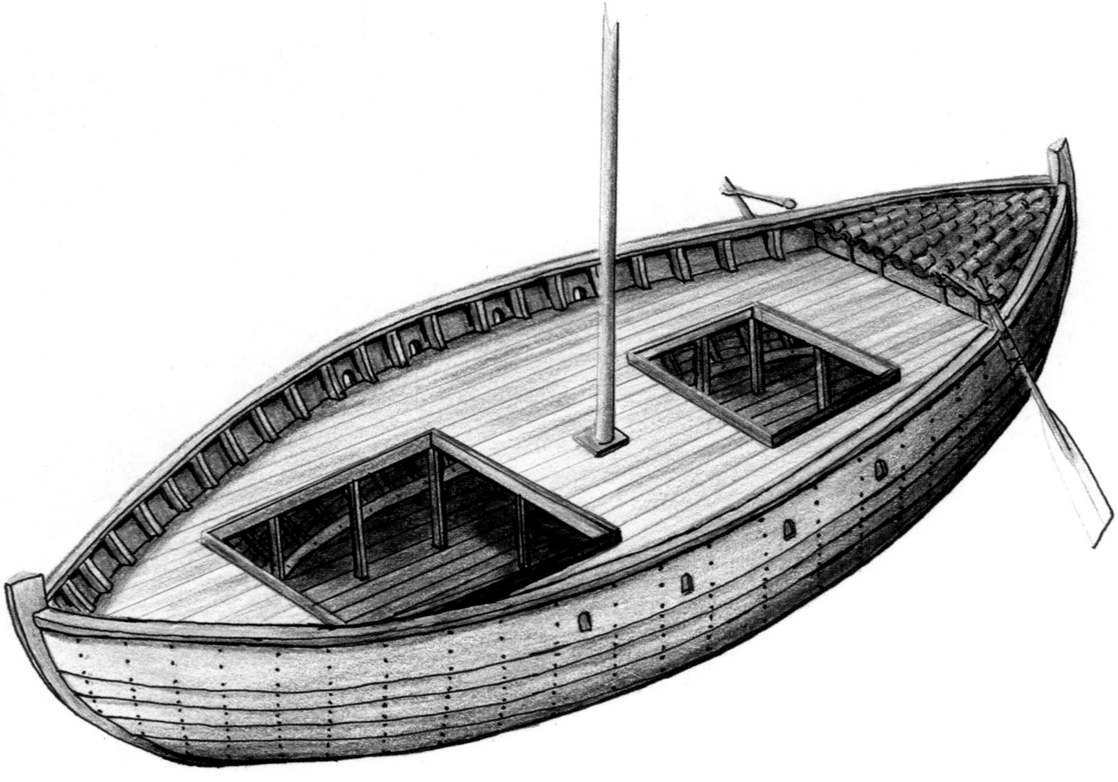

18 A Roman *Corbita*. See Appendix J.

19 Speculative illustration of the Claudian defences at Richborough. *See* Appendix J.

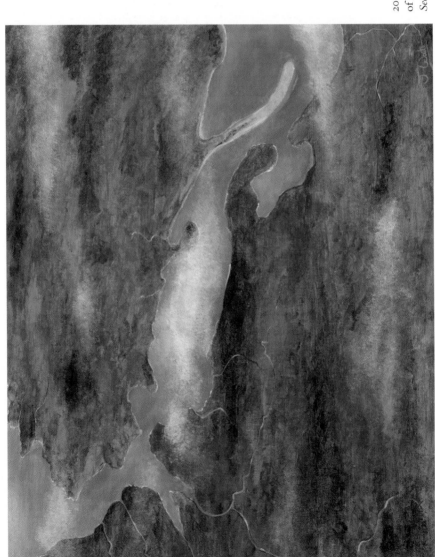

20 Speculative illustration of the Wantsum Channel. *See* Appendix J.

Of all these people, the most famed for valour are the Batavii; whose territories comprise but a small part of the banks of the Rhine, but consist chiefly of an island within it. These were formerly a tribe of the Chatti, who, on account of a civil war, removed to their present settlements and were thus destined to become a part of the Roman Empire. They still retain this honour, together with a memorial of their ancient alliance; for they are neither insulted by taxes, nor oppressed by farmers of the revenue. Exempt from levies and extraordinary contributions, and kept apart for military use alone, they are reserved, like a magazine of arms, for the purposes of war.[28]

The high regard in which Tacitus holds the Batavii speaks for itself and this admiration of these men, who the Romans held to be the very epitome of the warrior in both spirit and deed, is also evident in many other classical texts. Clearly these people produced a much prized fighting force and, as such, the Roman state believed it was prudent to extend to them such privileges as an exemption from tax or tribute in return for their continuing obligation to wage war in the name of Rome. However, it is hard to find a better example of Roman trust and respect for these warriors than the fact that they were subsequently charged with providing the emperor's personal bodyguard or horse guards which, as well as a clear sign of trust, must surely be regarded as a mark of high honour.

From their first encounters with Caesars forces through to the subsequent campaigns on the Rhine under commanders such as Tiberius and Germanicus, the Batavians consistently proved themselves worthy of Roman admiration. It therefore seems quite fitting, as they joined the legions and crossed the sea to Britain, that such an illustrious unit should be present at what would be one of Rome's most remarkable military accomplishments. Moreover, as will become clear later on in this work, it would also seem plausible to suggest that these warriors could well have represented a sizeable contingent of the auxiliary force.

A Common Attribute

Having now provided some background to the various units which we can identify as participating in Claudius' invasion of Britain, several things have become apparent. As well as some common history, the five units have one further thing in common which, for the purposes of this work at least, potentially provides us with a key reason why the early part of the invasion plan was executed so successfully.

The fact is that all of these units would have been very familiar with amphibious operations, or more particularly river-borne operations. Leaving aside for one moment the natural abilities of the Batavians, we have now established that, prior to their redeployment to Britain, all four legions were drawn from bases which dominated major rivers. Three had been based along the Rhine and the fourth, IX Hispana, had been operating from a base on the Danube prior to their redeployment. They probably accompanied Aulus Plautius as he left his post as governor of Pannonia and travelled west to assume overall command of the invasion operation.

The use of such major rivers to conduct patrolling operations and to facilitate the rapid movement of troops by boat were key to ensuring that the Roman military was able to dominate the area within the zones controlled by the respective garrisons. Therefore, the use of units experienced in conducting ship and river craft deployments would have to represent a vital requirement if the Romans were to ensure that the momentum of the early push inland was maintained.

There is a wealth of archaeology from the Rhine region which attests to the use of a variety of river assault craft which would have been used by the Roman military to maintain control of their territory. A number of reconstructed examples of these craft can be seen on display today at the ancient ship museum at Mainz, in Germany. The possible use of such craft, along with men who would have been responsible for operating them, namely the Classis Britannica Rome's northern fleet, is therefore something which we will discuss in a little more detail later.

Notes ·
1   A.R. Birley (2005), p. 21
2   A.A. Boyce (1942)
3   C. Scarre (1995), p. 44
4   Suetonius, *The Twelve Caesars – Claudius*, Chapter XXVI
5   Tacitus, *Annals*, Chapters VII, IV and XXII
6   *see* A.R. Birley (2005), p. 22
7   Eutropius, *Braeviarium Historiae Romanae*, 7. 13.2
8   E.W. Black (2000)
9   Cassius Dio, *Roman Histories – Book LX*, Chap XXIII, II
10 Ibid., *Book LIX* and *Book LX*, Chapter XXX
11 A.R. Birley (2005), p. 233
12 Flavius Josephus, *The Jewish Wars – Book III*, Chapter II
13 Suetonius, *The Twelve Caesars – Vespasian*, Chapter XX
14 Tacitus, *The Histories – Book III*, Chapter LXXV
15 Cassius Dio, *Roman Histories – Book LX*, Chapter IX
16 A.R. Birley (2005), p. 234
17 Suetonius, *The Twelve Caesars – Claudius*, Chapter XVII
18 R. Lanciani, *Pagan & Christian Rome* (1892), pp. 277–8
19 Julius Caesar, *The Gallic Wars – Book II*, Chapter XXIII
20 Ibid., *Book VIII*, Chapter VIII
21 Ibid., *Book VI*, Chapter XXXII
22 Ibid., *Book V*, Chapter XXIV
23 Cassius Dio, *Roman Histories – Book LV*, Chapter XXIII
24 L. Keppie (1984), p. 173
25 J. Peddie (1987), p. 181
26 Cassius Dio, *Roman Histories – Book LX*, Chapter XX
27 Julius Caesar, *The Gallic Wars – Book IV*, Chapter X
28 Tacitus, *The Germania*, Chapter XXIX

6

To Land an Army

A Question of Practicality

For the Romans, making sound choices was vital to the success of such a monumentally complex and important endeavour as the invasion of a territory which lay beyond the fringes of what was then the known world. So far, we have considered the importance of appointing a trusted and effective commander and then supporting him with a command team, each with the proven ability to successfully lead men to war. We have also discussed the choice of units involved and have offered some plausible explanations as to why these units, above any others, were the ones which were most likely to be chosen to make up the invasion army.

However, even though it would have been vitally important for the Claudian planners to make the right choices in respect of the army and its hierarchy, the risk of the operation failing would still have been very real if the wrong choice of landing site was made. Clearly, with an army numbering at least 40,000 men, it would have been of crucial importance to ensure that, wherever they landed, the troops could disembark with minimal difficulty and then establish a defended beachhead. In addition the optimum usage of the available campaigning time would have been of paramount consideration, so scheduling the right date for the start of the invasion would have been essential.

So too would be the ability of the army to make a rapid advance beyond the landing area and push quickly towards their initial objectives. It seems clear that, even before the outset of the campaign, the Romans recognised their chief opponents were going to be the Catuvellauni. Therefore the success of the mission hinged on the rapid decapitation of the tribe; neutralising its leadership and capturing its powerbase at Camulodunum (Colchester). Success in employing this strategy would not only defeat the most powerful opposition element, but the removal of the violently powerful and long-standing Catuvellaunian influence over its neighbours would serve to destabilise weaker tribes within the region of the south-eastern quarter of Britain, those who had allied themselves to the two princes – Togodumnus and Caratacus.

We should bear in mind that the task facing the Claudian planners differed from that which faced Caesar. His two invasions were launched from a Gaul which was highly unstable – given that it had yet to be fully pacified – forcing Caesar to implement additional plans to protect his interests while he was in Britain. Whereas the Claudian invasion was launched from a Gaul which had by then been fully integrated into the Roman Empire, providing a much more stable backdrop to the invasion. This does not detract from the enormity of the achievement by the architects of Claudius' invasion plans. They still needed to make crucial decisions, such as just how far away the army should sensibly be landed from its ultimate objective. A landing too close to the objective might allow the Britons to quickly muster a strong defensive force, a move which could prove disastrous as it would allow the native army the opportunity to push the Romans back into the sea before they had consolidated any early gains.

Rather than the image of the remote and mysterious island that Caesar had twice tried in vain to conquer, by AD 43 a clearer picture of Britain and its peoples had emerged for the Romans. For numerous reasons, in the ninety-seven years between the landings by Caesar and Claudius the tribes of southern Britain were now actively sending envoys and diplomatic missions to Rome itself. As Strabo tells us, Britons, with their distinctive physical characteristics, were by then to be seen walking the streets of Rome. What is more, there is no doubt that the Romans also sent their own representatives to the various tribal areas along the south and east coasts of Britain. After all, Rome would have viewed the internecine power struggles within the island and the aggressive posturing of the Catuvellauni towards Rome with keen interest. The senate would therefore be seeking to protect Roman interests by sending their own diplomatic missions to the various tribal factions. In doing so the Romans would have acquired an invaluable up-to-date insight into the prevailing political climate, the tribal areas themselves and the inhabitants.

Along with political and diplomatic contact, trade with Britain was also thriving due to Rome's closer proximity to Britain via a fully conquered Gaul. This would have meant that a wealth of further intelligence could be gathered from many more sources than those available to Julius Caesar. Consequently, the ability to plan an effective campaign strategy in much greater detail was now possible. Knowledge which had previously been denied to Caesar, such as the location of anchorages, navigable inland waterways and inland trade routes, had now become conveniently available. The Claudian planners must therefore have used this wealth of new and detailed intelligence as the foundations for their invasion plans.

As previously mentioned, this work will also base its re-examination of the Claudian invasion of Britain by more closely considering the alternative proposal as to the definite site of the landings; that the Romans actually landed at Chichester, as opposed to the coast of Kent. However, in considering this proposal it becomes apparent from the outset that many of those who favour Chichester as a landing site often appear to have been influenced more by what the archaeological evidence *seems* to tell us about the opening phase of the invasion, rather than what the evidence is actually capable of telling us when weighed alongside other vitally important factors. In certain circumstances, the basic truth of what an army needs to remain effective has clearly been over-looked. So too has the need to pause and consider whether the requirements of basic strategic necessity can sit comfortably alongside the interpretation which is being proposed. Often, it seems the temptation to over-interpret is also evident, given that some quite complex theories seem to have emerged from what often amounts to very little solid evidence.

Of course, reinterpretations and the proposal of new theories are always going to be vital elements in contributing towards establishing the truth of the matter. After all, it is these very things which prompt us to debate, question and research further in order to find answers. Yet the advancement of any new proposal should surely always rest squarely, not only upon the physical and scientific evidence from which it grew, but also on a careful examination of the practical considerations which must be applied in order to solve the problem at hand.

By way of some further explanation: it is important to bear in mind that if nothing else, the business of waging war is a profoundly practical enterprise, the basic tenets of which have not changed in thousands of years. Whilst this is clearly an inescapable truth it nevertheless seems that, certainly in putting the case for the Claudian landings taking place in Sussex, this factor is often either not taken fully into account or, in some instances, it seems to be regarded as lower in importance than the outcome of the wider scientific conclusions. If one is given to adopting an approach such as this, it will inevitably become hard to avoid the charge that insufficient care has been taken to applying a balanced approach. The end product can then lack sufficient credibility when placed under any real scrutiny.

It must therefore be reasonable to suggest then that when theorising about something as complex as a large-scale military campaign, about which very little is really known, to advance a plausible argument without properly weighing the archaeological and literary evidence against the timeless practicalities of waging war is difficult. Consequently, in the following parts of this chapter, whilst still having regard to the available evidence, we will examine the practicalities of the Roman invasion in some detail and then closely consider the suggestion of Chichester as a viable landing area. The validity of that proposal can then be tested by tempering modern archaeological thinking with an entirely pragmatic approach to the question of whether the Roman invaders would actually choose to come ashore there.

Food for Thought – A Practical Analysis of Supply & Demand

It was Napoleon Bonaparte who famously said that 'an army marches on its stomach'. Throughout the history of armed conflict, a fundamentally important principle of waging warfare is that no army can be expected to operate effectively beyond its line of supply, as to do so would ultimately render it unable to succeed in achieving its objectives. After all, an army can be made up of the finest, most well-equipped troops but if both men and beasts are left with empty stomachs, as history has repeatedly demonstrated, it is very likely they will quickly become little more than a disaffected rabble with a much reduced capacity or inclination to fight effectively. Therefore, the Roman planners would need to have ensured that they chose a landing area that could act as a key supply point in the first instance, feeding and equipping the army via vast lines of supply as it prosecuted its advance. Furthermore, any modern theory as to the location of the Roman landing area, regardless of the interpretation of archaeological data, would also need to be tested by the application of a wealth of practical questions before it could be considered to be a worthy suggestion for the location.

The ability to supply the advancing units, continuing to meet their basic daily needs as they moved further away from the landing areas, would be the key to the success of the overall undertaking. When planning an operation where it would be vital in the early phases to maintain a consistent forward momentum, too much time expended on foraging supplies from local sources would undoubtedly cause the early part of the advance to lose impetus. This could then allow the enemy to come off the back foot and afford them both time and opportunity to plan and execute a possible counter strike to the advance.

Furthermore, it is abundantly clear that any time spent on the business of foraging can present its own hazards. Indeed, we have already dealt with the issue of the vulnerability of Caesar's forces when we examined his first incursion in 55 BC, and more specifically how Legio XII were caught out by the Britons whilst engaged on such a mission. It therefore makes perfect sense to suggest that the Claudian planners would have been keen to minimise the necessity for carrying out such risky and time-consuming tasks.

In considering just how to supply such a large force as that deployed by Claudius, the very first thing that any planner would need to take into account would be not only how to procure and distribute the foodstuffs, but also to accurately calculate just how much food would have been needed to keep the army on the move. An interesting insight into the rations issued to a Republican era Roman soldier is provided by Polybius, writing in the second century BC. He describes the daily rations of infantry and cavalrymen as follows:

The allowance of corn to a foot-soldier is about two-thirds of an Attic medimnus a month, a cavalry-soldier receives seven medimni of barley and two of wheat. Of the allies the infantry receive the same, the cavalry one and one-third medimnus of wheat and five of barley, these rations being a free gift to the allies; but in the case of the Romans the quaestor deducts from their pay the price fixed for their corn and clothes and any additional arm they require.[1]

Polybius was a Greek, therefore he has naturally described the quantities of grain rations by reference to the principal dry measures used by his own culture. The *medimnus* was a volumetric measure used specifically for such foodstuffs as corn, and he has referred to the *Attic medimnus* as opposed to the *Aeginetan medimnus* or *Ptolemaic medimnus*, which were both greater in quantity. The Roman equivalent to the *Attic medimnus* was 6 Roman *modii*, which has a modern fluid equivalent of around 12 Imperial gallons (54.55 litres), or 1½ bushel as a dry measure.

Carrington asserts that the wheat ration referred to by Polybius equates to around 26.95 modern kilogrammes per head, per month.[2] This therefore represents a daily ration of around 0.86kgs. Carrington supports this by explaining that the discovery of a wheat issue record for a cavalry unit stationed at Carlisle during the first century AD seems to confirm that the same quantities referred to above were still being issued at that time. Whereas Peddie states that the corn ration referred to by Polybius equates to around 3 modern pounds (1.36 kg).[3]

In truth, the question of the supply and distribution of rations for an individual soldier is somewhat complex, and it is therefore expected that one is likely to encounter disparities among modern interpretations as to the various weights or types of dry ration issued to and carried by the Roman soldier. The Latin term for the dry ration is *frumentum*. However, this term does not refer to any specific type of ration, given that it is a generic descriptive which covers any type of grain such as corn, barley or wheat. Therefore, in order to keep matters as simple as possible, we will not enter into the debate as to how much of his rations a soldier would carry at any one time. Instead, we will approach the subject by assuming that the troops would have received a minimum daily amount of dry rations during the opening campaign phases. We will then calculate the need for a minimum daily ration requirement for both infantry and cavalry units, based on that amount.

Dependent on the type of ration, there are some variations in weight per volumetric measure. For instance, if we compare the bushel as a volumetric measurement against the actual weight of the various common grain rations, the weight differences are as follows:

Ration by 1 bushel	Weight in kgs	Weight in lbs
Barley	21.8	48
Corn	25.4	56
Oats	14.5	32
Wheat	27.2	60

In order to form some idea as to the total daily requirement of the various arms of the invasion force, we will now consider the total weight of rations which the Roman planners would need to requisition and distribute in order for the troops to remain effective. In the interests of maintaining a simple perspective we will focus on the supply requirements by referring to a generic amount in terms of all available dry rations and assume a realistic minimum requirement per man of 1kg (2.2lb) of dry rations per day.

Consequently, the daily requirement within the various elements of a full strength legion (see Appendix F) is as follows:

Unit	Weight in kgs	Weight in lbs	Weight in tons (approx.)
Contubernium (8 men)	8	17.6	–
Century (80 men)	80	176	–
Cohort (480 men)	480	1,056	0.47
Legion (5307 men)	5,307	11,675.4	5.2

Ton weights shown are in UK long ton.

As suggested, the figures shown are based on the full fighting strength of one Imperial legion. The figures do not take into account any abstractions through deaths, postings or secondments. A balance of sorts can be loosely applied in respect of those absences or losses by offsetting these against the sizeable retinue which would have accompanied a legion such as medical staff, supply operatives and clerks, and animal handlers such as grooms, muleteers and drovers. Nevertheless it should be borne in mind that the supply requirements which are about to be discussed relate more specifically to units in the field and their immediate support arms. No account has been taken in this work of the vast amount of personnel involved in the cultivation, manufacture and requisition of supplies and equipment, and the transportation of the same from its source of origin.

Assuming that auxiliary infantry would have more or less the same requirements as the legions, they would therefore require the following quantities of dry rations:

Unit	Weight in kgs	Weight in lbs	Weight in tons (approx.)
Auxiliary (quingenary – 500 men)	500	1,100	0.5
Auxiliary (milliary – 1,000 men)	1,000	2,200	I

Already we can see that the implementation of an effective plan for the daily supply and resupply of just one unit poses a significant issue, given the heavy demand it places on the supply chain. However, this is just in terms of human requirements and we have yet to factor in the needs of the mounts within a legion's cavalry contingent. In that respect, we therefore also need to make allowance for the fodder requirements of a mounted contingent of 120. This means that we should allow for a minimum of 240 horses, given that it would be extremely doubtful that each rider would not have at least one spare mount.

In order to calculate the requirement, a useful source of information has again been provided by Peddie, who used a table based on figures derived from Victorian military manuals, when pack and cavalry animals were still in widespread use.[4] The figures provided on the table show daily feed requirements for pack horses, mules (second class) and donkeys (second class).[5] Although the figures do not show a specific figure for a cavalry mount, it seems reasonable to assume that such an animal would have more or less the same daily nutritional requirements as a pack horse, given the levels of performance expected from each of these animals. Peddie does not create a separate table entry for pack horses, instead equating their daily fodder consumption to that of a mule. It is worth bearing in mind that the weights shown below may be slightly higher than those required by the Roman army, given that the pack horse employed by the Roman army would have been a little smaller than those of the British army of the Victorian era. It nevertheless seems reasonable to regard the final figures as very much within the boundaries of credibility.

Given that Peddie has supplied weights for both green and dry fodder we will, for the sake of simplicity once more, focus only on dry fodder. The reason for this is that green fodder is a foodstuff which would have been principally obtained by grazing. Unlike dry fodder, it is not therefore something which would likely need to be transported over significant distances in anything like the quantities required for dry fodder. As a consequence, it would be difficult to offer a plausible estimate as to just how much could be foraged and how much would need to be transported. We shall therefore complete our calculations based on the following daily requirement per horse:

Dry fodder = 5.9kgs (13lbs)
Salt = ½oz

Consequently, the daily animal fodder requirement of a legion cavalry contingent of 120 men using 240 mounts is as follows:

Dry fodder = 1421.6kgs (3,127.5lbs or approx. 1.4 tons)
Salt = 120oz (3.4kgs or 7.5lbs)

Consequently, the total daily weight of food which the fighting arm of a full-strength legion would need to remain effective in the field is: 6,726.4kgs (14,798.8lbs or approx. 6.62 tons).

Applying the same figures to auxiliary cavalry units therefore means that a quingenary unit (500 men), keeping one spare mount per rider, requires a total daily weight of food of 6,414.2kgs (14,111.2lbs or approx. 6.3 tons). A milliary unit (1,000 men), again keeping one spare mount per rider, therefore requires a total daily weight of food of 12,828.4kgs (28,222.4lbs or 12.6 tons).

Notwithstanding the fact that, on their own, these figures reveal one fighting unit will consume a massive quantity of basic foodstuffs per day, consideration still has to be given to the basic daily requirements of those animals used to transport the supplies to the forward areas. Therefore, having reference to Peddie's table once more, we will now calculate how much the animals within the supply column would consume on a daily basis.

Peddie provides us with data relating to the load capacity and speed of the various animals thus:

Type of animal	Load	Speed	Daily distance
Mules & pack horses	72.7kgs/160lb	3–4mph	20–25 miles
Donkeys	72.7kgs/160lb	2.5mph	15 miles
Oxen (Draught)	72.7kgs/160lb	2.5mph	15–20 miles

Again in order to simplify matters, we will choose one type of animal, in this instance the mule or pack horse given that these animals are the most practical; they are the fastest of the three choices and are also capable of covering the greatest daily distance. In choosing the mule or packhorse we are therefore confident that a supply column made up of these animals would be capable of matching the daily distance covered by a legion whilst marching at a forced pace.

At a normal pace, legionaries generally covered 20 Roman miles daily. However, at a forced pace they could be capable of 25 Roman miles a day. The Roman mile converts to the following modern units of measurement:

1 Roman mile = 0.92 Imperial miles (1.48 kms)

In order to keep pace with the legions, pack horses would therefore be an ideal choice for re-supplying rapidly advancing columns, given that the maximum amount of modern Imperial miles they would be required to cover daily would be 25 which, according to Peddie's table, is within acceptable parameters.

Consequently, based on the load capacity of each animal, it is possible to say that up to seventy-four animals would be needed to carry the minimum daily basic food ration to one entire legion. This therefore means that the additional weight of fodder required to sustain these animals is 437.6kgs (960.5lbs or approx. 0.4 tons) which, when added to the daily rations required by the legion itself, results in a grand total of 7,165.2kgs (15,763.4 lbs or approx. 7 tons). (For a full overview of grand total weights relating to unit types, see Appendix H.)

In order to better understand the scale of the logistical problems which the Roman planners faced, consideration must also be given to the forward planning concerning the cultivation and harvesting of the cereal crops which formed dry rations and the acreage of land required to do so. Again, for the sake of simplicity and in the interests of providing a basic understanding of the quantities of land needed to produce sufficient crops to feed the Roman army, the focus will be on one crop only: corn.

Modern estimates of corn yielded per acre vary, but a realistic average is around 150 Bushels. In weight this is expressed as 3,810kgs (8,382lbs or approx. 3.7 tons). Consequently, to issue 1kg of corn to each individual in a full legion of 5,307 men, it would take the corn yield of around 1.3 acres of land, or just over ½ a hectare. However, it should be remembered that the figures shown above relate to estimates of modern yields, which are much more productive than ancient crop yields. The amount of land which the Romans would have required would therefore have been significantly greater than the above quoted figures.

Given the above analyses it is not really difficult to see that, the physical risks posed to foraging armies aside, the ability to source just one type of dry supply from the local environs upon landing would have clearly presented huge problems. The influx of around 40,000 soldiers and their attendant entourage, including animals, would have made a significant and instant impact upon local supplies, both in the landing areas and spreading out along the lines of advance. Therefore, if the Romans had taken the decision to supply themselves largely from local sources, the resulting serious depletion of local stocks would not only pose potential problems for the coming year but may also have set potentially friendly sections of the population against the Roman army – especially once they had realised they were facing a winter of hunger caused solely by the demands of the invading Romans.

There is no doubt that the Romans would have tapped into the local supply reserves to some degree. However, the extent to which that happened and how judiciously it took place would logically determine whether they would be able to conduct a swift advance, or whether they would have to prosecute a slower advance; diverting resources to the procurement of supplies and dealing simultaneously with what would likely be considerable unrest resulting from the excessive depletion of local stocks.

In that regard, it should be borne in mind that the greater part of the armies used by the Britons during this period were comprised of tribal levies which were raised from ordinary peasants owing loyalty to a particular lord. It stands to reason, therefore, that they would be more likely to heed a call to arms if they felt that the presence of the Roman invaders would carry no benefits and were likely to drive them to starvation unless stopped.

It must surely, however, be some form of indicator to allow us to confidently assume that a large reserve of food supplies had actually been amassed in various locations on the European mainland, particularly northern Gaul, and then shipped over. Especially when we consider that the opening part of the campaign, which culminated in the fall of Colchester, was concluded relatively quickly. This has to indicate that the Romans were able to concentrate on making a rapid, well-supplied advance, at least to the south side of the Thames, without the need to gather large amounts of food en route.

We also need to consider that the dry rations discussed above, although staple requirements, would not be sufficient for an army to exist upon exclusively. The dry rations themselves would provide an adequate base diet for the various animals used by the army and would also allow soldiers to make such basic dishes as gruels, porridge, bread and *bucellatum* (hard tack biscuits). Nevertheless, it would also be necessary to supplement these supplies with fresh meat rations and dairy products such as cheeses. Also required would be salt and dried, smoked or salted meats, along with beer or wine. This last item would have been particularly important, given that local supplies of water, albeit plentiful, may either not have been fit for consumption for whatever natural reason, but could also even have been deliberately polluted by the retreating Britons in order to deny the supply to the Romans. The Roman planners must therefore have seen the need to have portable reserves available.

Probably the most versatile of these liquid supplies would have been wine, although we do need to understand that the Roman army would have been unable to avail themselves of anything as palatable as a modern table wine. In fact, the most likely variety available to the average soldier was a wine sometimes referred to as *acetum*, which, as the name may suggest, was a very basic acidic wine almost akin to vinegar which required heavy dilution before it was palatable. A reserve supply of this wine could therefore be augmented by adding it to good or mildly substandard water supplies. This would in turn render the water safer to drink, given its anti-bacterial properties. Indeed, this wine has been recorded as also being used by Roman medics to clean wounds.

An interesting commentary has been produced by Richard Thomas of the University of Leicester concerning the archaeological evidence of food and supply at a Roman fortress lying close to the town of Alchester in Oxfordshire.[6] The site itself is of a large fortress, capable of housing a unit of troops comparable in size to a full legion. Dating evidence indicates that the site itself was occupied by the Romans as early as AD 43 and as such the archaeological evidence which can be recovered from it is a valuable insight into the activities of the Roman army immediately after the invasion. However, on a cautionary note, the site of the fortress lies just north of the Thames, at a considerable distance inland from either of the suggested landing sites and, although the recovered finds are therefore broadly reflective, they may not be fully representative of what supply strategies were being employed by the Romans during the opening phase of the invasion. Indeed, the location would seem more to suggest that the fortress was established during the advances made by the Romans after the fall of Colchester.

Studies of the animal remains recovered from the site show that, by and large, the occupants of the fortress had adopted a dietary profile which was consistent with that of the indigenous population. Broadly speaking this would mean the large-scale importation of livestock from further afield was not something the Romans were engaged in by this time. However, the data from the recovered animal remains also showed that the remains of wild species were scarce, indicating that the garrison had no need to resort to hunting to supplement their food stocks, as meat derived from domesticated livestock was plentiful. Interestingly, excavations did recover oyster shells on site and also showed that there were a higher percentage of pig bones than would be expected in a local, late Iron Age context. The presence of the oyster shells indicates quite conclusively that some goods were being imported from further afield, as these were more of a luxury item and could not be considered to be a military staple.

Although pig bones were recovered from the site – the quantities of which suggest that consumption of pork was higher than expected in the context of the local diet – Thomas notes they are not there in sufficient enough numbers to suggest that such stock was either being imported as 'bone in' meat cuts, or whole carcasses. However, as mentioned, the evidence of the oyster shells proves the importation of goods from much further afield was taking place. Therefore, if importation of a variety of bulk stocks and supplies such as livestock or meat was also taking place, one must consider a possible reason for why evidence of this is not showing up in the archaeological record. Thomas accounts for this in part by explaining that, due to local soil conditions, smaller bones and those of younger animals may have decomposed long since. Also, that animal by-products which were useful in the production of various other items, such as bone, would have been removed for working and processing and therefore disposed of elsewhere. Nevertheless, if we reflect upon the weight of supplies needed to feed the army then another explanation logically emerges.

It is commonly accepted that the Roman army had a preference for pork. The reason for this preference is more likely to lie within the context of logistical considerations, rather than any cultural or personal preferences, given that pigs are able to bear two litters a year and are able to produce their first litter at around one year of age. This therefore makes the pig somewhat like the ancient equivalent of fast food, given that a high yield of good quality meat can be produced in a shorter space of time compared to other domesticated species. However, the pig is not without its drawbacks and moving large numbers of pigs over any sort of distance would be extremely difficult due to their essentially un-cooperative temperament. Combined with the pig's natural urge to root, the task of quickly moving even small groups of pigs over any sort of distance would prove almost impossible. Consequently, the only option available to anybody wishing to transport large quantities of pork is to slaughter and butcher the carcasses first and then transport the meat.

This probably brings us to the next good reason as to why pork was a preferred choice for the Roman army, in that it lends itself very well to food preservation processes. Pork can be salted, dried and smoked in order to keep it edible. Indeed, it is acknowledged that Roman soldiers did carry dried or smoked cuts of bacon which were capable of being stored in their marching packs. Consequently, a possible reason for the absence of larger quantities of pork bones from the archaeological record at Alchester is because pork was being supplied in processed cuts which had been pre-boned to reduce weight, thereby reducing the transportation demand.

There is of course absolutely no reason to suppose that the Romans were supplying themselves exclusively by an extended line of supply. Indeed, it is sensible to believe that they would have been drawing all kinds of fresh supplies from the local environment and populace by a number of means. Yet it would also be sensible to suggest that the Romans would have identified that they would need to take a balanced approach to how they went about this. Ultimately, given the above alternative explanation, it is clear that the absence of evidence on this occasion does not prove conclusively that large-scale importation of meat was not taking place.

Chichester – A Strategic and Logistical Appraisal

Unlike with Caesar, in reaching a decision on where to land their army we can be confident that the Claudian planners would have been in possession of much more detailed local intelligence about Britain. We have already noted Caesar's comments concerning a lack of useful intelligence about Britain and the fact that he could not even glean that much useful information from the mariners and traders who sailed to the island at that time. Nevertheless, in the years that separated the last of Caesar's raids from the Claudian invasion, it is clear that Rome's awareness of Britain and its inhabitants had changed dramatically.

The trade between Britain and the Roman Empire via Gaul would have meant that Rome was familiar with all of the island's major ports and anchorages, particularly along the south and east coasts. The Romans would have therefore put that knowledge to good use in order to decide where it would be most practical to land a large invasion army. Certainly, in the case of Chichester, the advantages of securing such a very large natural harbour area are obvious, particularly when there was a primary need to secure an anchorage for a large fleet of ships. However, whilst clearly an important consideration, Chichester would have to fulfil a number of other practical requirements before it could be deemed suitable to receive the invasion force.

It has been claimed that one of the reasons why the Roman army may have wanted to land at Chichester is because there was already a strong Roman presence in southern Britain and because the Romans already had an established military base at Chichester. Manley has explored this possibility and provides it some support within his discussion of archaeological evidence in Chichester prior to AD 43.[7] The evidence for a strong military presence is not compelling, however. Although it seems reasonable to argue that there was some form of Roman military presence in the area prior to the invasion, the archaeological evidence for a substantial military presence prior to AD 43 has not yet been discovered. Furthermore, there appears to be an issue with the dating evidence, relative to small finds such as pottery, which has been recovered from the area and which proves to be problematic when settling on a likely interpretation of its presence.

A study of the forms of pottery, such as Arretine ware, may either indicate that there was some form of Roman presence from perhaps the very end of the first century BC, continuing into the early decades of the first century AD. Equally the remains could suggest increased trade with the continent in such wares. Yet if we are content to accept that there is sufficient evidence to suggest there was some form of Roman military presence in Chichester, then how might we interpret the purpose of that presence? The answer to that question may well lie with the power struggles that were going on within the tribes affected by Catuvellaunian expansionism around the turn of the millennium and, in particular, Tincommius' flight to Rome to seek sanctuary with Augustus after he was ousted in AD 5 as ruler of the southern Atrebates by his brother, Eppillus. (See Appendix A.)

Interestingly, Eppillus exercised full control over the tribe from Calleva Atrebatum (Silchester) until AD 15 when he was in turn ousted from power by Verica, who ruled from Noviomagus (Chichester) until he was forced to flee to Rome around AD 42 and appeal to Claudius for his assistance. Given this sequence of events and the archaeological remains available, it seems that the Romans had, by the turn of the millennium, developed lucrative trade and diplomatic links with the Atrebates. Consequently, we can assume that the expulsion of Tincommius may have threatened Roman interests in the region and that this may then have prompted Augustus to send a diplomatic mission to the territory, possibly under the protection of a small detachment of Roman troops. This in turn could then have developed into a localised Roman military presence by the time Verica took control of the tribe. The purpose of which was to provide a degree of military support and assurance to an ally who was experiencing an increasing threat from Catuvellaunian aggression but whose future political and strategic benefits and trading revenues were far too valuable to just abandon.

Currently, the available archaeological evidence is unable to sustain an argument for a larger Roman military presence than this. Furthermore, historic evidence, specifically Dio's account of the landings, lends absolutely no support to the idea that a significant part of southern Britain was already under the control of Rome by the time the invasion force landed. (See Appendix G). This is because Dio is clearly describing an event which is no less than an armed invasion on a large scale, not the mass movement of redeployed troops into an already subdued territory. In addition, if the movement of such a large force of troops was merely a reinforcement of a pre-existing significant Roman presence in southern Britain, why would Dio comment on the troop's reluctance to board the ships and sail for Britain? Surely, if the southern kingdoms were already under Roman control, the Roman troops would have no reason to be so fearful of venturing into a land that even Dio describes as being beyond the limits of the known world. Indeed, if southern Britain was already under Roman control the only thing the troops would realistically need to fear would be the chance of a rough sea crossing to another Roman territory.

The notion of a full-scale invasion is furthermore supported by Suetonius when he delivers his own very brief account of the Claudian invasion.[8] Suetonius confirms that Claudius' motivation was to earn a Triumph from the conquest of Britain, something which had not been attempted since Caesar's day. How then, could a Roman emperor suppose that he could earn so important an honour as a Triumph from an already partially Romanised land?

As a further thought, it is also worth considering that if the Romans had been a significant presence in southern Britain for some time before the invasion, why is there not any evidence of a developing infrastructure, such as roads, prior to the date of the invasion? Within a year of the invasion of AD 43 the Romans had completed major civil engineering projects. They had laid down miles of roads, constructed bridges and built aqueducts and bath houses. Obviously these things were primarily for their own advantage, but as well as statements of power and control, they also came to act as a powerful incentive to the native peoples to accept Romanisation as a benefit. It therefore seems highly implausible to suggest that the Romans would have stayed in southern Britain for upwards of four decades without starting to develop a considerable infrastructure, the modern-day evidence for which should surely be more evident yet is currently conspicuous by its absence.

As we have previously acknowledged, the use of such a large anchorage as that provided by Chichester Harbour would have proven to be extremely advantageous to the Romans, given their apparent need to accommodate such a large fleet. On the other hand, the Romans may not have needed such a large anchorage as that offered by Chichester Harbour as they may never have intended to anchor their entire fleet at any one time. In addition, it must also be borne in mind that the distance between ports would certainly need to be considered when choosing a landing site.

It has been suggested that the Romans sailed from up to three points on the coast of Gaul, which may account for Dio's description of the fleet sailing in three waves. However, Dio does not directly name either a port from which the fleet sailed, or the port from which Claudius crossed to Britain. This information is instead provided by Suetonius, who tells us that when summoned by Plautius, Claudius sailed to Britain from Gaesoriacum, which is now the modern French port of Boulogne.[9] Then, as now, the port was a major maritime centre and it also has another Latin name, Portus Itius, which was also the departure point for both of Caesar's expeditions to Britain.

Given that Caesar tells us that he assembled a fleet of over 600 ships for his second expedition to Britain, it is clear that even in the earlier phases of Roman occupation Portus Itius offered a harbour which was capable of accommodating a sizeable fleet of ships.[10] Caesar confirms that the crossing to Britain itself was a run of around 30 [Roman] miles. Therefore, if we assume that the Claudian fleet did indeed depart from this point, the total distances involved in sailing to either Chichester or Richborough are as follows:

Boulogne to Richborough:
Approx. 38 nautical miles or 43.7 miles (47.5 Roman miles or 70.3kms)

Boulogne to Chichester:
Approx. 94 nautical miles or 108.1 miles (117.5 Roman miles or 173.9kms)

If nothing else, these figures demonstrate that any fleet bound for Chichester would need to spend considerably more time at sea than one bound for

Richborough, which in turn poses an increased risk to the fleet of sustaining damage or loss at sea. This therefore leads us to ask: would the Romans be prepared to take the increased risk of losing men, shipping and supplies when they could make a quicker landing on the shores of Kent? Particularly when this would be an alternative which would allow them to not only shorten their sailing time, but also allow them to consider sending military aid to any friendly British tribes once they were safely ashore and established.

Furthermore, the advantages of using the large natural harbour at Chichester are soon outweighed by the disadvantages of landing an army in that area when one begins to consider the countryside beyond the area of the port. Hind explains that the distance from Chichester to the lower Thames area, via Stane Street, is 56 miles (60.8 Roman miles or 90.1kms).[11] Hind also points out that this distance is less than that which the Roman army would have needed to cover between Richborough and London. However, this is somewhat misleading when considering the overall distances involved in travelling from both Chichester and Richborough to the ultimate destination, Colchester.

Consequently, in order to gain a clearer perspective, we need to consider the approximate overall distances for each journey, which are as follows:

Chichester to Colchester:
119 miles (129.3 Roman miles or 19.5kms)

Richborough to Colchester:
104 miles (113 Roman miles or 167.3kms)

Already it becomes apparent that there is a clear disadvantage in marching from Chichester, given that it lays the best part of a day's march further away from Colchester than Richborough. In addition, the route up from Chichester poses more problems than the route from Richborough, given that troops marching from Richborough would be able to make use of part of the North Downs Way, at least up to the River Medway. However, marching from Chichester meant that the Romans would either have needed to penetrate the Weald, or make a lengthy detour to skirt round it, to avoid the difficult terrain or ambushes. As history shows us, the Roman army was always more effective when fighting in open ground and it seems very unlikely that they would have wished to invite a repeat of the Varus disaster of AD 9. Clearly, by attempting to march through miles of totally unfamiliar and heavy woodland, this would be just what the Romans would potentially be inviting.

As a result, the necessity to find a safer, less arduous route would have markedly increased the overall distance between their starting point of

Chichester and their ultimate destination of Colchester. In addition, any increase in distance would need to be weighed against the daily supply requirements of the army; the greater the distance travelled, the greater the burden on the supply chain would become.

Hind's suggestion that the Romans actually landed in Chichester is based in part on Dio's reference to a section of the Bodunni tribe offering their allegiance to the Romans, prior to their arrival in their territory.[12] Hind supports the now widely held view that the tribe in question were in fact the Dobunni, a tribe whose territory lay to the north-west of the Atrebatean capital. Hind reinforces this belief by explaining that, if it is the case that Dio is actually referring to the Dobunni, then the events described by Dio discount any logical explanation for a landing in Kent. However, whilst we will discuss Dio's description of the opening phases of the Roman advance later, it appears that Hind does not seem to have taken into consideration certain other options, the first of which being that Dio could have been mistaken in naming this particular tribe.

Barrett has questioned the accuracy of Dio's account in relation to the chronology of Claudius' visit to the island to claim victory over the Britons.[13] He sets out a persuasive argument which, as he rightly recommends, should at the very least cause us to treat Dio's account with some degree of caution. It is not therefore unreasonable to suggest that, in the light of Barrett's criticisms regarding the accuracy of Dio's account (even if only from a chronological point of view), Dio's sources may be flawed and he could therefore also have been incorrect when he included a reference to a tribe called the 'Bodunni', when in fact he actually should have been referring to another tribe. Consequently, if one supports the case for a landing in Kent; the tribe in question would be the Cantiaci.

That said, it would be somewhat disingenuous to offer an interpretation which places a high reliance on the greater part of Dio's account, only to dismiss this part alone as clearly wrong. Another plausible alternative exists: that Dio's reference does indeed relate to the Dobunni. But, in seeking to strengthen the argument for a landing in Chichester, Hind has in fact sought to dismiss the possibility that although their territory was not within the area of the landings, they nevertheless decided it would be wise to throw their lot in with the Romans at an early stage of the invasion.

Of course, this does not fit with Dio's account when he refers to the Romans leaving a garrison in place after receiving the surrender of the 'Bodunni'. However, it may not be so straightforward as to interpret this as meaning that the Romans left a garrison in the territory of the 'Bodunni'. This is because the opening lines of Chapter XX also tell us that, prior to the surrender of the tribe, Plautius had encountered and routed both Caratacus and Togodumnus.

Consequently the telling of this part of the account seems not to be entirely clear in its meaning, given that it runs directly into the reference concerning the 'Bodunni'. Thus it may be possible that Dio was actually saying that the garrison in question was left at the site of one of the encounters with the two princes and not in the territory of the 'Bodunni' as Hind suggests.

Nevertheless, if we stay with Hind's interpretation for the moment, we next need to look at the suggestion that the Romans, in an attempt to lend military aid to the Dobunni, could have sent a 'flying column' up to the tribal capital at Corinium (Cirencester) (See Fig. 9). In examining this suggestion, the first thing that should be considered would be the likely strength of any force required to undertake a lengthy march into potentially hostile territory, with the capability to provide sufficient punch on their arrival to drive off any hostile forces sent against the Dobunni. It would therefore seem sensible to suggest that a legion battle group – comprising one full legion, a minimum of 500 cavalry, a further 3,000 auxiliary infantry and a cohort of 500 archers – would be needed. This force therefore represents a total of around 9,300 men. That is to say around a quarter of the force which it is generally accepted the Romans landed with. These numbers seem high at first glance, but it must be remembered that the battle group would need to be able to operate entirely separately of the main force and be easily capable of defending itself. Any lesser force could risk being overwhelmed and annihilated by the Britons with the inevitable consequence that the invasion force would have lost a large part of its strength for potentially no good reason.

The next matter to consider is the distance that the troops would need to travel in order to complete their mission. Hind suggests that once Cirencester had been secured, the column could have returned to Chichester. From Chichester to Cirencester it is approximately 79 miles (85.8 Roman miles or 127.1kms). If we assume that the Romans would have been travelling at a forced pace of 25 Roman miles a day, then this means that it would take the column around three and a half days to complete the march. However, this is only if we are content to accept that the march would be completed without any delays, such as attacks upon the column en route.

The next factor to bear in mind is that the column would have to be supplied by a trailing supply column; constantly ferrying supplies overland between the head of the column and the supply base at Chichester. This is because there are no navigable waterways close to the proposed line of march which would have allowed the Romans to transport supplies up from Chichester by boat. This means that, for the column to complete the march to Cirencester, the Romans would need to commit a minimum of four days' supplies to feed the entire column. This represents a total weight of dry rations alone of 69.2 tons. Of course,

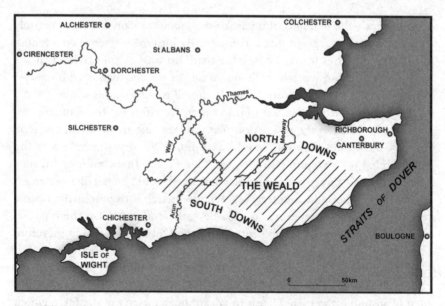

Fig. 4 The south-east quarter of Britain showing the key locations discussed, which provides a clear geographical perspective with regard to Roman landings carried out at either Chichester or Richborough and any inland advances carried out afterwards.

we then need to recognise that these mileage figures and minimum weight of supplies then need to be doubled, in order to fit with Hind's suggestion that the force quickly returned to Chichester once their objective had been completed.

Taking all of this into consideration, one must surely be prompted to ask: why would the Romans wish to risk committing so many men to such a venture? Especially when it is clear that the battle group could only be supplied by a trailing column which would be moving back and forth through Catuvellaunian-controlled territory. This would leave it highly vulnerable to repeated attacks and far removed from any immediate aid. Even if the idea of the flying column crossed the Roman planners' minds, they would have quickly identified that the plan was fraught with risk and would provide no real advantage, given that the invasion force would be much better placed to attempt relief operations once it had secured all of its primary objectives.

The next point to make concerns Hind's suggestion that once their mission to 'liberate' Cirencester had been completed the whole column would have returned to Chichester in order to take part in the march on Colchester. However, to do so would have been to make nonsense of the entire operation. This is because the column, or at least a greater part of it, would have needed to remain in the town to prevent its recapture. Otherwise there would have been little point in penetrating so deep into territory which the enemy still had the ability to dominate.

We have now established that, beyond the great natural harbour, there seem to be no real advantages to a landing at Chichester from either a strategic or a logistical point of view. Even from a political point of view, there seems to be no sound reason why the Romans would feel compelled to over-reach themselves militarily in order to lend support to a potential ally, particularly when that support could be provided more effectively at a later juncture. Effectively, we have therefore now established that the location itself not only represents a greater sailing distance for the fleet but places the invasion force at a significantly further distance from the primary objective of Colchester than any landing at Richborough. Furthermore, the ground which the troops would need to cover would be more difficult to traverse given the natural barrier of the Weald, and the only supply option open to the army would have been via trailing overland supply columns with absolutely no opportunity for shipping support until the Thames was reached.

In summary, given the points we have discussed above, there is only one logical conclusion which can be drawn as to the suggestion that Chichester was the landing site for the invasion. That is to say that it is highly unlikely that one of the most efficient and tactically adept armies in history would deliberately choose to risk the outcome of the entire invasion by placing itself in such a poor position. By landing at Chichester the Roman invasion army would have only created huge and clearly unnecessary logistical problems for itself, in order to secure what would only amount to fairly insignificant short-term political gains. Consequently, until such time as solid evidence is available to show that Chichester did indeed play host to the invasion force, it no longer seems either viable or sensible to propose that the Claudian invasion force would ever have chosen to land there.

Cogidubnus and the Invasion

Much has been said about the possible part played by Tiberius Claudius Cogidubnus (also referred to as Togidubnus) in the invasion and after the Romans had landed. Barrett, for instance, provides a detailed discussion on the various possibilities relating to how Cogidubnus fitted into the plans for invasion and his rule over the Atrebates as a client king of Rome after the Claudian invasion.[14] From what Barrett tells us it is clear that we are dealing with a man whose origins are uncertain and for whom various interpretations of his role and origins can be applied. For instance, it is as plausible to suggest that he returned to the kingdom after fleeing to Rome as a child with Tincommius, as it is to suggest that he was already in place as a ruler allied to the Catuvellauni after Verica's flight to Rome and then later switched his allegiance to Claudius.

There are only two ancient references to Cogidubnus, one of which is a reference to him in Tacitus' *Agricola*, as follows: 'Certain domains were presented to

King Cogidumnus [sic], who maintained his unswerving loyalty right down to our own times – an example of the long-established Roman custom of employing even kings to make others slaves.'[15] The other reference is given in a badly damaged inscription on Purbeck marble which was recovered whilst workmen were excavating the cellar of a house in Chichester in 1723.[16] The only decipherable part of the name, which is now almost universally held to be that of Cogidubnus, is '*gibubni*'. The suggested reconstruction of the inscription reads:

[N]EPTVNO ET MINERVAE
TEMPLVM
[PR]O SALUTE DO[MUS] DIVINAE
[EX] AVCTORITAT[E TI] CLAVD
[CO]GIDUBNI R[EGIS] LEGA[TI] AVG[VSTI] IN
BRIT[ANNIA]
[COLLE]GIUM FABROR[UM] ET QUI IN EO
[SUN]T D[E] S[UO] D[EDERUNT] DONANTE AREAM
[...]ENTE PUDENTINI FIL[IO]

To Neptune and Minerva, for the welfare of the Divine House by the authority of Tiberius Claudius Cogidubnus, king, imperial legate in Britain, the guild of smiths and those therein gave this temple from their own resources, ...ens, son of Pudentinus, presenting the site.

This translation has been disputed by Bogaers, who calls into question the interpretation of Cogidubnus' actual status.[17]

That aside, the issue of Cogidubnus has, it seems, produced somewhat of a diversionary red herring in the context of the invasion. Academics and historians alike have become caught up in the importance of Cogidubnus, relative to the invasion and the period shortly afterwards. However, even if we suppose that Claudius had actually reacted positively to Verica's entreaties and decided to send an invasion force solely to free the Atrebates from the control of the Catuvellauni, this does not automatically mean that the Romans would be obliged to land within the territory of the Atrebates. After all, what good would the Roman presence be to the Atrebates if they were tactically disadvantaged by landing their forces in the kingdom, creating significant logistical problems for themselves and not being able to secure early gains against the Catuvellauni? Similarly, if Cogidubnus was already in power by the time the Romans landed, it does not automatically follow that the Romans would have landed their troops in his territory, just because he had made friendly overtures to the Romans in exchange for their military support.

It has been suggested that Cogidubnus may even have been placed in control of the Atrebates by the Catuvellauni after Verica fled to Rome. His friendly overtures may not therefore have been completely trustworthy as far as the Romans were concerned, as it seems most unlikely that the possibility of treachery on the part of Cogidubnus could not, at that juncture, be totally discounted. On that basis it would be more sensible to make a landing in a more readily accessible place where early advantages could be gained and a strong logistical and tactical advantage had been established. Then, as we have already suggested, the Romans could think about moving further afield with a view to lending assistance to such possible allies as Cogidubnus and the Atrebates.

There is no contemporary evidence which survives which demonstrates that Cogidubnus was a significant figure in the historical record of the invasion. However, this changes in the period immediately after the invasion: he is amongst that highly select list of native British rulers who Roman historians mention as still holding some form of power after the invasion. Cogidubnus is nonetheless still a shadowy figure whose later curriculum vitae seems to have grown largely out of the theories put forward by academics. In reality, we know nothing solid about Cogidubnus, nor can we say with absolute certainty that Tacitus' Cogidubnus is the same man as the '*gidubni*' referred to on the inscription recovered from Chichester. Furthermore, we are as yet unable to say whether Tacitus' Cogidubnus or the '*gidubni*' from the inscription were ever resident at the fabulous palace at Fishbourne, let alone that it was built for either of them.

The question of Cogidubnus and his role in the early years of Roman administration in Britain is likely to be the subject of extensive further debate in years to come. Given what little Tacitus actually has to say about him, it seems a fair assumption to make that he could have been an existing ruler who was granted extra power and title from the Romans. However, for the purposes of this work it seems wiser to confine oneself to the fact that there is little definite to say about him, rather than the fact he seems to be no more than a part of the local nobility who was astute enough to realise that the old order was soon to disappear. He ultimately turned himself into an instrument of the Roman state in order to preserve his own power and status. And on that note, we will venture to say no more about him.

A Question of Timing

If there is a further important point to be learnt from Julius Caesar's British incursions, it is that deciding on the correct timing for the landings in Britain was a crucial part of the overall plan. As such, it seems highly unlikely that the Claudian planners would have overlooked the well-documented consequences of staging what amounted to poorly planned and rushed missions carried out at the wrong end of the campaigning season.

In Caesar's accounts of his raids on Britain he has helpfully provided us with sufficient information to allow us to identify the times of the year when both raids took place. However, the classical accounts that have survived to our times and which refer to the Claudian invasion require a little more scrutiny in order to provide us with an approximate date for the sailing of the invasion fleet.

By now, any reader of this work should have realised that the thrust of any argument put forward has always originated from consideration of what the practicality of the situation dictates that the invasion plan should be, rather than labouring overlong on the results of academic hypotheses alongside the interpretation of historical and archaeological evidence. Therefore, the starting point for any suggestions made in this work as to when the Roman army may have landed in Britain has to primarily be driven once more by the practical considerations linked to the timing of the landings.

It is clear that there could be no errors in deciding when to stage the landings if Claudius' army was to make a safe crossing of the Fretum Gallicum (Straits of Dover) with minimum loss. The landings would therefore need to be carried out early enough in the year to allow the invasion force to comfortably complete its primary objectives. Seasonal weather trends would also be a key factor to consider, both to allow the soldiers to campaign as effectively as possible and to allow the chain of supply to operate as unhindered by poor conditions as possible. Therefore, finding the right window of opportunity was paramount.

As has been documented by Caesar's accounts of his own raids, sailings made too late in the year forced him to abandon his advance and return to Gaul in order to avoid the fierce storms which blew up around the time of the autumnal equinox and which would batter the Straits of Dover throughout the winter. However, a sailing too early in the year could also invite disaster as fierce storms can still rise up in the channel, even after the tidal levels change again with the *vernal* (spring) equinox. With so many men, ships and supplies at sea at any one time, it would only take one powerful storm to catch the Romans off guard and not only could the greater part of the invasion fleet be decimated, but Rome's military capability in the northern reaches of the empire would be seriously affected too.

The spring equinox generally falls around 20 March, so we can say with some certainty that the Romans would not have risked a large-scale crossing of the Straits of Dover so close to this date. However, they would nevertheless have wished to sail as soon as practicable after that date in order to make best use of the available campaigning season. The intended sailing times would also need to take account of when the army could actually be fully assembled for embarkation. Had the majority of the force been assembled in Gaul prior to the onset of winter, they could have over-wintered in tented camps close to the point of embarkation and then been ready to sail as soon as the weather window allowed. However, this seems an unlikely option for the majority of the force given that a winter spent *sub pellibus* (under leather) would have been dangerous for morale; the troops would have been forced to endure prolonged periods of poor winter weather in inadequate accommodation, probably without sufficient work to keep them fully occupied. It would therefore seem more reasonable to suggest that only an advance party over-wintered close to Boulogne in order to make preparations for the arrival of the fleet and the rest of the invasion force, which would march into the area once weather conditions had sufficiently improved.

The evidence for the increased presence of the Roman army in the area is a difficult thing to locate, however. Given that the presence was only ever going to be on a temporary basis, no permanent buildings would have been erected to accommodate the men. They instead would have bivouacked in large marching camps, the archaeological footprint of which is hard to find given that it generally consists of little more than perimeter ditches and the occasional remains of bread ovens. Indeed, the elusive nature of such encampments is also an encumbrance when locating the actual line of march which the Romans took after moving out from the landing area to advance on Colchester.

Barrett has discussed the timing of the invasion alongside Dio's account and identified certain chronological errors created by the account.[18] The first and less important error demonstrates well why the accuracy of Dio's writings should not be accepted at face value without first carrying out some further verification work. Dio tells us that, upon his departure for Britain, Claudius left his fellow consul, Lucius Vitellius, in charge of affairs at home.[19] Dio also tells us that Claudius and Vitellius held the consulship for *semenstris* (six months). However, the consular *fasti* (calendar) show that Claudius and Vitellius were succeeded by the suffect consuls, Lucius Pedanius Secundus and Sextus Palpellius Hister, whose terms of office began in March of AD 43. This date is supported by a ritual purification of the city which was described by Pliny the Elder as taking place on 7 March of that year, during the suffect consulship of Secundus and Hister.[20] This therefore means that Claudius and Vitellius could actually only have served a *bimenstris* (two-month term) in consular office.

Barrett tells us that corroboration for this is given in Suetonius' account of the life of Claudius, who tells us that all of Claudius' consulships were *bimenstris*, apart from his fifth term as consul in AD 51 which was *semenstris*.[21] However, this in itself is not accurate as Claudius' second term as consul was in AD 42 when he served for a full term alongside his second consul, Caius Caecina Largus. Perhaps here then is where Dio, and it would appear Suetonius too, have become a little confused as to the length of Claudius' consular terms.

The second error which Barrett describes is actually more serious as it concerns the chronological anomalies which had been created by Dio's assertion that Claudius, having been summoned to Britain by Plautius, was away from Rome for six months. Barrett points out that if the reading of Dio is to be taken at face value, it is difficult to see how the events he describes could fill a period of six months when it is more likely that they would be completed in around two. Nevertheless, as we shall now discuss, Dio's description of Claudius' absence from Rome is very helpful in allowing us to begin to plot a possible date of embarkation for the invasion army. Furthermore, the date arrived at fits extremely well with the allowances which would need to be made in order to time the sailing of the fleet to the best advantage.

Dio is not alone in describing Claudius' absence from Rome as a period of six months, as Suetonius also tells us that Claudius was away from Rome for this period of time.[22] Of course, it is entirely possible that both Suetonius and Dio used the same reference sources to compile their accounts, possibly the lost books of Tacitus' *Histories*. It is even possible that Dio may have used part of Suetonius' work as a reference, given that his work was the earlier account.

In Dio's account, he mentions that Claudius returned to Rome during the consulship of Caius Sallustius Crispus Passienus and Titus Statilius Taurus. Both men were in office in early AD 44. However, whilst Taurus' term was *semenstris*, commencing in January of that year, Passienus' term was only *bimenstris*, again commencing in January. (See Appendix I.) Therefore, if Dio's account is accurate in this regard Claudius could not have returned to Rome any later than early March of AD 44.

The two corroborating classical accounts of Claudius' absence from Rome, and the reference to the consular term during which Claudius made his return to Rome, are very useful. With these we are able to identify an approximate date for when Plautius summoned Claudius to join him in Britain. Consequently, if we accept the relative accuracy of the information provided in the accounts and work six months back from the consular term mentioned, we are able to say that Plautius sent for Claudius somewhere between early July and late August/early September of AD 43. That said, it seems unlikely that Plautius sent for Claudius in the later part of this time bracket as the deterioration in sea conditions on the approach to the autumn would represent an unacceptable risk to Claudius' safety.

A further clue exists in Dio's account which not only allows for a more precise calculation of when Plautius summoned his master, but also for more closely predicting when the invasion fleet actually sailed.[23] Dio mentions that, having initially been blown back on their course, the Romans were heartened by an auspicious event: a flash of light crossed the night sky from east to west, the same direction as the fleet were sailing. In dealing with this part of the account, there are two ways to evaluate its significance. The first is to identify it as a *topos*, a literary device which Dio frequently injects into his work to add support to his account. However, in this instance there is a second possible explanation beyond the use of *topoi*, which allows us to identify a known celestial event and which also provides us with a clear date range. The event in question is the meteor shower known as the Eta Aquariids.

This meteor shower occurs annually as a result of Earth passing through the particles left by Halley's Comet as it travels around our solar system. The shower begins in late April and grows in intensity before concluding in early to mid-May. The radiant point from which the meteors travel is the constellation of Aquarius, hence the name given to the shower. The timing of the shower within the calendar is significant, given that it is only one of three showers which would plausibly tie in with the six-month period of absence mentioned in the accounts by Suetonius and Dio. However, the other two events, the Pi Puppids and the Lyrids, seem to be unlikely candidates.

The Lyrids are another annual shower which occurs in mid to late April, but they are fast-moving meteors which are radiant from the constellation of Lyra. As such they would travel on an east-to-north-east axis and would not, therefore, fit with the description given by Dio as travelling from east to west. The Pi Puppids, meanwhile, are completely unsuitable as a possibility. They emanate from the constellation Puppis and appear in late April, but in the southern sky. However, even were they visible in northern latitudes they are not an annual event and appear as bright and slow moving, a description which, at any rate, seems not to match Dio's description of a 'flash' of light.

Given that we can therefore effectively discount the Pi Puppids, there are only two meteor showers which could be possible candidates for the flash of light described by Dio; by date reference the next nearest meteor shower events do not fit into the chronology we have now established. The Quadrantids are too early, as they occur in early January, and the Arietids are too late as they occur in mid-June.

Of course, there is nothing to suggest that what the Roman fleet saw was something other than a meteor or similar event. However, in respect of the Eta Aquariids, there is a further piece of evidence which Dio has provided which also supports the suggestion that it was in fact a meteor from this particular shower which the fleet observed. As we have mentioned previously, the meteors of the Eta Aquariids are radiant from the constellation of Aquarius. What is interesting about this fact is that this part of the sky is not visible until the hours just before dawn. This fits very well with Dio's description that, during the course of the night sailing, the fleet had been driven back on its course. It is therefore clear that the event had not been viewed during the earlier part of the night crossing, whilst the ships were still battling the weather and the constellation of Aquarius had not yet risen into view.[24]

On the basis of the above conclusions, it is therefore possible to suggest that a late April–early May crossing was made by the invasion fleet, and after around two months of campaigning Plautius summoned Claudius to be present for the final part of the campaign.

If we accept the fact that the fleet indeed sailed around early May, then the historical accounts begin to make even more sense. This is because Dio has again assisted us with some further information which allows us to tighten down key dates within the invasion even further.[25] Dio tells us that Claudius spent only sixteen days in Britain. Furthermore, in Chapter XXI of the book, he tells us that Claudius 'hastened' back to Rome.

Barrett questions the use of this description and takes it to mean that Claudius was not necessarily in a hurry to return to Rome. He took it instead to mean that Claudius hastened to leave Britain. However, Barrett makes no detailed examination of this point and instead ventures to conclude that it may be impossible to provide a chronological reconstruction that eliminates the difficulties thrown up by Dio's account. This conclusion is unfortunate in that it appears somewhat ill judged – given that the evidence is contained predominantly in Dio's account – to allow us to construct a plausible timeline not only for the invasion but also for Claudius' involvement in the campaign.[26]

By sailing the invasion fleet by early May, and then adding around two months of campaigning, this takes us to around early July, at which point we are told that Plautius halted his advance, set about consolidating his gains and sent for Claudius to join him. It seems reasonable that we should allow Claudius about a month and a half to reach Britain given that we need to allow perhaps two weeks for Plautius' message to reach him and for him to assemble his entourage before he commenced his journey. This would mean his departure from Rome was around mid-July. We then need to allow for a sea voyage from Ostia, Rome's ancient sea port, to Massilia, which is now the modern French port of Marseilles. This may have taken at least a further week: Suetonius explains that Claudius' ship was nearly wrecked twice during this leg of the journey, which may very well have delayed Claudius.[27]

Dio states that Claudius then made his way from Massilia to Portus Itius (Boulogne) both by land and river routes. However, Suetonius states that Claudius marched through Gaul. If then, for arguments sake, we accept that Claudius marched the entire route, we must recognise that his entire entourage could only have moved at the pace of his infantry escort, with whom his cavalry would be obliged to keep pace. Therefore, if we accept that the column could cover an average of 20 Roman miles a day, the journey of 445 Roman miles (410 miles or 659.8kms) would take just over twenty-two days to complete. This therefore takes us to around mid-August.

There is no reason to doubt that the reinforcements which Claudius took to Britain with him had not already been assembled and were ready to depart as soon as Claudius arrived at the port. Therefore, assuming that conditions were favourable for an immediate sailing, Claudius would have made the journey across the channel and landed in Kent after a comfortable day's sail. Consequently, after a stay in Britain of sixteen days, Claudius was ready to start the return journey by early September.

It is here that the above chronology ties in particularly well with the events described. Firstly, Claudius' aides would have been anxious to get Claudius back across the channel at this point as the autumnal equinox, typically falling around 22–23 September, was approaching and, as discussed earlier, sea conditions were deteriorating. Therefore, in order to ensure the safety of the emperor, a rapid departure from Britain was essential. Secondly, the suggested chronology allows for all the events described within the invasion to take place in one campaigning season. Thirdly, adding six months to the suggested date for Claudius' departure from Rome would mean that Claudius would arrive back in Rome around mid-January, as Dio says, during the consular offices of Taurus and Passienus. The assertion made by Barrett as to the difficulties in producing a plausible chronology for the campaign seems, consequently, somewhat inaccurate.

The Classis Britannica and Claudius' Invasion

Most commentators agree that the Classis Britannica was formed shortly before the Claudian invasion of Britain, probably for the primary purpose of facilitating the landing of the invasion force and then keeping it supplied as the campaign gained impetus. As an organisation this body remains relatively obscure, however, with comparatively little archaeological evidence to draw on and almost nothing in existence by way of classical accounts to assist our understanding of the way the navy was organised and how it actually operated. We can therefore only speculate at this time as to the exact remit of this organisation. Consequently, our comments on the role of the fleet will again focus only on practical considerations, rather than making reference to any academic papers which, at any rate, seem to be fairly scarce on this particular subject.

Physical evidence, other than the coastal bases and inland installations attributable to the Classis Britannica, is most often represented by the wealth of brick and tile stamps which have been recovered over the years. However, the way the navy was operated is only really hinted at by Tacitus in the *Agricola*, and it needs to be borne in mind that the type of operations he briefly described, such as landing marines and settlement raiding along the Scottish coast, occurred some forty years after the Claudian landings and are likely to be roles which steadily evolved from the fleet's originally intended purpose as a transport and supply arm.[28]

Although the capability to mount attacks and land troops may have been something which the Classis Britannica developed in later years, it seems reasonable to suggest that the ability to transport and land troops to both coastal and inland locations formed part of their early role. That capability becomes even more plausible when one considers our earlier point that all of the legions which took part in the invasion's earliest phases were drawn from bases close to large, navigable rivers, such as the Rhine and the Danube. The legionaries that took part in the Claudian invasion would therefore have been fully conversant with river operations and competent in making the best use of shipping to support campaigns.

The name Classis Britannica implies that the fleet operated exclusively in British waters. However, this is not strictly true as its first main base was the great Gallic naval base at Portus Itius (Boulogne) and its area of operations saw it sailing not only in the waters around Britain but also along the coastline of northern Europe.

Thanks largely to 1950s and '60s Hollywood film productions which featured the Roman world, most people visualise a typical image of a Roman fleet as a body of vessels, almost exclusively comprised of sleek warships, equipped with multiple banks of oars and having the capability to sink or disable opposing vessels with bronze rams fitted to the bow. However, although a small number of typical Roman warships may have formed part of the invasion fleet, it is more likely that the backbone of the fleet was formed by a variety of cargo type vessels. These would have been capable of transporting men and horses, as well as food and equipment. The most typical form of vessel used were therefore likely to have been variants of the *Corbita*. These vessels varied in size and load capacity and were ideal for the transportation of a wide variety of cargos, dependent on the size of the vessel itself. (See colour plate.) Ships of this type fit closely with the descriptions of the bespoke vessels which Caesar describes as being built for his second raid on Britain.[29]

However, it certainly seems unreasonable to suppose that the entire invasion fleet had been assembled prior to the onset of the winter of AD 42, given that so many ships moored in one port area would be difficult to manage and maintain and therefore at significant risk of storm damage over the course of the winter. In addition, the amount of ships required for the invasion were likely to be well in excess of the levels of shipping normally operated by the fleet which would eventually become the Classis Britannica. It therefore seems more reasonable to suggest that, as with Caesar's shipping requirements, these additional ships were constructed over the winter months at a variety of locations, both in ports and on major rivers and then sailed on to Boulogne. There they would begin to amass during the weeks prior to the intended departure date.

With regard to the number of vessels that were initially involved in the invasion, Caesar tells us that in order to transport four legions and 800 cavalry, without baggage train, he had assembled a fleet of 600 transports and 28 war-ships.[30] However, it should be considered that, during both of Caesars incursions, he elected to beach the majority of his ships for the duration of the campaign.

Peddie provides comment on the shipping requirement required by the Claudian invasion force by discussing the actual numbers of men and animals required to be shipped, along with their supplies.[31] He estimates that the total fleet requirement would have been upward of 1,000 ships. However, without knowing the actual sizes, types and carrying capacity of the vessels used, placing an estimate on the total shipping requirement is problematic. Although it does seem worth pointing out that if Caesar needed over 600 ships to transport four legions and 800 cavalry, without their attendant baggage train, it seems unlikely that the 1,000 ships which Peddie suggests would have been sufficient to transport around double that number in one sailing.

Nevertheless, if we are content to accept that the Classis Britannica numbered in excess of 1,000 vessels at this point we have to make the logical assumption that the Romans would not just allow so many ships to remain at anchor whilst the invasion took hold ashore. It is far more likely that they would make best use of these resources and that a large proportion of the fleet returned to Gaul on the first available tide, in order to begin shuttling across the massive quantities of supplies needed to keep the army moving. Consequently, as was suggested earlier in this work, this tactic would negate the need for a harbour capable of accommodating that many vessels at one time.

Whilst this was happening, shore parties from the Classis Britannica, probably with the assistance of the legions' engineers, would begin to establish the very first Roman supply ports in Britain. At the same time the small number of warships we previously mentioned could have been used to carry out patrolling in the area, securing the seaways. Once the initial landings had taken place and the establishment of supply bases had been completed, the next phase of naval operations would have been well underway. They would involve navigating the coast and entering navigable waterways which would enable the fleet to penetrate towards inland locations. This in turn would then allow the fleet to

Fig. 5 Classis Britannica stamp on a Pila brick found at Folkestone, Kent. (*RIB*, Vol. II, Fascicule V, Instrumentum Domesticum, 2481.22)

transport supplies to forward units, removing the need for them to rely solely on trailing lines of supply carried by pack animals.

The support that such a capability could provide to the army would be vital to the success of the campaign, as it would ensure a constant flow of equipment and provisions to a quickly advancing army. However, as vital as this support would be, it could only be offered if the right choice of landing area was made. In the opening part of the next chapter, we will discuss exactly why it is that a landing in the Richborough area could be the only real option open to the Romans. Particularly if they were to succeed in their initial goal of a rapid landing in force, followed by the defeat of Caratacus and Togodumnus and the capture of Colchester.

Notes

1 Polybius, *The Histories – Book VI*, Chapter 39, pp. 12–14
2 Carrington, in S. Stallibrass & R. Thomas (2008), p. 22
3 J. Peddie (1987), p. 30
4 'Animal Management', *Veterinary Department for the General Staff, War Office* (1901, Reprinted 1914)
5 J. Peddie (1987), p. 31
6 S. Stallibrass & R. Thomas (2008), pp. 31–49
7 J. Manley (2002), pp. 111–28
8 Suetonius, *The Twelve Caesars – Claudius*, Chapter XVII
9 Ibid.
10 Julius Caesar, *The Gallic Wars – Book V*, Chapter II
11 J.G.F. Hind (1989), p. 12
12 Ibid., p. 16
13 A.A. Barrett (1980), pp. 31–3
14 A.A. Barrett (1979), pp. 227–42
15 Tacitus, *Agricola*, Chapter XIV
16 *RIB* 91, p. 25
17 J. Bogaers (1979), pp. 243–54
18 A.A. Barrett (1980), pp. 31–3
19 Cassius Dio, *Roman Histories – Book LX*, Chapter XXI
20 *Natural History – Book X*, Chapter XXXV
21 Suetonius, *The Twelve Caesars – Claudius*, Chapter XIV
22 Ibid., Chapter XVII
23 Cassius Dio, *Roman Histories – Book LX*, Chapter XIX
24 Meteor shower research conducted online at: www.meteorshowersonline.com
25 Cassius Dio, *Roman Histories – Book LX*, Chapter XXIII
26 A.A. Barrett (1980), p. 33
27 *Suetonius, The Twelve Caesars – Claudius*, Chapter XVII
28 Tacitus, *Agricola*, pp. 10, 25, 29–30 and 38
29 Julius Caesar, *The Gallic Wars – Book V*, Chapter I
30 Ibid., Chapter II
31 J. Peddie (1987), pp. 38–41

7

INVASION

Kent – A Practical Perspective

If Chichester as a landing site offered very little by way of a tactical and logistical advantage to the Romans, then Richborough represents a total opposite. Therefore, in this section we will deal with just what it was about the location which would have made a landing in Kent so attractive to the Romans.

We have already discussed the relative distances involved, both in sailing from Boulogne to Chichester and to Richborough, and marching from Chichester and Richborough to Colchester. Though we have now identified that there are clearly disadvantages in respect of those distances involving a march from Chichester, the argument for Kent is further reinforced by a number of other practical considerations.

Advocates for the case for Kent cite a number of archaeological finds which supposedly lend strong support for the view that the Romans made their advance from the Kent coast and then moved towards the Thames – where they subsequently crossed and moved on to capture Colchester. However, some of the better known archaeological finds and features which are presented as evidence for invasion activity, such as the Bredgar Hoard and the discovery of early military features from the excavations at the villa site in Eccles in Kent, are far too circumstantial in nature. Indeed, they are unable to conclusively demonstrate a strong evidential link with the initial inland advance of the Roman army. That being so, this cannot be said of Richborough: it is, in contrast, extremely difficult to ignore the wealth of strong archaeological evidence that has been recovered from this area. Even on its own, and because of its very nature, Richborough asserts a strong case for a large-scale troop landing at precisely the right date. Therefore, whilst we will examine the significance of the archaeology at Richborough, the chief discussion point of this part of the work will focus on the everyday requirements for supporting the invasion and how that is facilitated by the local topography.

As we have seen, much has been said about the supposed influence of the Atrebates as a factor in choosing Chichester as a landing site; from Verica's flight to Rome to the later involvement of Cogidubnus as a client ruler. However, if proponents of the Chichester case can present the argument that

Rome had acted to support Verica, then those in favour of a Kentish landing can reasonably also offer the same argument: that Adminius could have presented himself as a useful ally to the Romans by asking them to restore him to rule in Cantium in return for the local support he may have been able to command, thereby providing an initial degree of stability to assist the Roman occupation. After all, the only resistance the Roman army met in Kent, as we shall discuss later, was a clash with Caratacus and Togodumnus close to Canterbury and a decisive two-day battle on what appears to be the River Medway.

Whilst there is scope for proposing each of these arguments, the plain fact is that neither one has any real strength. No evidence exists to say conclusively what happened to either Verica or Adminius after they had sought the protection of Rome. Consequently, any theories which seek to provide a possible role for either of these rulers during or immediately after the invasion can really only be regarded as unsubstantiated speculation. Again then, it seems more appropriate that practical considerations should form the basis of any argument for the landing site, rather than unsupported supposition.

One has only to study the coastline and inland topography of the south-eastern quarter of the British Isles in AD 43 to appreciate just how well it lends itself to a large-scale landing, followed by a fully supported advance to Colchester. (See Fig. 4.) Even if we look at a modern map it is not hard to see how easy it would have been for the Romans to have received naval support while they marched through the top of Kent and then crossed the Thames close to its estuary. The next leg of the advance could then also have been provided with naval support as shipping took full advantage of major Essex rivers such as the Crouch, Blackwater and finally the Colne, which would have allowed the Romans to sail their ships right into Colchester.

In examining the merits of Chichester as a landing area we have already made a strong case for a landing area closer to Gaul, given the huge amount of supplies that the Romans would have needed to ship in from the continent in order to keep the army fed. In contrast, upon first consideration of Richborough, it seems difficult to resolve how the original site would have been big enough to accommodate such a vast amount of men and supplies. Nevertheless, as we consider the site and its immediate environs more closely, an explanation emerges for just how well suited the site is for not only the landing of a large number of troops but also for its secondary and more important role as a key component of the re-supply operations which the Romans would need to run in order to support the military advance.

Given that the very first action carried out by the troops as they landed was to establish a strong defensive position, it seems sensible to consider initially just what further interpretations we can draw from the archaeological evidence for this earliest of phases and then attempt to reconcile this with the fact that in excess of 40,000 troops landed here before making the push inland.

Referring the original 1949 excavation reports of J.P. Bushe-Fox, Webster relates that the two parallel ditches that are associated with the Claudian landings ran for a distance of 644m (705 yards) in an almost north–south orientation.[1] Where the northern end of the defences terminates with the Richborough stream, at the southern extremity there are the beginnings of a curve to the feature. This indicates that the defences may have enclosed a site approximately 10 acres (4.5ha) in area. There is also evidence for a single gateway, around 3.35m (11ft) in width. Webster points out that a site of this size would not have been big enough to accommodate the entire invasion force as this would have required a site with a surface area of around 150 acres (60.7 ha). He does, however, suggest that it may instead have been the camp of an initial task force of several thousand men. He also offers the theory that the smallness of the early camp may serve as evidence to confirm the existence of the first of the three waves of the invasion forces, as referred to by Dio in his account of the invasion,[2] as a smaller initial landing of troops would have only needed to establish a smaller fortification. Furthermore, Webster offers the possible explanation that the site itself, which was clearly very short-lived in purpose, was actually there to defend the original anchorage for the fleet.

Manley explores the possibilities of just what size the initial camp area may have been, prior to the erosion that has occurred in the nearly two millennia since the Romans came ashore.[3] He postulates that if around 100m of the surface area to the east, north and central extremities of the site had been lost to erosion then the original surface area contained within the defences would be more in the order of 43.2 acres (17.5 ha).

As referenced by Manley, Gilliver refers to the treatises by the supposed Roman military surveyor, Pseudo-Hyginus,[4] on building and fortifying camps or surveying camps.[5] Based on the figures which Pseudo-Hyginus provides, we are told that a hectare would accommodate a recommended troop density of 1,174 men. If we accept that figure as a standard troop density per hectare of camp, then the surface area which Manley estimates may have been occupied by the camp in AD 43 would have only been capable of accommodating around 20,500 men. Manley also suggests that the available shoreline at Richborough which the defences would have protected would only have been capable of accommodating around sixty-two tightly packed vessels at any one time. Consequently, we are left with a defensive compound which is incapable of accommodating the full invasion force and which would also be unable to protect the vast numbers of shipping required by the Romans.

However, far from ruling Richborough out as a landing site, we are in fact able to offer a very plausible argument for just why the site was almost certainly the landing area and also why the earliest defensive structures had no need to accommodate the entire invasion army and the vast number of ships that would have transported and supplied it.

This argument commences with Peddie's observations: he states that the first wave of troops to land would have taken possession of and then fortified key areas of ground whilst other troops pushed inland to locate the Britons.[6] This means that, within a very short space of time, the amount of troops which the earliest defence works would have needed to protect at Richborough was greatly reduced, given that a large contingent of the troops quickly advanced inland. After all, with no Britons to impede the advance it would have been absolutely unthinkable that the Romans would initially content themselves with the toe hold on Britain that they had so far achieved, and fail to take full advantage of the situation by making a rapid push inland. It would have been absolutely plain to Plautius and his staff that any delay in expanding their early gains would risk inviting a strong counter attack, which could push them straight back into the sea.

Peddie also hypothesises that Plautius would have sought to gain control of the Wantsum Channel and the Isle of Thanet. He supports this by referring to the archaeological evidence for the early occupation of Regulbium (Reculver) at the northern mouth of the Wantsum Channel by a garrison of around 250 men. Peddie explains that by taking control of these three key locations, Plautius would then have direct control of a strategic navigable waterway. He would therefore have secured himself not only a large and safe anchorage which could easily accommodate vast numbers of ships, but he would have also taken possession of a waterway which would provide him with a safer, much shorter route through towards the Thames Estuary. This would remove the need for shipping to negotiate the more dangerous waters of North Foreland, off the north-east coast of Thanet.

The navigability of the Wantsum Channel has been the focus of some debate in the past. However, this issue has been recently addressed by Moody, who has commented on the development of the channel from its initial formation up to the point when it finally silted-up in more recent times.[7] Moody explains that the north and south creeks which eventually joined to form the channel were probably linked up in the early Bronze Age. Once fully open, the channel would then have been scoured out by tides flowing through it from the direction of the Thames Estuary. Moody also states that the channel was likely to have been at its deepest between the Roman and late Anglo-Saxon periods. The channel was therefore navigable until around the eleventh century when the deposition of silt began to choke it, eventually separating the northern and southern inlets before blocking the channel completely.

Fig. 6 The coastline of north-east Kent and Thanet during the Roman period, as suggested by Moody. (Illustration adapted from G. Moody (2008), p. 51)

The fact that Thanet was separated from the Kentish mainland by a tidal channel is interesting, not only from the point of view that it provided the Romans with a shortcut to the Thames, but also because it provided a natural defensive barrier which could only be effectively overcome by the use of shipping. Therefore anyone wishing to assault Thanet would need to have use of an efficient navy in order to quickly land sufficient numbers of troops on the island. Certainly the Romans had this capability. The Britons, however, did not, as although they had limited access to shipping, they had nothing that constituted a navy at their disposal.

In order to gain a clear tactical and logistical advantage, it consequently seems logical to assume that the second of Dio's three waves initially landed on Thanet and quickly subdued whatever opposition they encountered,

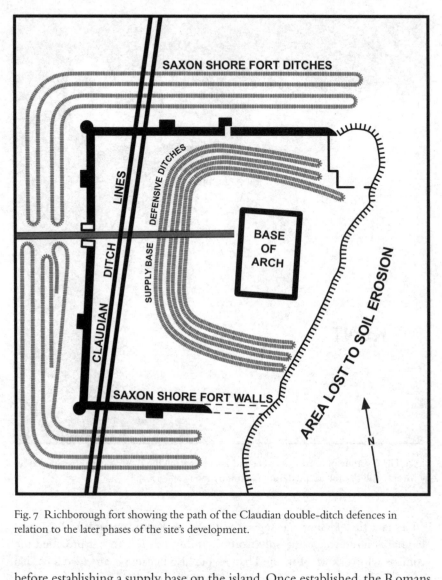

Fig. 7 Richborough fort showing the path of the Claudian double-ditch defences in relation to the later phases of the site's development.

before establishing a supply base on the island. Once established, the Romans would then have been able to receive shipping in a sheltered harbour, with the facility to offload cargo in a totally safe environment. Effectively, the south-western parts of the island could then have been used as a reception for re-supply drops; acting almost like an ancient-world version of the Mulberry harbour systems used by the allies in the 1944 Normandy landings. This would have afforded the Romans the capability of distributing provisions and equipment, initially by shipping them across the short stretch of water between Thanet and Richborough. There would therefore have been no need to create an area significantly bigger than the early defensive enclosure which has been identified at Richborough, as the base would have effectively only been required to provide an early function as a smaller secondary reception area; receiving incoming supplies which were to be sent out on a trailing supply line.

Even during the early part of the inland advance it seems reasonable to propose that, as the ground was swept clear of opposition, the Classis Britannica switched from their original task of providing transport for the invasion army to their next phase of operations: that of importing and distributing supplies. As soon as the advance had gained ground the fleet would have been needed to sail into the Wantsum Channel and travel as far down the Little and Great Stour rivers as they could go; supporting the troops as they closed on Canterbury and opening up multiple lines of supply. This meant the advancing troops could then avoid reliance on a single trailing column out of Richborough for their daily supply requirements. (See Fig. 12.)

The early part of the advance we are referring to could have been carried out by the third wave of troops mentioned by Dio. As this part of the army pushed its way inland this would, in turn, have negated the necessity to have a larger base at Richborough as it clearly did not need to accommodate vast numbers of ships and troops at any one time. If such is the case, there is no need to question the size of the original Claudian defences at Richborough as there is clearly a sound reason why the defensive enclosure did not need to be any bigger.

In truth, there is as yet no conclusive evidence to support the theory that the Romans effectively used Thanet as a large offshore supply base. Yet it should be borne in mind that there is an abundance of finds to attest to the presence of the Roman military on the Thanet side of the Wantsum at the time of the invasion. There are also many archaeological features on Thanet which have yet to be properly investigated and interpreted, and any number of these could in the future support the above suggestion. It is nevertheless difficult to refute the fact that the above argument is incredibly sound from a tactical and logistical point of view, as it is one which makes complete sense of why the Romans had no need to accommodate the entire fleet at one time, or erect defences sufficient to protect the entire invasion army in one particular place.

The Military Campaign Commences

Prior to the invasion army setting sail for Britain, there appears to have been a strong degree of unrest amongst the troops. The men seem to have been gripped by what may have been a combination of superstitious dread and a fear of what lay beyond the fringes of the known world. According to Dio, it was only the intervention of Narcissus, the freedman secretary of Claudius, which finally persuaded the troops to follow Plautius to Britain.[8] Dio also mentions that although the fleet sailed, this was done late in the season. However, given what we have previously discussed about the sailing dates, it seems more logical to interpret this as meaning that the fleet actually sailed later than intended in the campaigning season.

Having landed on the shores of Britain, we are nevertheless told that the Roman forces met with no opposition. Dio explains that this is effectively because the Britons had spies or agents across the channel in Gaul who had reported back the unrest and refusal of the troops to sail. Hearing this, Caratacus and Togodumnus had decided not to muster their armies as they believed that the invasion had been called off. Subsequently, the tribal levies had remained in their farms and homesteads, making it impossible to muster the army in time to mount a defence against the landings when they did finally happen. There is a clear irony here given the fact that, by exhibiting such disobedience and uncharacteristic fear, the Roman army was subsequently gifted with a tremendous early advantage culminating in them being able to achieve a stunning victory – even by their standards.

Dio's account then records that, although the Briton's did manage to assemble their army, the Romans could not engage them in open battle. Dio appears to suggest that the Britons instead chose to adopt guerrilla-style tactics, as they did in Caesar's day; preferring to harass rather than engage in great numbers. However, the next part of Dio's account is significant, given that he tells us that Roman forces actually encountered and defeated both Caratacus and Togodumnus, then afterwards received the surrender of the 'Bodunni' (an event which was discussed earlier in this work).[9] Having defeated both, the Romans then left a garrison behind whilst the rest of the army continued its advance.

As with Caesar's campaigns, the Romans' first contact with any major British settlement would have been in the Canterbury area. In Caesar's time it was the hill fort at Bigbury, just to the west of the modern town. However, by the time of the Claudian invasion, Bigbury had long been abandoned and the new settlement was now in the area of Durovernum Cantiacorum (Canterbury). This was the tribal *oppidum*, or capital of the Cantiaci tribe, which logically seems to be an appropriate location for the Britons to mount an early defence against the advancing Romans. Interestingly, there is archaeological evidence that the Romano-British settlement is pre-dated by the remains of Roman military occupation, giving further weight to the theory that this was indeed the place at which Plautius chose to leave a garrison before continuing his advance west.

Here it seems as though history repeats itself somewhat, as, just had been the case at the time of Caesar's raids, the Britons chose not to engage the Roman army and instead pulled back to defend a strategic river crossing. However, before dealing with that part of the campaign it seems worth some further reflection as to just how much fighting preceded the landmark battle on the River Medway. This is because Dio states very clearly that, prior to this event, Plautius defeated Caratacus first and then Togodumnus. This clearly tells us that there were not one, but two significant clashes with native forces prior to the battle on the Medway. This may suggest that, rather than adopting guerrilla-style tactics at the outset, the Catuvellaunian princes were initially more willing to give conventional battle to the Romans than may have previously been believed. After all, the Catuvellauni had been carrying on a ruthless and successful campaign of expansionism since the time of Cassivellaunus. Confidence in their own military capability must therefore have been extremely high when Claudius' forces came ashore.

The possibility of some sort of battle occurring in the Canterbury area seems likely, although it would be impossible to give a definitive view as to the scale of the clash. That being said, given what Dio tells us about the Britons' early difficulties in mustering their army, it would seem unlikely that either of these early encounters amounted to anything along the lines of a large-scale battle. Had such been the case, it seems more likely that a writer such as Dio, with his more sensationalist style, would have made greater literary capital from the clashes.

As to the likely site of any second battle, the only source of information for this (Dio) is simply too vague to provide any assistance. Furthermore, unless archaeological evidence can be detected of an assault on a town or settlement, the chances of finding evidence for any ancient-world battle which took place on open ground are negligible. This is because clean-up operations which would have been carried out after the battle to remove both the dead and weapons and equipment generally mean that such sites are almost sterile, archaeologically speaking. Consequently, unless there is something such as the chance find of a mass grave for instance, the site of the second battle is unlikely to ever be identified.

The Battle on the Medway

It is not possible to say how well Caratacus and Togodumnus emerged from their opening clashes with the Roman invaders. We do not know if they were wounded in the fighting and we do not know how many of their men survived, only to face the Romans once more in the far more decisive battle to come. However, if Dio's account of the battle is accurate then we are able to say that, by the time the Roman forces had reached the river, the Briton's had been able to amass a considerable army to prevent a crossing and had taken the opportunity to ready themselves to receive the Romans at what both sets of protagonists had identified as a key crossing point on the river.

As we shall discuss in more detail later, the Romans did have forces available which were capable of fording even deep, fast-flowing rivers. However, the available numbers of these troops would have been nowhere near sufficient to cross in such a quantity that would have given them any hope, on their own, of taking on the massive army assembled by the Britons without being quickly cut to pieces. If there is any doubt about this, we only need to consider the fact that Dio describes a battle during which the Britons were able to put up a hard fight against perhaps three legions, and their attendant auxiliary forces, for two days. This is very significant because, in the context of ancient warfare, a two-day battle is a rare occurrence. This therefore provides ample testimony not only to the ferocity of the fighting, but the immense scale of the battle itself.

Consequently, we can only conclude that however effective in battle the auxiliary troops that initially crossed the river were, they could never have stood on their own against such overwhelming force. The purpose of the next part of this work is therefore to identify a precise location for the battle by identifying the strategies which both sides adopted both before and at the outset of the battle. This will include an explanation for the use of the troops, universally accepted to be Batavian auxiliaries, to ford the river ahead of the main force.

The Medway is a major river, rising initially from a spring as a trickling stream at Turner's Hill in East Sussex, before winding its way through Sussex and Kent for around 70 miles. It is currently navigable for around 50 miles of its length and is tidal down to Allington Lock, just north of Maidstone, Kent. The river's long journey ends at the mouth of the Thames Estuary, where it discharges into the Thames between the Isle of Grain and Sheerness.

Although it has been previously suggested that the Roman army achieved its crossing of the Medway close to Rochester, the river is extremely wide at this point and, despite the obvious skills of the Batavians, its width would certainly prove to be prohibitive to the success of the mission described by Dio. Furthermore, even though the river shoals at low tide above the modern Rochester Road Bridge, the low-tide water depth is still around 1m. Consequently, combined with the sucking river mud they would have had to deal with, this depth of water would have made it practically impossible for heavily armed and armoured legionaries to ford at this point.

Many scholars and historians who refer to Dio's description of the invasion campaign believe that the river crossing which Dio noted was made around the area of Snodland. This is around 2½ miles from Aylesford, Kent, and lies near to the route of the North Downs Way, which runs close to the east bank of the river. This part of the route is alternatively referred to as the Pilgrims Way and on the bank of the Medway, opposite Snodland on the Burham side of the river, a memorial stone has been erected which commemorates the river crossing and battle.

Though the proposal of the location as the battle site has been previously questioned, one needs only to visit this part of the Medway, particularly at low tide, to understand just what an excellent fording opportunity this part of the river would have presented to the Romans, and why the Britons defended the location which such a large force.

From the Britons' point of view, it was vital that they maintained control of this point. Certainly, once Caratacus and Togodumnus had been able to gauge the offensive capabilities of the Romans in their earlier encounters they must have rapidly drawn the conclusion, just as Cassivellaunus had so many years previously, that set piece battles were unlikely to succeed against an army of this type. Therefore, the best way to tackle the advance was to attempt to hold the Romans at a point of their choosing. Having failed to achieve anything with their action close to Canterbury, the two princes must subsequently have realised that the next objective for the Roman army was to quickly cross the Medway in order to maintain momentum.

They must have eventually reached the conclusion that the best way to halt the advance and perhaps regain some military advantage was to mount a defence of the fording point at Snodland. Clearly, they would have known this would be the nearest location to allow a rapid crossing in force as they had no doubt used the same fording point previously and may well have ordered the destruction of any existing bridges downstream. The theory must have been that if the fording point was defended by a large and imposing army the Romans would not risk a crossing en masse, only to have to throw themselves into the midst of such a large host after barely clearing the water. The hope then must surely have been to avoid an immediate and massive battle by deterring a crossing and thereby slowing the Roman advance. This may then have allowed the Britons time to develop a counter to the Roman push into Kent.

The Medway in the area below and between Burham and Snodland takes a number of sharp turns in its course, forming almost a hairpin-like bend as it turns away from Burham and travels for around a hundred yards or so towards Snodland. It is because of the way the river turns through these courses that gravel is deposited on the river bed. The gravel has built up, causing the river to become extremely shallow at low tide and also providing a firmer crossing by foot, given that the river bed is gravel and not mud at the stretch directly between the two villages. Furthermore, at low tide, the river is no more than knee deep along this stretch, making it perfect for a large amount of soldiers and horses to quickly and safely cross the river at this point. In short, from a strategic point of view it was vitally important to both the Britons and the Romans that they controlled this point on the Medway.

Nowadays the eastern bank of the river is augmented by a flood defence in the form of a high earthen bank which closely traces the course of the riverbank and is no doubt designed to prevent the inundation of the flood plain next to the river, which now serves predominantly as grazing land. In AD 43 the bank would not have been present and, apart from the probable presence of tall marsh reed beds, the Britons on the western bank of the Medway would have had an uninterrupted view of the flood plain, right up to the ridge of hills that rise in the east, overlooking the flood plain and the course of the river. The Roman army would not, therefore, have been able to approach the fording point without the waiting Britons having ample warning of their presence.

However, whilst the native defenders on the west bank obviously held a clear tactical advantage in their choice of position, the Romans were gifted with the advantage of high ground in the form of the aforementioned ridge of hills. These rose gently up from the flood plain, offering commanding views over the entire area, including the course of the river. Consequently, combining the information they had gathered from their cavalry scouts with what they could see from the various vantage points along the ridge line, the Romans would then have been able to tell exactly where the Britons had arrayed their forces and the numbers they faced. They would also have developed a full understanding of the behaviour of the river and the course it followed. Their information

Fig. 8 The memorial stone erected close to Snodland, Kent in 1997 to commemorate the battle on the Medway between the defending Britons and the advancing Roman army. (Photograph by John Olden, reproduced by kind permission)

would have therefore been fully current as to the disposition of the Britons, right up to the point that they decided to implement their plans. In the end, it would be this detailed and fully up-to-date knowledge of both the enemy and the local topography which would prove to be the fatal flaw in the defence of the crossing point by the Britons.

Dio tells us that the Britons had camped out in careless fashion on the opposite side of the river to the Roman forces, as they were apparently confident that the Romans could not cross without the use of a bridge. In discussing what happened next, we must therefore take this to more clearly mean that the Britons knew there were no bridges the Romans could avail themselves of, and that they had control of the only crossing point. As a result, with such a small stretch of river under threat of attack they were clearly confident that the Romans could not rush across in sufficient numbers to weaken or breach their defence. Equally, Plautius would have recognised that any attempt to mount a direct assault via the fording point would potentially cost him a lot of men. Too many casualties for no gain at this point could jeopardise his entire mission. He would therefore need an alternative plan which would serve to dilute the massive show of force which awaited his men on the other side of the river.

The key to the success of Plautius' plan would rely on two things: knowledge of when the river was at its lowest point and the rapid deployment of a perfectly timed diversionary flank attack on the assembled Britons. The first could be accomplished via the observations of scouts, combined with the intelligence which could be gathered from locals who were disposed towards assisting the Roman forces. However, the second element would require the use of specialised troops, capable of crossing the Medway without the need to use a bridge, fording point or boat.

Whilst some dispute that they were present during the Roman landings, it is widely accepted that the troops that carried out this crucial role were Batavian auxiliaries. Dio describes these troops as having the capability to cross fast-flowing water whilst still equipped in full armour. Certainly this ability is cited by Hassall, who makes a strong case for their use during the invasion of AD 43.[10] This ability to cross stretches of water impassable to more conventional troops and then emerge ready for combat is well recorded in various classical accounts of the Batavians in combat.

In order to understand how effective the use of these troops were, we must form a view of the battlefield, relative to the Medway at Snodland and taking into account the kind of forces assembled in the area. The Britons must have assembled on the western side of the Medway in the immediate area of the ford, in order to present a dense obstacle to deter any crossing attempts. Therefore, Plautius would need to try to fragment that assembly before he could even start

Fig. 9 The River Medway as it traces its way between the two modern settlements of Burham and Snodland. The buildings in the background are industrial premises on the Snodland side of the river. (Author's photograph)

to attempt a crossing. By assembling his available legions very conspicuously on the eastern side of the Medway, close to the ford, the Britons would be obliged to hold at that position – convinced that an attack could come from nowhere else than across the ford. It is therefore likely that they chose not to patrol the river elsewhere with scouts as they saw no need to do so.

Dio tells us that Vespasian was present, along with Sabinus. If we accept that each man commanded a legion battle group that would mean that Plautius could array two legions with their attendant auxiliary forces on the flood plain, close to the ford. Dio also tells us that Gnaeus Hosidius Geta joined the battle the next day. It therefore seems reasonable to assume that his legion was kept back as a second wave and these may have been grouped close to the ridge of hills overlooking the ford. With his forces in place Plautius would wait for around midday, when the river tide was at its lowest, before ordering the Batavians to cross at a discrete distance downstream and after the river straightens its course after winding past Snodland.

An equally mixed force of Batavian infantry and cavalry, perhaps totalling 2,000 in number (four quingenary cohorts) would then challenge the northernmost flank of the native host, instantly causing a fragmentation of the force as the host spontaneously turned to engage the new threat and sent out its cavalry and chariots to counter the shock appearance of so many Roman troops on the wrong side of the river. As Dio tells us, the result was carnage as the auxiliaries concentrated not on conventional combat but on targeting the enemy horses. This would have had the immediate effect of shattering the Britons' charge and greatly reducing the overall mobility of the warrior elite within the army. This in turn would deplete the threat to the legion battle groups waiting to cross the river.

At the same time as the Batavian auxiliaries mounted their surprise flank attack, it is very likely that the Romans would have deployed cohorts of archers to rain waves of arrows onto the narrow spit of land on the opposite bank. This would have caused devastating casualties among the waiting Britons, forcing them back and providing a window of opportunity for the legionaries to attempt a crossing of the fording point. The Auxiliary forces, their task completed, would then have had the choice of withdrawing back across the river, with their cavalry covering the infantry retreat, or skirting the main body of the native army in an attempt to link with the legion battle groups who had by then seized the moment and stormed across the river, quickly taking control of the bank area. However, given that remaining on the field would carry a significant risk of sustaining heavy casualties within the ranks of the Batavians, it seems more likely the Batavians withdrew back across the river in order to take part in a later phase of the battle.

Once on the opposite bank, the legions commanded by Vespasian and Sabinus engaged in a ferocious battle, the legions fighting to take ground and the Britons striving to push the Romans back into the river. As daylight had begun to fade, however, the Britons had probably been pushed further north and the Romans would then have secured plenty of ground on the western side of the Medway. Meanwhile, Geta's force, as a reaction to the progress made by the Roman spearhead, was no doubt moved forward by Plautius in readiness for a renewal of hostilities the next day.

An uneasy night must surely have followed as both armies rested out in the open on the field of battle. Hostilities would then have renewed with the dawn; the battle to control the ground erupting once more with neither side managing to secure any significant advantage over the other. The battle would then have intensified as Geta's troops crossed the ford as soon as possible – around midday – and entered the fight, taking on the role of the main offensive formation and allowing the legions of Vespasian and Sabinus to adopt a support role. This suggestion is supported by the fact that Dio mentions that, at this point, Geta is almost captured. However, the entry of his legion into the battle proved so decisive that Geta was subsequently awarded *ornamenta triumphalia* for his part in the fighting. The enemy then broke from the fight and fled north, towards the Thames. Consequently, Plautius was left in possession of a vitally important strategic location on the Medway.

To the Thames and Beyond

Dio's account does not provide us with a report of what happened between the site of the Medway battle and the Roman advance to the Thames. What is certain is that, upon reaching the Thames, the Roman forces had effectively secured control of the territory around the tidal reaches of the Medway. This meant that the Romans were now able to open the great river up to the supply operations of the Classis Britannica. Now their ships were able to sail significant distances inland, again creating opportunities to establish multiple supply points and thereby reducing the burden on supply columns using pack animals. This would mean that supplies and equipment could be more quickly shipped to end users such as small garrisons left to control pacified areas and parties of engineers conducting such operations as road or bridge building. It would also represent the most efficient and economical use of resources.

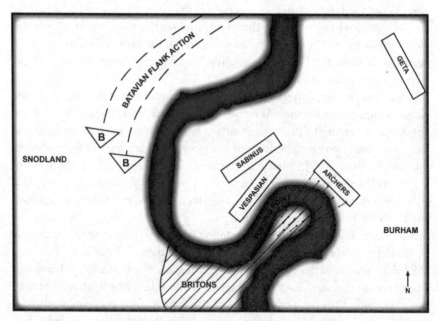

Fig. 10 Phase 1. The course of the Medway as it runs past the modern villages of Snodland and Burham, whose approximate locations have been included in order to aid orientation. The battle started with a surprise flank attack from the north by mixed cohorts of Batavian auxiliaries which drew the British cavalry and chariots out from the main force. At this point Roman archers rained down arrows on the Britons waiting on the opposite bank in order to clear the ground for the legion battle groups to ford the river.

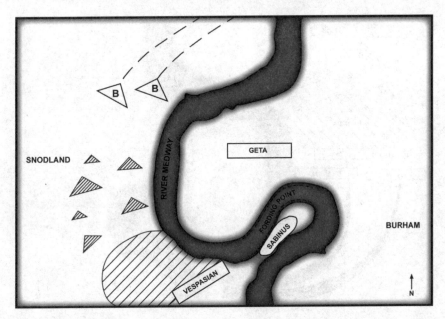

Fig. 11 Phase 2. The legions were able to make a successful crossing of the fording point and once on the other side engaged the main body of Britons. As Geta moved his legion down in preparation to cross the river the fighting intensified, raging for the rest of the day with no decisive advantage gained by either side.

Another thing which Dio neglects to mention is what happened when the Romans had followed the retreating Britons as far as Durobrivae Cantiacorum, which is now modern Rochester. This town was the second largest settlement in Cantium (Kent) at the time and the literal translation of its name means 'the walled town of bridges'. Whilst there is no archaeological evidence to confirm this, the name of the town strongly suggests that there were a number of bridges at the location which, as we have previously suggested, the Britons had no doubt felt it expedient to destroy in order to prevent the Romans from crossing the Medway at this point.

The fact that Dio's account suggests that fighting took place around the Canterbury area, whilst making no mention of what happened when the Romans reached Rochester, is interesting. Indeed, we could perhaps take this to mean that precisely nothing happened when the Romans arrived, perhaps because the inhabitants of the town had fled upon hearing the news that the Roman army had crossed the Medway and were heading straight for them. Of course, there is also the possibility that the Roman army made directly for the crossing at Brentford, which was discussed previously in the context of Caesar's campaign against Cassivellaunus. However, as was also mentioned in

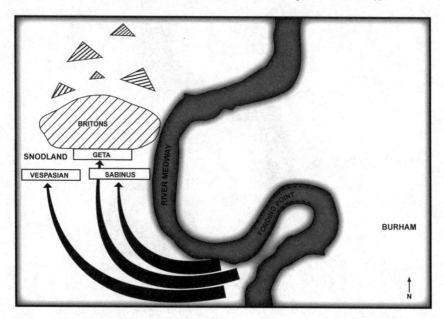

Fig. 12 Phase 3. As fighting resumed on day two of the battle, Geta's legion became lead formation and Vespasian and Sabinus supported the advance. The Britons were pushed further north until their formation finally broke and the Britons fled towards the Thames, leaving the victorious Roman army in control of the ford.

that section of the work, there is an alternative Thames fording point which has been suggested by Thornhill.[11] Indeed, the strong argument he has put forward for this location would mean that it would have been almost impossible for the Romans to have avoided Rochester on their way to the Thames, given the close proximity of the fording point to the town.

Thornhill points out that, by 1930, Sir Mortimer Wheeler had been able to establish that the level of the Thames in Roman times was around 15ft lower than its present-day levels. He also states that the description offered by Dio, of a point where the river enters the sea and forms a large pool at high tide, effectively rules out a crossing at any point along the Thames which is west of Gravesend. The possibility that the Claudian forces crossed at Brentford is therefore clearly defunct.

Thornhill suggests that the evidence for a now submerged fording point can be found between Lower Higham in Kent and East Tilbury in Essex. He points out that an ancient ferry previously existed at this location, which suggests that as the level of the Thames rose, a ferry replaced the ford in order to allow the continued use of the important routes which converged upon the crossing point on either bank. Thornhill also points out that this is the only known ancient ferry across the Thames below Gravesend.

Circumstantially, these are interesting points to consider. However, the case for a crossing point existing at this location in Roman times becomes more solid when Thornhill reveals that excavations carried out on the Mucking Escarpment, close to modern Thurrock in Essex, have revealed not only the existence of a Bronze Age hill fort but also showed that the Romans built a small fort of their own on the site of the more ancient fort. The Roman site, covering some 1½ acres, had a single entrance and a rectangular, partly double-ditched enclosure, which indicated something more than a temporary usage. Dating evidence in the form of a bronze armour component from a first century Roman legionary's armour was also discovered. Thornhill argues that the existence of both forts, which stand close to the road approaching the ferry site, must emphasise the importance of the road – which itself is a convergence point for other routes – and its relationship to the crossing point.

If, as seems highly likely, a fording point had existed at this location then, as Thornhill points out, it would be consistent with what Dio has to say about the Romans' pursuit of the Britons across the Thames. Dio mentions that the Britons crossed without difficulty due to their knowledge of the firm ground and easy passages. However, the Roman troops were less successful in their crossing as, without such local knowledge, they experienced some difficulty and were forced to cross the Thames via a bridge further downstream whilst the Batavian auxiliaries swam across. Thornhill believes that this last action suggests that because the Batavians were forced to swim, the Romans may have been caught out by a rising tide.

Nevertheless the Romans eventually managed to cross the Thames and our dateable evidence for their presence on the Essex side of the Thames is amply supported by the existence of the aforementioned fort at Mucking. At this stage of the advance the Roman army, having crossed the Thames, had re-engaged the fleeing Britons and it appears they were able to inflict significant casualties on them before getting into difficulties in the marshes and losing a number of men. By this time the Roman army was around 40 miles away from its ultimate objective of Colchester, and it is here that Thornhill suggests that they took advantage of the high ground over the river while Plautius halted the advance and summoned Claudius to come and claim his victory.

Dio explains that there were a number of reasons why Plautius stalled the advance at this point. It seems that a key factor had to do with the death of Togodumnus. Having successfully crossed the Thames, the Romans had continued to do battle with the Britons as Dio tells us that Togodumnus perished at around this time, presumably killed in battle. His death then seems to have galvanised the Britons who began to hit back hard at the Romans in order to exact revenge for their fallen leader. We are then told that a fearful Plautius decided he would go no further and instead would consolidate his gains and send for Claudius before continuing the advance.

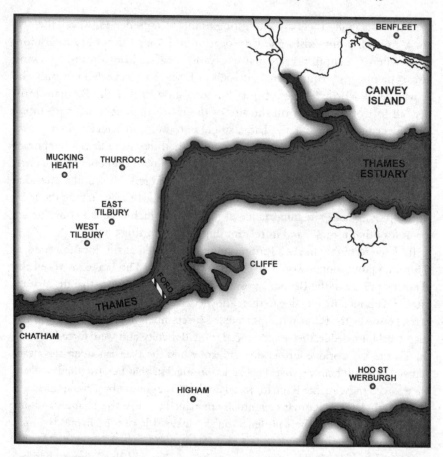

Fig. 13 The modern Thames showing the position of the ancient ford, as described by Thornhill, crossing between Lower Higham in Kent to East Tilbury in Essex.

When considering Dio's account at this point it seems evident that the decision made by Plautius was not a tactical decision which he made in isolation, but was instead something which had been pre-arranged and which was more probably a detail which had already been factored into the original invasion plan. In fact, Dio is very specific when he recounts that Plautius had been ordered to summon Claudius in the event that he encountered particularly stubborn resistance. Furthermore, we are told that the Romans had already assembled men and equipment ready to support the campaign when needed. It is therefore evident that the necessity to minimise the risks had clearly been considered and precise rules had been laid down in respect of this.

Claudius' determination for the campaign to succeed is consequently very evident at this point. After all, if his forces could achieve the conquest of Britain for him, then his so far unremarkable reign would be transformed and his tenuous grip on Imperial power would become much stronger. One has to wonder at this point what would have happened if it had been a general more like Caesar, rather than Plautius, commanding the Roman army. Would such a commander have sensed victory and forged on for Colchester regardless? Or would he instead have taken stock of his gains, as it appears Plautius did, choosing instead to consolidate those gains, strengthen his position and allow his men to catch their breath after a lightening advance? Certainly, from the point of view of the army, it seems reasonable to suggest that the pace of such a campaign would have proven testing to even the most seasoned of veterans. Consequently, the opportunity to regroup and switch to a more defensive role for a time would have no doubt been very welcome.

So it was that the Roman army dug in and waited for the arrival of their emperor. In giving the matter some further consideration, this part of Dio's account can also provide us with some further insights as to the conduct of the invasion commander at this point.[12] Firstly, it seems erroneous on Dio's part to describe Plautius as fearful of pressing ahead to Colchester without waiting for Claudius to arrive with reinforcements. After all, Plautius had so far conducted an enormously successful campaign and had made significant gains. Although clearly still a determined adversary, the Britons were by now definitely on the back foot. It therefore seems extremely doubtful that Plautius was wary of the prospect of further engagements with the Britons.

It is instead far more likely that the thing that Plautius feared more was the consequences of making a successful push for Colchester without Claudius being there to claim victory over the Britons. After all, this was a huge event, almost on a modern par with the NASA moon landings. Imperial protocol would dictate that only the emperor was worthy of claiming such a victory and for a general to even consider claiming that accolade for himself would be unthinkable. No doubt if he had decided to attempt it, the decision would have almost certainly proven fatal. Consequently, Plautius must have resolved himself to the fact that discretion was indeed the better part of valour and instead stuck rigidly to the plan to summon his master.

In addition, the notion that Plautius was actually wary of further large-scale clashes with the Britons does not really sit well against his decision to summon Claudius. After all, why would Plautius decide to summon Claudius to a remote and dangerous land such as Britain if he still felt that the Roman grip on Britain was weak and there was a risk that the Britons could mount any sort of effective counter-offensive against his army? It seems most unlikely that Plautius would have had the confidence to summon Claudius unless he was not absolutely sure that he could, at the very least, hold the ground he had gained.

The other interesting point to be drawn from this part of Dio's account is that he clearly states that the army made no further territorial gains. If such is the case, we can be sure that the available fighting strength of the army was either holding in Kent or in the area of the Essex marshes on the southern side of the Thames. Holding both banks at this point would have been crucial as it would have allowed Plautius to dominate the crossing points of the ford and the aforementioned bridge on the lower reaches of the Thames. This would create an effective buffer zone while allowing the army in Kent to strengthen their position. It would also open up the mouth of the Thames to the Classis Britannica who would then be able to sail supplies directly to the troops on the Essex side of the Thames.

The notion that the entire army remained concentrated in Kent and the area of the Thames crossing would effectively mean that Vespasian had not yet separated from the army and marched Legion II Augusta and its associated units down towards the south coast to begin his campaign against the southern tribes. However, we shall discuss this issue in more detail a little later on.

In the previous chapter we proposed a chronology which was based predominantly on what Suetonius, and more particularly Dio, have to tell us about Claudius' personal involvement in the campaign. If we accept the strength of the argument for that chronology then the period between early July and mid-August would have proven extremely useful to Plautius; allowing him to greatly strengthen the position of his various units and fully establish a supply infrastructure as he tasked his army with the building of roads and forts, establishing basic port facilities at various locations and undertaking the construction of bridges at key river crossings.

Although it is impossible to say just who it is that is being referred to, Suetonius tells us that Claudius' Triumph following his return to Rome was witnessed by 'certain exiles'.[13] If we presume that the exiles he refers to are in fact the kings mentioned as fleeing from Britain, then it may be possible that one of these was Adminius, older brother to both Caratacus and Togodumnus and the former ruler of Cantium (Kent). Although pure speculation, it is nevertheless worth considering that Adminius may have had a hand in the initial phases of the invasion. Certainly, as one-time ruler of the kingdom where the landings would take place, his influence would have been invaluable whilst Plautius consolidated and waited for Claudius. His previously established links to the nobility of the Cantiaci could have greatly assisted the Roman invaders to gain support and a degree of credibility among the local populace. Particularly if they could see that their former king had returned willingly at the head of a powerful foreign army and was willing to support the presence of these troops as they ousted his brothers and returned him to power.

As we now know, that power would come with strict limitations. It seems extremely unlikely that Adminius would not have been fully aware of how the Romans dealt with such matters. Therefore, if Adminius had returned home with the support of a Roman army, it would be indicative of the fact that he had resigned himself to the realisation that he would have no real autonomy over his former kingdom. He no doubt would have viewed this as better than no power at all, or worse, ending up dead as a result of resisting Rome.

Assisted by Adminius or not, Plautius' army now had control of a significant foothold in Britain, and by the time Claudius arrived with reinforcements during August the scene was set for one last push which would finally see the fall of Colchester.

The Birth of a Province

Though we cannot say for sure exactly where Claudius landed, from what Dio tells us it does seem that it was in Kent where the emperor first set foot in Britain and not in Essex. Dio tells us that, having joined his waiting legions, he then crossed the Thames and engaged with the waiting Britons.[14] However, this part of the account becomes somewhat confused as what Dio has to tell us about this part of the campaign does not fit with either the chronology we have now established or the timings referred to by either Suetonius or Dio himself, which tell us that Claudius stayed in Britain for only sixteen days.

From Dio's account we are able to deduce that the Britons had assembled an army, ready to make one last effort to check the Roman advance to Colchester. However, this force was defeated and Colchester subsequently fell to the conquering Romans, completing a major objective of the invasion by shattering the rule of the Catuvellauni and seizing their seat of power. Where Dio's account begins to lose credibility is where he mentions that, having taken Colchester, Claudius then secured the surrender of numerous other tribes, either by capitulation or force of arms. Having achieved this, Claudius then disarmed the tribes and left Britain for Rome, instructing Plautius to complete the subjugation of the remainder of the island.

Whilst there is no problem with accepting that Claudius would have received tribal envoys who would have offered the surrender of their tribes, the notion that he used force to subdue other tribes is highly improbable. Having taken Colchester, Claudius now had immediate control over the lands of the Cantiaci, the Trinovantes and the Catuvellauni. Therefore, in order to personally subdue any other tribes he would need to have travelled over a much larger area. This is clearly something which would have taken Claudius a lot longer to achieve than the sixteen days that we are told he remained in Britain. Thus it seems highly unlikely that Claudius was present at anything other than the fall of Colchester and the formalities that followed.

What seems to be a more likely scenario is that which is suggested in Suetonius' account of the invasion. Suetonius tells us that Claudius fought no battles and suffered no losses, but reduced a large part of the island to submission. His description is very similar to the inscription on the Triumphal Arch erected in Rome which records Claudius' campaign. The inscription, a substantial piece of which is now on display at the Capitoline Museum in Rome, records the surrender of eleven British kings as follows:

> The Roman Senate and People to Tiberius Claudius Caesar Augustus Germanicus, son of Drusus, Pontifex Maximus, Tribunician power eleven times, Consul five times, Imperator 22 times, Censor, Father of the Fatherland, because he received the surrender of eleven kings of the Britons defeated without any loss, and first brought barbarian peoples across the Ocean into the dominion of the Roman people.[15]

Presumably the reference to achieving the surrender without loss refers to the fact that no Roman units were entirely destroyed during the campaign. After all, Dio specifically tells us of losses during the Thames crossing. Furthermore, it is impossible to accept that the invasion army would not have received some fatalities as it battled through Kent and pushed for Colchester.

A more probable result for this part of the invasion is that Claudius' presence was necessary only to formalise the surrender of the tribes, and that he took no active part in the fighting. Certainly he landed in Britain with reinforcements for Plautius, but to suggest that an emperor with an entirely academic background and with no real military experience or acumen would lead his army into such a crucial battle is unrealistic. It is instead more likely that Plautius conducted the remainder of the campaign whilst Claudius looked on and then facilitated the emperor's reception of the suppliant kings. Once Claudius had begun his journey back to Rome, Plautius would have then made preparations for the approach of winter and planned the next steps in achieving the overall conquest of the island.

The last point that we need to deal with in terms of Claudius' involvement in the campaign is his prolonged absence from Rome. If we accept that he left Britain by late August or early September then we need to account for why he does not appear to have arrived back in Britain until January of AD 44. Dio tells us that Claudius sent Magnus and Silanus, his son-in-laws, ahead of him to take news to Rome of the victory. At the very least this implies that he was not going to be rushing back to Rome.

Barrett follows this up by suggesting that there was indeed no rush on Claudius' part to return to Rome.[16] This is because he believes that a reference by Pliny the Elder infers that Claudius was already engaging in some preliminary Triumphal celebrations as he passed through Gaul and entered Italy.[17] The passage Barrett refers to states that Claudius sailed from the mouth of the Po river near Ravenna, out into the Adriatic. Barrett believes this is a reference to some form of Triumphal celebration, although he does concede that this could have happened after Claudius returned to Rome. It nevertheless seems a perfectly reasonable suggestion to make that Claudius could well have been delayed due to celebrations in his honour as he made his way back to Rome. However, we must also take into consideration the change in seasons as the deterioration of the weather going into winter would have also played a part in delaying the emperor's progress. Consequently, a return leg of the journey of around four months does not seem to be that unreasonable.

Having taken Colchester, the Roman army would soon move its operations out over a much wider area, and it is perhaps appropriate that we should now consider when it was that Vespasian took Legio II Augusta down to the south coast to begin his campaign against the southern tribes. In order to fit in with the chronology that we have suggested and, based upon the assumption that Vespasian and his legion remained in the Kent area for the push on Colchester, it seems that Vespasian would have not been able to commence his own part of the invasion campaign until the late summer of AD 43. However, based upon the conclusions set out in a paper by Sauer it is possible to make a suggestion as to how Vespasian commenced his campaign against the southern tribes.[18]

Sauer's paper deals with the discovery of the fragmentary remains of a legionary's tombstone at the site of the legion fortress at Alchester, just to the southwest of the modern Oxfordshire town of Bicester. This is the site which was discussed previously in relation to the provision of foodstuffs to the army. Sauer argues that the inscription on the tombstone of Lucius Valerius Geminus is evidence that the Alchester fortress was the first permanent base for Legio II Augusta. He points out that the inscription shows Geminus to be a veteran of the second Augustan legion and, as such, this means that the site is almost certainly the base of the legion in which he served. Sauer supports this argument by pointing out that there are no known instances of legion veterans being buried at any location other than the bases, or *colonia*, of their particular legions. However, since the article's publication a counter argument has arisen, arguing that the inscription may not actually say that Geminus served with II Augusta. Consequently, this calls into question the identification of the site as the base for the legion.

Nevertheless, Sauer's argument does seem persuasive. If his argument is correct then due to the fact that the earliest phases of the fortress can be dated to AD 43, it would show that, having been present at the fall of Colchester, Vespasian and his legion then marched directly west. Then, having established a permanent base at Alchester, the legion marched directly south, crossing the Thames and commencing a campaign, which, as Suetonius points out, saw Vespasian fight thirty battles, subjugate two warlike tribes and capture twenty towns, as well as capturing the Isle of Vectis (the Isle of Wight).[19]

The overall success of the invasion campaign would ultimately mean that Britain was destined to become a part of the Roman Empire for the best part of the four centuries which followed the landings. Rome's dominance of the island would never be entirely complete, however. In the years after the land-ings the Roman army, under successive governors, would struggle to exert their control as they pushed west. Indeed, for around the next eight years, one man would rally fierce British resistance to the Romans as he fought not only a guerrilla campaign but also engaged the legions in open battle.

That man was Caratacus, survivor of the fall of Colchester and the last of the Catuvellaunian royal line.

Notes

1 G. Webster (1993), p. 96
2 Cassius Dio, *Roman Histories* – *Book LX*, Chapter XIX, IV
3 J. Manley (2002), pp. 108–09
4 *De munitionibus castrorum / de metatione castrorum*
5 C.M Gilliver (1999), pp. 86–7
6 J. Peddie (1987), pp. 55–6
7 G. Moody (2008), pp. 35–52
8 Cassius Dio, *Roman Histories* – *Book LX*, Chapter XIX, II
9 Ibid., Chapter XX
10 M.W.C Hassall (1970), pp. 131–6
11 P. Thornhill (1976), pp. 119–28
12 Cassius Dio, *Roman Histories* – *Book LX*, Chapter XXI
13 Suetonius, *The Twelve Caesars* – *Claudius*, Chapter XVII
14 Cassius Dio, *Roman Histories* – *Book LX*, Chapter XXI
15 *CIL*, Vol. VI, 920-923=31203-4
16 A.A. Barrett (1980), p. 33
17 *Natural Histories* – *Book III*, Chapter XVI, 119
18 E. Sauer (2005), pp. 101–33
19 Suetonius, *The Twelve Caesars* – *Vespasian*, Chapter IV

THE ATREBATEAN ROYAL LINE BETWEEN CAESAR AND CLAUDIUS

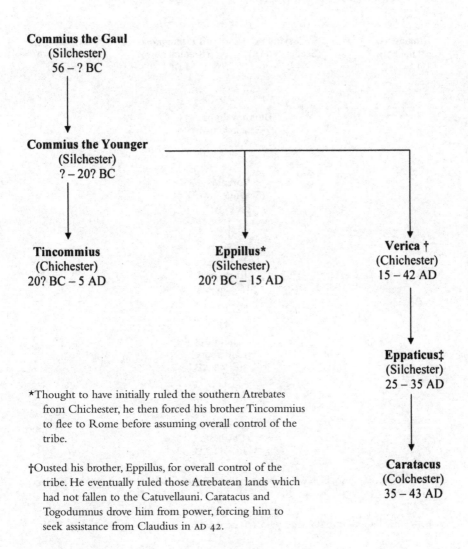

Commius the Gaul
(Silchester)
56 – ? BC

Commius the Younger
(Silchester)
? – 20? BC

Tincommius
(Chichester)
20? BC – 5 AD

Eppillus*
(Silchester)
20? BC – 15 AD

Verica †
(Chichester)
15 – 42 AD

Eppaticus‡
(Silchester)
25 – 35 AD

Caratacus
(Colchester)
35 – 43 AD

*Thought to have initially ruled the southern Atrebates from Chichester, he then forced his brother Tincommius to flee to Rome before assuming overall control of the tribe.

†Ousted his brother, Eppillus, for overall control of the tribe. He eventually ruled those Atrebatean lands which had not fallen to the Catuvellauni. Caratacus and Togodumnus drove him from power, forcing him to seek assistance from Claudius in AD 42.

‡Seized control of northern Atrebatean lands for the Catuvellauni and governed from Silchester.

THE CANTIACAN ROYAL LINE BETWEEN CAESAR AND CLAUDIUS

Cingetorix
(Seat unknown)
54 BC – ?

Carvilius
(Seat unknown)
54 BC – ?

Taximagulus
(Seat unknown)
54 BC – ?

Segovax
(Seat unknown)
54 BC – ?

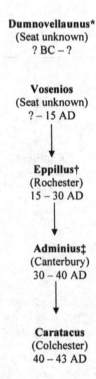

Dumnovellaunus*
(Seat unknown)
? BC – ?

Vosenios
(Seat unknown)
? – 15 AD

Eppillus†
(Rochester)
15 – 30 AD

Adminius‡
(Canterbury)
30 – 40 AD

Caratacus
(Colchester)
40 – 43 AD

*Previously, erroneously, believed to be the same person as the Trinovantean king of the same name.

†The former king of the Atrebates who was deposed by his brother, Verica.

‡Thought to be the eldest son of Cunobelin and appointed to administer Catuvellaunian rule over the territory.

Appendix C

The Catuvellaunian Royal Line between Caesar and Claudius

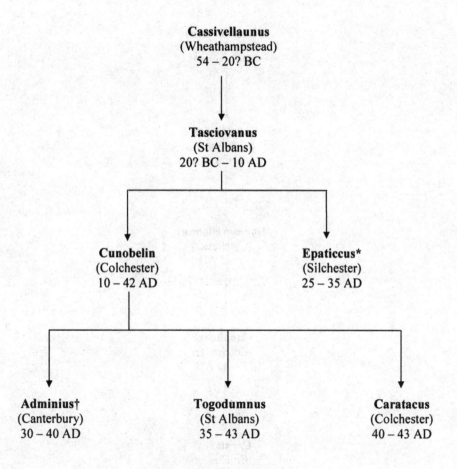

Cassivellaunus
(Wheathampstead)
54 – 20? BC

Tasciovanus
(St Albans)
20? BC – 10 AD

Cunobelin
(Colchester)
10 – 42 AD

Epaticcus*
(Silchester)
25 – 35 AD

Adminius†
(Canterbury)
30 – 40 AD

Togodumnus
(St Albans)
35 – 43 AD

Caratacus
(Colchester)
40 – 43 AD

*Brother to Cunobelin, who forced Tincommius to flee to Rome, taking control of northern Atrebatean lands and ruling from Silchester.

†Believed to be the eldest son of Cunobelin. Took control of Cantium (Kent) from Eppillus and subsequently fled to Rome around AD 40.

Appendix D

The Trinovantean Royal Line between Caesar and Claudius

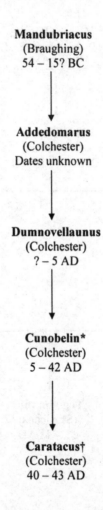

Mandubriacus
(Braughing)
54 – 15? BC

Addedomarus
(Colchester)
Dates unknown

Dumnovellaunus
(Colchester)
? – 5 AD

Cunobelin*
(Colchester)
5 – 42 AD

Caratacus†
(Colchester)
40 – 43 AD

*Permanent control of the tribe passes to Catuvellaunian rulers at this point.

†It is possible that power was ceded to Caratacus, prior to Cunobelin's death, due to the old king's illness or infirmity.

STRUCTURE OF THE CURSUS HONORUM

Republican Era		Imperial Era	
Appointment	**Minimum Age**	**Appointment**	**Minimum Age**
		Vigintivir	18
Military service		Military Tribune	20
Quaestor	30	Quaestor	25
Aedile or Tribune	37	Aedile or Tribune	27
Praetor	40	Praetor	30
		Prefect	
		Propraetor	
		Proconsul	
		Legatus Legionis	
Consul*	43	Consul*	32
		Praefectus Urbi	
Censor		Propraetor	
		Proconsul	

*Should an elected consul not complete his full term of office (one year) then a suffect consul was elected to take his place for the remainder of the term of office.

Typical Command Structure and Organisation of an Imperial Legion

Senior Commanders
Legatus Legionis (Legion Commander – Legate)
Tribunus Laticlavius (Broad Stripe Tribune – Senatorial Appointment)
Praefectus Castrorum (Camp Prefect)
Tribuni Angusticlavii x 5 (Narrow Stripe Tribunes)

Optimum Fighting Strength
Cohort I★ – 5 x double strength centuries of 160 men – total strength 800
Primus Pilus (First Spear Centurion) commanding the first century of the first cohort, along with four other Primi Ordines (First Ranks) to command each of the other centuries.

Cohorts II to X – Each cohort comprised of six centuries of 80 men – total strength **4,320**
Seniority of centurions within each cohort is as follows: Pilus Prior, Pilus Posterior, Princeps Prior, Princeps Posterior, Hastatus Prior and Hastatus Posterior.
   Each century is comprised of 10 *contubernia* (section) of 8 men.

Equites Legionis (Legionary Cavalry) – total strength **120**

Overall legion strength – 5,307

The figure includes the sixty-seven command ranks but does not include attendant personnel such as animal handlers etc, or the veteran contingent.

★As mentioned by Keppie, (1984, pp. 174) the existence of double-strength centuries in early Imperial legions is well demonstrated by the layout of the legionary fortress at Inchtuthil in Scotland. However, it is possible that this may have been a Flavian innovation, not in use at the time of the Claudian invasion. If such was the case, this would have made no difference to the actual strength of the cohort and would merely require that the above arrangement be substituted with six normal sized centuries in **Cohort I**, along with the addition of an extra centurion of Hastatus Posterior rank.

DIO'S ACCOUNT OF THE CLAUDIAN LANDINGS

XIX. – While these events were happening in Rome, Aulus Plautius, a senator of great renown, made a campaign against Britain; for a certain Bericus, who had been driven out of the island as a result of an uprising, had persuaded Claudius to send an army thither. **2** Thus it came about that Plautius undertook this campaign; but he had difficulty in inducing his army to advance beyond Gaul. For the soldiers were indignant at the thought of carrying on a campaign outside the limits of the known world, and would not yield him obedience until Narcissus, who had been sent out by Claudius, mounted the tribunal of Plautius and attempted to address them. **3** Then they became much angrier at this and would not permit Narcissus to speak a word, but suddenly shouted with one accord the familiar cry, 'Io Saturnalia' (for at the festival of Saturn the slaves don their masters' dress and old festival), and at once right willingly followed Plautius. Their delay, however, had made their departure late in the season. **4** They were sent over in three divisions, in order that they should not be hindered in landing,– as might happen to a single force,– and in their voyage across they first became discouraged because they were driven back upon their course, and then plucked up courage because a flash of light rising in the east shot across to the west, the direction in which they were sailing. So they put in to the island and found none to oppose them. **5** For the Britons as a result of their inquiries had not expected that they would come, and had therefore not assembled beforehand. And even when they did assemble, they would not come to close quarters with the Romans, but took refuge in the swamps and the forests, hoping to wear out the invaders in fruitless effort, so that, just as in the days of Julius Caesar, they should sail back with nothing accomplished.

XX. – Plautius, accordingly, had a deal of trouble in searching them out; but when at last he did find them, he first defeated Caratacus and than Togodumnus, the sons of Cynobellinus, who was dead. **2** (The Britons were not free and independent, but were divided into groups under various kings.) After the flight of these kings he gained by capitulation a part of the Bodunni, who were ruled by a tribe of the Catuellani; and leaving a garrison there, he advanced farther and came to a river. The barbarians thought that Romans would not be able to cross it without a bridge, and consequently camped in rather careless fashion on the opposite bank; but he sent across a detachment of Germans, who were accustomed to swim easily in full armour across the most turbulent streams. **3** These fell unexpectedly upon the enemy, but instead of shooting at any of the men they confined themselves to wounding the horses that drew their chariots; and in the confusion that followed not even the enemy's mounted warriors could save themselves. Plautius thereupon sent across Flavius Vespasian also (the man who afterwards became emperor) and his brother Sabinus, who was acting as his lieutenant. **4** So they, too, got across the river in some way and killed many of the foe, taking them by surprise. The survivors, however, did not take to flight, but on the next day joined issue with them again. The struggle was indecisive until Gnaeus Hosidius Geta, after narrowly missing being captured, finally managed to defeat the barbarians so soundly that he received the ornamenta triumphalia, though he had not been consul. **5** Thence the Britons retired to the river Thames at a point near where it empties into the ocean and at flood-tide forms a lake. This they easily crossed because they knew where the firm ground and the easy passages in this region were to be found; **6** but the Romans in attempting to follow them were not so successful. However, the Germans swam across again and some others got over by a bridge a little way up-stream, after which they assailed the barbarians from several sides at once and cut down many of them. In pursuing the remainder incautiously, they got into swamps from which it was difficult to make their way out, and so lost a number of men.

XXI. – Shortly afterwards Togodumnus perished, but the Britons, so far from yielding, united all the more firmly to avenge his death. Because of this fact and because of the difficulties he had encountered at the Thames, Plautius became afraid, and instead of advancing any farther, proceeded to guard what he had already won, and sent for Claudius. **2** For he had been instructed to do this in case he encountered any particularly stubborn resistance, and, in fact, extensive equipment, including elephants, had already been got together for the expedition.

When the message reached him, Claudius entrusted affairs at home, including the command of the troops, to his colleague Lucius Vitellius, whom he had caused to remain in office like himself for a whole half-year; and he himself then set out for the front. **3** He sailed down the river to Ostia, and from there followed the coast to Massilia; thence, advancing partly by land and partly along the rivers, he came to the ocean and crossed over to Britain, where he joined the legions that were waiting for him near the Thames. **4** Taking over the command of these, he crossed the stream, and engaging the barbarians, who had gathered at his approach, he defeated them and captured Camulodunum, the capital of Cynobellinus. Thereupon he won over numerous tribes, in some cases by capitulation, in others by force, and was saluted as imperator several times, contrary to precedent; **5** for no man may receive this title more than once for one and the same war. He deprived the conquered of their arms and handed them over to Plautius, bidding him also subjugate the remaining districts. Claudius himself now hastened back to Rome, sending ahead the news of his victory by his sons-in-law Magnus and Silanus.

XXII. – These on learning of his achievement gave him the title of Britannicus and granted him permission to celebrate a triumph. They voted also that there should be an annual festival to commemorate the event and that two triumphal arches should be erected, one in the city and the other in Gaul, because it was from that country that he had set sail when he crossed over to Britain. **2** They bestowed upon his son the same title as upon him, and, in fact, Britannicus came to be in a way the boy's regular name. Messalina was granted the same privilege of occupying front seats that Livia had enjoyed and also that of using the carpentum.

Cassius Dio, Roman Histories – Book LX, Chapters XIX–XXII

Appendix H

Overview of Daily Dry Fodder Requirements Per Unit

Unit and groups	Kgs	Lbs	Tons (approx)
Legion			
5,307 Men	5,307	11,675.4	5.2
240 Horse	1,421.6	3,127.5	1.4
74 Pack Horses/Mules	436.6	960.5	0.4
Total Requirement	**7,165.2**	**15,763.4**	**7.0**
Auxiliary Infantry			
Quingenary (500 Men)	500	1,100	0.5
7 Pack Horses/Mules	41.3	90.9	★
Total Requirement	**541.3**	**1,190.9**	**0.5**
Milliary (1,000 Men)	1,000	2,200	1
14 Pack Horses/Mules	82.6	181.8	★

Unit and groups	Kgs	Lbs	Tons (approx)
Total Requirement	**1,082.6**	**2,381.8**	**I**
Auxiliary Cavalry			
Quingenary (500 Men)	500	1,100	0.5
1,000 Mounts	5,900	12,980	5.8
88 Pack Horses/Mules	519.2	1,142.2	0.5
Total Requirement	**6,919.2**	**15,222.2**	**6.8**
Milliary (1,000 Men)	1,000	2,200	I
2,000 Mounts	11,800	25,960	11.6
176 Pack Horses/Mules	1,038.4	2,284.4	I
Total Requirement	**13,838.4**	**30,444.4**	**13.6**

*Denotes weight less than ½ ton

APPENDIX I

CONSULS AND SUFFECT CONSULS
OF THE FIRST CENTURY AD

Year	First Consul	Second Consul
I	C. Iulius Caesar	L. Aemilius Paullus
suff.		M. Herennius Picens
2	P. Vinicius	P. Alfenus Varus
suff.	P. Cornelius Lentulus Scipio	T. Quinctius Crispinus Valerianus
3	L. Aelius Lamia	M. Servilius
suff.	P. Silius	L. Volusius Saturninus
4	Sex. Aelius Catus	C. Sentius Saturninus
suff.	C. Clodius Licinus	Cn. Sentius Saturninus
5	L. Valerius Messalla Volesus	Cn. Cornelius Cinna Magnus
suff.	C. Vibius Postumus	C. Ateius Capito
6	M. Aemilius Lepidus	L. Arruntius
suff.		L. Nonius Asprenas
7	Q. Caecilius Metellus Creticus Silanus	A. Licinius Nerva Silianus
suff.	Faustus (II) Cornelius Sulla	Lucilius Longus
8	M. Furius Camillus	Sex. Nonius Quinctilianus
suff.	L. Apronius	A. Vibius Habitus
9	C. Poppaeus Sabinus	Q. Sulpicius Camerinus
suff.	Q. Poppaeus Secundus	M. Papius Mutilus
10	P. Cornelius Dolabella	C. Iunius Silanus
suff.	Ser. Cornelius Lentulus Maluginensis	Q. Iunius Blaesus
11	M'. Aemilius Lepidus	T. Statilius Taurus
suff.	L. Cassius Longinus	
12	Germanicus Iulius Caesar	C. Fonteius Capito
suff.		C. Visellius Varro
13	C. Silius	L. Munatius Plancus
suff.	A. Caecina Largus	
14	Sex. Pompeius	Sex. Appuleius

15	Drusus Iulius Caesar *(Jan.–Dec.)*	C. Norbanus Flaccus *(Jan.–June)*
suff.		M. Iunius Silanus *(July–Dec.)*
16	Sisenna Statilius Taurus	L. Scribonius Libo
suff.	P. Pomponius Graecinus	C. Vibius Rufus
17	L. Pomponius Flaccus	C. Caelius Rufus
suff.	C. Vibius Marsus	L. Voluseius Proculus
18	Ti. Caesar Augustus III *(Jan.)*	Germanicus Iulius Caesar II *(Jan.–Apr.)*
suff.	L. Seius Tubero *(Feb.–July)*	Livineius Regulus *(May–July)*
suff.	C. Rubellius Blandus *(Aug.–Dec.)*	M. Vipstanus Gallus (Aug.–Dec.)
19	M. Iunius Silanus Torquatus *(Jan.–Dec.)*	L. Norbanus Balbus *(Jan.–Apr.)*
suff.		P. Petronius *(May–Dec.)*
20	M. Valerius Messala Barbatus Messalinus	M. Aurelius Cotta Maximus Messalinus
21	Ti. Caesar Augustus IV	Drusus Iulius Caesar II
22	D. Haterius Agrippa	C. Sulpicius Galba
23	C. Asinius Pollio	C. Antistius Vetus
suff.		C. Stertinius Maximus
24	Ser. Cornelius Cethegus *(Jan.–June)*	L. Visellius Varro *(Jan.–June)*
suff.	C. Calpurnius Aviola *(July–Dec.)*	P. Cornelius Lentulus Scipio *(July–Dec.)*
25	Cossus Cornelius Lentulus *(Jan.–Aug.)*	M. Asinius Agrippa *(Jan.–Dec.)*
suff.	C. Petronius (Sept.–Dec.)	
26	Cn. Cornelius Lentulus Gaetulicus	C. Calvisius Sabinus
suff.	L. Iunius Silanus	C. Vellaeus Tutor
27	L. Calpurnius Piso	M. Licinius Crassus Frugi
suff.	P. Cornelius Lentulus	C. Sallustius Crispus Passienus
28	Ap. Iunius Silanus	P. Silius Nerva
suff.	L. Antistius Vetus	Q. Iunius Blaesus
29	C. Fufius Geminus *(Jan.–June)*	L. Rubellius Geminus *(Jan.–June)*
suff.	A. Plautius *(July–Dec.)*	L. Nonius Asprenas *(July–Dec.)*
30	M. Vinicius *(Jan.–June)*	L. Cassius Longinus *(Jan.–June)*
suff.	L. Naevius Surdinus *(July–Dec.)*	C. Cassius Longinus *(July–Dec.)*
31	Ti. Caesar Augustus V *(Jan.–May 9)*	L. Aelius Seianus *(Jan.–May 9)*
suff.	Faustus Cornelius Sulla *(May 10–Sept.)*	Sex. Teidius (*or* Teidius) Valerius Catullus *(May 10–June)*
suff.		L. Fulcinius Trio *(July–Dec.)*

suff.	P. Memmius Regulus *(Oct.–Dec.)*	
32	Cn. Domitius Ahenobarbus *(Jan.–Dec.)*	L. Arruntius Camillus Scribonianus *(Jan.–June)*
suff.		A. Vitellius *(July–Dec.)*
33	L. Livius Ocella Ser. Sulpicius Galba *(Jan.–June)*	L. Cornelius Sulla Felix *(Jan.–June)*
suff.	L. Salvius Otho *(July–Dec.)*	N.N. *(July–Dec.)*
34	Paullus Fabius Persicus *(Jan.–June)*	L. Vitellius *(Jan.–June)*
suff.	Q. Marcius Barea Soranus *(July–Dec.)*	T. Rustius Nummius Gallus *(July–Dec.)*
35	C. Cestius Gallus *(Jan.–June)*	M. Servilius Nonianus *(Jan.–June)*
suff.	D. Valerius Asiaticus *(July–Dec.)*	A. Gabinius Secundus *(July–Dec.)*
36	Sex. Papinius Allenius *(Jan.–June)*	Q. Plautius *(Jan.–June)*
suff.	C. Vettius Rufus *(July–Dec.)*	M. Porcius Cato *(July–Dec.)*
37	Cn. Acerronius Proculus *(Jan.–June)*	C. Petronius Pontius Nigrinus *(Jan.–June)*
suff.	C. Caesar Augustus Germanicus *(July–Aug.)*	Ti. Claudius Nero Germanicus *(July–Aug.)*
suff.	A. Caecina Paetus *(Sept.–Dec.)*	C. Caninius Rebilus *(Sept.–Dec.)*
38	M. Aquila Iulianus *(Jan.–June)*	P. Nonius Asprenas *(Jan.–June)*
suff.	Ser. Asinius Celer *(July–Dec.)*	Julius Africanus *(July–Dec.)*
39	C. Caesar Augustus Germanicus II *(only Jan.)*	Cn. Domitius Corbulo *(Jan.–June)*
suff.	A. Didius Gallus *(Feb.–Dec.)*	Cn. Domitius Afer *(July–Dec.)*
40	C. Caesar Augustus Germanicus III	*sine collega*
suff.	C. Laecanius Bassus	Q. Terentius Culleo
41	C. Caesar Augustus Germanicus IV *(1.–13. Jan.)*	Cn. Sentius Saturninus
suff.	Q. Pomponius Secundus *(for Caligula)*	
suff.	Q. Futius Lusius Saturninus *(in office on 17 July 41)*	M. Seius Varanus *(in office on 17 July 41)*
42	Ti. Claudius Caesar Augustus Germanicus II	C. Calpurnius Piso
43	Ti. Claudius Caesar Augustus Germanicus III *(Jan.–Feb.)*	L. Vitellius II *(Jan.–Feb.)*
suff.	Sex. Palpellius Hister *(Mar.–July)*	L. Pedanius Secundus *(Mar.–July)*
suff.	A. Gabinius Secundus *(Aug.–Sept.)*	N.N. *(Aug.–Sept.)*

suff.	Q. Curtius Rufus *(Oct.–Dec.)*	Sp. Oppius *(Oct.–Dec.)*
44	C. Sallustius Crispus Passienus II *(Jan.–Feb.)*	T. Statilius Taurus *(Jan.–June)*
suff.	P. Calvisius Sabinus Pomponius Secundus *(Mar.–June)*	
45	M. Vinicius II *(Jan.–Feb.)*	T. Flavius Sabinus *(Jan.–June)*
suff.	Ti. Plautius Silvanus Aelianus *(Mar.–Dec.)*	T. Statilius Taurus Corvinus *(July–Dec.)*
46	D. Valerius Asiaticus II *(Jan.–Feb.)*	M. Iunius Silanus *(Jan.–Dec.)*
suff.	Camerinus Antistius Vetus *(Mar.)*	
suff.	Q. Sulpicius Camerinus *(Mar.–June)*	
suff.	D. Laelius Balbus *(July–Aug.)*	
suff.	C. Terentius Tullius Geminus *(Sept.–Dec.)*	
47	Ti. Claudius Caesar Augustus Germanicus IV	L. Vitellius III
suff.	C. Calpetanus Rantius Sedatus *(Mar.–Apr.)*	M. Hordeonius Flaccus *(Mar.–Apr.)*
suff.	Cn. Hosidius Geta *(July–Dec.)*	T. Flavius Sabinus *(July–Aug.)*
suff.		L. Vagellius *(Sept.–Oct.)*
suff.		C. Volasenna Severus *(Nov.–Dec.)*
48	A. Vitellius *(Jan.–June)*	L. Vipstanus Poplicola *(Jan.–June)*
suff.	L. Vitellius *(July–Dec.)*	G. Vipstanus Messalla Gallus *(July–Dec.)*
49	C. Pompeius Longus Gallus	Q. Veranius
suff.	L. Mammius Pollio *(Mar.–June)*	Q. Allius Maximus *(Mar.–June)*
50	C. Antistius Vetus	M. Suillius Nerullinus
51	Ti. Claudius Caesar Augustus Germanicus V	Ser. Cornelius Scipio Salvidienus Orfitus
suff.		L. Calventius Vetus C. Carminius *(Sept.–Oct.)*
suff.		T. Flavius Vespasianus *(Nov.–Dec.)*
52	Faustus Cornelius Sulla Felix	L. Salvius Otho Titianus
suff.		Q. Marcius Barea Soranus *(June–Aug.)*
suff.		N.N. *(Sept.–Oct.)*
suff.		L. Salvidienus Rufus Salvianus *(Nov.–Dec.)*

53	D. Iunius Silanus Torquatus *(Jan.–June)*	Q. Haterius Antoninus *(Jan.–June)*
suff.	N.N. *(July–Aug.)*	N.N. *(July–Aug.)*
suff.	Q. Caecina Primus *(Sept–Oct.)*	P. Trebonius *(Sept.–Dec.)*
suff.	P. Calvisius Ruso *(Oct.–Dec.)*	
54	Cossos Cornelius Lentulus	M. Asinius Marcellus
55	Nero Claudius Caesar Augustus Germanicus *(Jan.–Feb.)*	L. Antistius Vetus *(Jan.–Apr.)*
suff.	N. Cestius *(Mar.–Apr.)*	
suff.	L. Annaeus Seneca *(May–Oct.)*	P. Cornelius Dolabella *(May)*
suff.		M. Trebellius Maximus *(Aug.)*
suff.		P.(?) Palfurius *(Sept. / Oct.)*
suff.	Cn. Cornelius Lentulus Gaetulicus *(Nov. / Dec.)*	T. Curtilius Mancia *(Nov. / Dec)*
56	Q. Volusius Saturninus	P. Cornelius Scipio
suff.	L. Iunius Gallio Annaeanus *(July / Aug.)*	T. Cutius Ciltus *(July / Aug.)*
suff.	NN. *(Sept. / Okt.)*	NN. *(Sept. / Okt.)*
suff.	L. Duvius Avitus *(Nov. / Dez.)*	P. Clodius Thrasea Paetus *(Nov. / Dez.)*
57	Nero Claudius Caesar Augustus Germanicus II *(whole year?)*	L. Calpurnius Piso *(Jan.–June)*
suff.		L. Caesius Martialis *(July–Dec.)*
58	Nero Claudius Caesar Augustus Germanicus III *(Jan–Apr.)*	M. Valerius Messalla Corvinus *(Jan.–June)*
suff.	C. Fonteius Agrippa *(May / June)*	
suff.	A. Petronius Lurco *(July–Dec.)*	A. Paconius Sabinus *(July–Dec.)*
59	C. Vipstanus Apronianus *(Jan.–June)*	C. Fonteius Capito *(Jan.–June)*
suff.	T. Sextius Africanus *(July–Dec.)*	M. Ostorius Scapula *(July–Dec.)*
60	Nero Claudius Caesar Augustus Germanicus IV	Cn. Domitius Afer II
61	P. Petronius Turpilianus *(Jan.–June?)*	L. Iunius Caesennius Paetus *(Jan.–June?)*
suff.	Cn. Pedanius Fuscus Salinator *(July / Aug.)*	L. Velleius Paterculus *(July / Aug.)*
62	P. Marius *(Jan.–Apr.?)*	L. Afinius (Asinius) Gallus *(Jan.–June)*
suff.	P. Petronius Niger *(Juli / Aug.)*	Q. Manlius Ancharius Tarquitius Saturninus *(July / Aug.)*
suff.	Q. Iunius Marullus *(Sept.–Dec.)*	N.N. *(Sept.–Nov.)*

suff.		T. Clodius Eprius Marcellus *(Nov.–Dec.)*
63	C. Memmius Regulus *(Jan.–June)*	L. Verginius Rufus *(Jan.–June)*
64	C. Laecanius Bassus *(Jan.–June)*	M. Licinius Crassus Frugi *(Jan.–June)*
suff.	C. Licinius Mucianus? *(July–Oct.)*	Q. Fabius Barbarus Antonius Macer? *(July–Oct.)*
suff.	N.N. *(Nov./Dec.)*	N.N. *(Nov./Dec.)*
65	A. Licinius Nerva Silianus *(Jan.–June)*	M. Iulius Vestinus Atticus *(Jan.–Apr.)*
suff.		P. Pasidienus Firmus *(May–June)*
suff.	C. Pomponius Pius *(July/Aug.)*	C. Anicius Cerialis *(July/Aug.)*
suff.	N.N. *(Sept.–Dec.)*	N.N. *(Sept.–Dec.)*
66	C. Luccius Telesinus *(Jan.–June?)*	C. Suetonius Paullinus *(Jan.–June?)*
suff.	M. Annius Afrinus *(July/Aug.)*	C. Paccius Africanus *(July/Aug.)*
suff.	M. Arruntius Aquila *(Sept.–Dec.)*	M. Vettius Bolanus *(Sept.–Dec.)*
67	L. Iulius Rufus	Fonteius Capito
suff.	L. Aurelius Priscus *(Mar./Apr.?)*	Ap. Annius Gallus *(Mar./Apr.?)*
68	Ti. Catius Asconius Silius Italicus	P. Galerius Trachalus
suff.	Imp. Nero Claudius Caesar Augustus Germanicus V *(Apr.?–June)*	*sine collega*
suff.	N.N. *(July/Aug.)*	N.N. *(July/Aug.)*
suff.	C. Bellicus Natalis *(Sept.–Dec.)*	P. Cornelius Scipio Asiaticus *(Sept.–Dec.)*
	Cingonius Varro *(designated)*	
69	Ser. Galba Imp. Caesar Augustus II *(Jan.)*	T. Vinius (Rufinus?) *(Jan.)*
suff.	M. Otho Caesar Augustus *(Jan. 22–Feb. 28)*	L. Salvius Otho Titianus II *(Jan. 22–Feb. 28)*
suff.	L. Verginius Rufus II *(Mar–Apr. 22)*	T. Flavius Sabinus *(Mar.–Apr. 22)*
suff.	A. Marius Celsus *(May–Aug.)*	Cn. Arrius Antoninus *(May–Aug.)*
suff.	Fabius Valens *(Sept.–Oct.)*	A. Caecina Alienus *(Sept.–Oct. 30)*
suff.		
suff.	C. Quintius Atticus *(Nov.–Dec.)*	Cn. Caecilius Simplex *(Nov.–Dec.)*

70	Imp. Caesar Vespasianus Augustus II	T. Caesar Vespasianus
71	Imp. Caesar Vespasianus Augustus III	M. Cocceius Nerva
suff.	Caesar Domitianus	Cn. Pedius Cascus
72	Imp. Caesar Vespasianus Augustus IV	T. Caesar Vespasianus II
73	Caesar Domitianus II	L. Valerius Catullus Messallinus
74	Imp. Caesar Vespasianus Augustus V	T. Caesar Vespasianus III
suff.	Ti. Plautius Silvanus Aelianus II	L. Iunius Vibius Crispus II
suff.	Q. Petillius Cerialis Caesius Rufus II	T. Clodius Eprius Marcellus II
75	Imp. Caesar Vespasianus Augustus VI	T. Caesar Vespasianus IV
suff.	Caesar Domitianus III	L. Pasidienus Firmus
76	Imp. Caesar Vespasianus Augustus VII	T. Caesar Vespasianus V
suff.	Caesar Domitianus IV	
77	Imp. Caesar Vespasianus Augustus VIII	T. Caesar Vespasianus VI
suff.	Caesar Domitianus V	Cn. Iulius Agricola
78	D. Iunius Novius Priscus	L. Ceionius Commodus
79	Imp. Caesar Vespasianus Augustus IX	T. Caesar Vespasianus VII
suff.	Caesar Domitianus VI	
80	Imp. T. Caesar Vespasianus Augustus VIII *(Jan. 1–14)*	Caesar Domitianus VII *(Jan. 1–14)*
suff.	L. Aelius Lamia Plautius Aelianus *(Jan. 14 until June)*	A. Didius Gallus Fabricius Veiento II *(Jan. 14–Feb. 11)*
suff.	Q. Aurelius Pactumeius Fronto *(Mar.–May)*	
suff.	C. Marius Marcellus Cluvius Rufus *(June–?)*	
suff.	M. Tittius Frugi *(?–Dec.)*	T. Vinucius Iulianus *(?–Dec.)*
81	L. Flavius Silva Nonius Bassus *(Jan.–Feb.)*	L. Asinius Pollio Verrucosus *(Jan.–Feb.)*
suff.	C. Iulius Iuvenalis *(Mar.–Apr.)*	M. Roscius Coelius *(Mar.–Apr.)*
suff.	L. Vettius Paullus *(May–June)*	T. Iunius Montanus *(May–June)*
suff.	N.N. *(July–Aug.)*	N.N. *(July–Aug.)*

suff.	L. Carminius Lusitanicus (Sept.–Oct.)	M. Petronius Umbrinus (Sept.–Oct.)
82	Imp. Caesar Domitianus Augustus VIII	T. Flavius Sabinus
suff.	N.N.	Servaeus Innocens
suff.	N.N.	L. Salvius Otho Cocceianus
suff.	N.N.	(? C. Arinius) Modestus
suff.	L. Antonius Saturnius *(July–?)*	P. Valerius Patriunus *(July–?)*
83	Imp. Caesar Domitianus Augustus IX	Q. Petillius Rufus II
suff.	L. Tettius Iulianus	Terentius Strabo Erucius Homullus
84	Imp. Caesar Domitianus Augustus X	C. Oppius Sabinus
suff.	L. Iulius Ursus	
suff.	C. Cornelius Gallicanus *(Sept.–?)*	C. Tullius Capito Pomponians Plotius Firmus *(Sept.–?)*
85	Imp. Caesar Domitianus Augustus XI *(Jan.–Feb.)*	T. Aurelius Fulvus II *(Jan.–Feb.)*
suff.	Q. Gavius Atticus	L. Aelius Oculatus
suff.	M. Annius Herrenius Pollio (July–Aug.)	P. Herrenius Pollio *(July–Aug.)*
suff.	D. Aburius Bassus *(Sept.–Oct.)*	Q. Iulius Balbus *(Sept.–Oct.)*
suff.	C. Salvius Liberalis Nonius Bassus *(Nov.–Dec.)*	... Orestes *(Nov.–Dec.)*
86	Imp. Caesar Domitianus Augustus XII (Jan.)	Ser. Cornelius Dolabella Petronianus *(Jan.–Apr.)*
suff.	C. Secius Campanus *(Jan.–Feb.)*	
suff.	N.N.	Q. Vibius Secundus *(Mar.–Apr.)*
suff.	Sex. Octavius Fronto *(May–?)*	Ti. Iulius Candidus Marius Celsus *(May–?)*
suff.	A. Bucius Lappius Maximus *(Sept.–?)*	C. Octavius Tidius Tossianus L. Iavolenus Priscus *(Sept.–?)*
87	Imp. Caesar Domitianus Augustus XIII *(Jan.)*	L. Volusius Saturninus *(Jan.–Apr.)*
suff.	Calpurnius Piso Crassus Frugi Licinianus *(Feb.–Apr.)*	
suff.	C. Bellicus Natalis Trebanianus *(May–Aug.)*	C. Ducenius Proculus *(May–Aug.)*
suff.	C. Cilnius Proculus *(Sept.–Dec.)*	L. Neratius Priscus *(Sept.–Dec.)*

88	Imp. Caesar Domitianus Augustus XIV *(Jan.)*	L. Minicius Rufus *(Jan.–Apr.)*
suff.	D. Plotius Grypus *(Jan–Apr.)*	
suff.	Q. Ninnius Hasta *(May–Aug.)*	L. Scribonius Libo Rupilius Frugi Bonus *(May–Aug.)*
suff.	M'. Otacilius Catulus *(Sept.–Dec.)*	Sex. Iulius Sparsus *(Sept.–Dec.)*
89	T. Aurelius Fulvus *(Jan.–Apr.)*	M. Asinius Atratinus *(Jan.–Apr.)*
suff.	P. Sallustius Blaesus *(May–Aug.)*	M. Peducaeus Saenianus *(May–Aug.)*
suff.	A. Vicirius Proculus *(Sept.–Dec.)*	M'. Laberius Maximus *(Sept.–Dec.)*
90	Imp. Caesar Domitianus Augustus XV	M. Cocceius Nerva II
suff.	L. Cornelius Pusio Annius Messala (replaced Domitian)	
suff.	L. Antistius Rusticus	Ser. Iulius Servianus
suff.	Q. Accaeus Rufus	C. Caristanius Fronto
suff.	P. Baebius Italicus	C. Aquillius Proculus
suff.	L. Albius Pullaienus Pollio	Cn. Pinarius Aemilius Cicatricula Pompeius Longinus
suff.	M. Tullius Cerialis	Cn. Pompeius Catullinus
91	M'. Acilius Glabrio	M. Ulpius Traianus
suff.	Cn. Minicius Faustinus	P. Valerius Marinus
suff.	Q. Valerius Vegetus	P. Metilius Sabinus Nepos
92	Imp. Caesar Domitianus Augustus XVI	Q. Volusius Saturninus
suff.	L. Venuleius Montanus Apronianus	
suff.	L. Stertinius Avitus	Ti. Iulius Celsus Polemaeanus
suff.	C. Iulius Silanus	Q. Iunius Arulenus Rusticus
93	Sex. Pompeius Collega	Q. Peducaeus Priscinus
suff.	T. Avidius Quietus	Sex. Lusianus Proculus
suff.	C. Cornelius Rarus	Tuccius Cerialis
94	L. Nonius Calpurnius Torquatus Asprenas *(Jan.–Apr.)*	T. Sextius Magius Lateranus *(Jan.–Apr.)*
suff.	M. Lollius Paullinus D. Valerius Asiaticus Saturninus	C. Antius A. Iulius Quadratus
suff.	L. Silius Decianus	T. Pomponius Bassus
95	Imp. Caesar Domitianus Augustus XVII *(Jan.)*	T. Flavius Clemens *(Jan.–Apr.)*
suff.	L. Neratius Marcellus *(Jan.–Apr.)*	

suff.	A. Bucius Lappius Maximus II *(May–Aug.)*	P. Ducenius Verus *(May–Aug.)*
suff.	Q. Pomponius Rufus *(Sept.–Dec.)*	L. Baebius Tullus *(Sept.–Dec.)*
96	C. Manlius Valens *(Jan.–Apr.)*	C. Antistius Vetus *(Jan.–Apr.)*
suff.	Q. Fabius Postuminus *(May–Aug.)*	T. Prifernius Paetus *(May–Aug.)*
suff.	Ti. Catius Caesius Fronto *(Sept.–Dec.)*	M. Calpurnius […]icus *(Sept.–Dec.)*
97	Imp. Nerva Caesar Augustus III *(Jan.–Feb.)*	L. Verginius Rufus III *(Jan.–Feb.)*
suff.	Cn. Arrius Antoninus II *(Mar.–Apr.)*	L. Calpurnius Piso *(Mar.–Apr.)*
suff.	M. Annius Verus *(May–June)*	L. Neratius Priscus *(May–June)*
suff.	L. Domitius Apollinaris *(July–Aug.)*	Sex. Hermentidius Campanus *(July–Aug.)*
suff.	Q. Glitius Atilius Agricola *(Sept.–Oct.)*	L. Pomponius Maternus *(Sept.–Oct.)*
suff.	P. Cornelius Tacitus *(Nov.–Dec.)*	M. Ostorius Scapula *(Nov.–Dec.)*
98	Imp. Nerva Caesar Augustus IV *(to Jan. 12)*	Imp. Caesar Nerva Traianus II *(Jan.–June)*
suff.	Cn. Domitius Tullus II *(Jan. 13–Jan. 31)*	
suff.	Sex. Iulius Frontinus II *(Feb.)*	
suff.	L. Iulius Ursus II *(Mar.)*	
suff.	T. Vestricius Spurinna II *(Apr.)*	
suff.	C. Pomponius Rufus Priscus Coelius Sparsus *(May–June)*	
suff.	A. Vicirius Martialis *(July–Aug.)* C. Pomponius Rufus Acilius	L. Maecius Postumus *(July–Aug.)* Cn. Pompeius Ferox Licinianus
suff.	(Tu?)scus Coelius Sparsus *(Sept.–Oct.)*	*(Sept.–Oct.)*
suff.	P. Iulius Lupus *(Nov.–Dec.)*	N.N.
99	A. Cornelius Palma Frontonianus	Q. Sosius Senecio
suff.	Sulpicius Lucretius Barba	Senecio Memmius Afer
suff.	Q. Fabius Barbarus Valerius Magnus Iulianus	A. Caecilius Faustinus
suff.	Q. Fulvius Gillo Bittius Proculus	M. Ostorius Scapula
suff.	Ti. Iulius Ferox	N.N.

Appendix J

Narrative Descriptions of Images

Plate 10

A reproduction Roman *gladius* (short sword) and a *pugio* (dagger) from the author's own collection; two of the primary weapons of the Roman legionary. By the time of the invasion of AD 43 the *gladius* of the type shown, the Pompeii pattern, was in common use. The blade form had evolved from the original *Gladius Hispaniensis* type, which the Roman army had previously adopted, to the pure functionality of the straight-edged blade shown here. The weapon was predominantly used to deliver well-placed stab wounds, with the intention of inflicting fatal injuries by use of the minimum of physical effort in wielding the weapon. This method of deployment is completely opposite to the use of longer-bladed slashing swords, which required much more physical effort from the user but which were more likely to deliver survivable wounds.

The example of the *pugio* shown here is a heavy iron dagger with a cast-bronze hilt. This weapon seems to have retained the 'waisted' shape of the older type *Gladius Hispaniensis* sword blades, again making it predominantly a stabbing weapon. (Author's photograph)

Plate 11

This weapon is also from the author's own collection and shows the top two-thirds of the Roman *pilum* (javelin). This was a weapon which was typically deployed at around 20 or 30 yards from its target. Although it could be used as a hand-held defensive weapon in a variety of formations, it was principally designed for use as a hand-thrown missile, delivered either individually or in timed volleys. Its slim iron tip, wrought in square section, provided formidable penetration and once lodged into such things as shields it was difficult to remove, often forcing the user to discard the shield and thereby leaving themselves exposed to further incoming volleys. Once thrown, any weapons with bent tips which were recovered from the field after battle could be replaced by knocking out the two rivets shown in the shank socket. This allowed the tip to be quickly replaced with very little effort. The old tip could then be quickly repaired by legion blacksmiths working either in the field or at rear bases. (Author's photograph)

Plate 12

The helmet shown is a reproduction of the Imperial Gallic Type H from the author's own collection. Gallic pattern helmets were in widespread use by AD 43 and represent the pinnacle of Roman helmet design. Aesthetically the helmet shown is very impressive and as a functional piece it possesses excellent attributes. The ridged designs chased out of the flat metal, such as the 'eyebrows' on the front of the helmet bowl and the embossing on the cheek pieces, greatly increase the strength of the metal by adding rigidity. A thick iron brow guard protected against weapon strikes intended to collapse the front of the bowl, and the broad cheek pieces provided excellent protection to both the wearer's face and the blood vessels in the neck. The broad neck guard at the rear protects the wearer from decapitating blows to the nape of the neck, while bronze flanges riveted to the side of the helmet protect the ears but still allow sound to reach the wearer. (Author's photograph)

Plate 13

Photograph of a large marble sculpture of Emperor Claudius, currently on display in the Vatican Museum, Rome. Claudius is depicted as the god Jupiter in this sculpture and has been portrayed with a classically heroic body of perfect aesthetic proportions. However, although the facial features are no doubt broadly representative of the emperor, it must be borne in mind that the primary objective of creating such imagery is a form of personal propaganda. It was essentially created to project a powerful image and to show the subject in the most favourable manner possible. Consequently, it is very doubtful that we can say that the sculptor's rendition of the emperor's body is as accurate as the facial features may be, particularly given the descriptions of Claudius which have been given by writers such as Suetonius, who speaks of Claudius possessing a number of obvious bodily deformities. (Author's photograph)

Plate 14–15

The reproduction legionary *scutum* (shield) shown is from the author's own collection and is an example of a type common to the Claudian invasion period. This example is painted with the markings of Legio XIIII Gemina. The shield is hemicylindrical in section, allowing the user to pull it close into his body to resist hard impacts and also to use the large surface area of the shield to ram opponents. Bronze or brass edge trims and a heavy iron *umbo* (boss) also provide the shield with offensive qualities as the edge of the shield can be applied to body targets and the boss used for facial strikes. The body of the shield is made from laminated strips of thin wood, similar as a design concept to modern plywood. This is then covered with a thin layer of goatskin, followed by a layer of coarse linen which is glued on and then painted with the required design. The back of the shield is reinforced with thin wooden strips and the single handle runs horizontally, allowing the user to more easily hold the shield in various positions. (Author's photograph)

Plate 16

The reconstruction of the legionary shown here is representative of the equipment in use at the time of Caesar's raids in Britain. Common helmet types in use at that time were the early Coolus variants and the Montefortino type, as depicted here. The variant shown here is a Montefortino Type C, fabricated in bronze, which is fitted with a detachable horsehair crest.

The *lorica hamata* (mail shirt) during this period is designed primarily to defend against slashing weapons, such as long-bladed swords, hence the shoulder doublings which provide added protection from downward strikes. Shirts of this period were significantly longer than early Imperial period variants but became notably shorter by the first century AD as the armour took on proportions more akin to a modern T-shirt.

The weapons carried by the legionary are the *pilum* and a *gladius* which, at this time, would have been a sword of the Mainz pattern. This blade form was very similar in shape to the original *Gladius Hispaniensis* from which it evolved, with a broad waisted blade which tapered into a long thin point. This was ideally suited to penetrating mail shirts, in common use with Rome's enemies. The example shown here is slung directly from a waist belt with no baldric fitted to the scabbard.

The shield is an early form of *scutum*, which is a wooden form with a hemicylindrical section. It is reinforced with a central spine and two wooden strips applied close to the edges. Bronze-edge trims are fitted along with an iron boss, both of which add to its offensive qualities. Shields of this type were adopted from Gallic/Celtic designs and are very similar to those carried by the Britons of the period. (Author's illustration)

Plate 17

By the Claudian period there had been some pronounced changes in the styles of equipment which the legionary carried. The mail shirt had now been shortened to around hip length, although shoulder doublings were still in use. *Lorica segmentata*, another body armour type, had evolved by this time and was a system of thin iron plates articulated on leather straps. Helmets had also seen significant design advances and the type carried here is an iron helmet of the Gallic variants. Here the legionary has suspended it from around his neck by using the cords which secure the cheek guards when the helmet is worn. He also carries a Pompeii pattern *gladius* and a bronze-handled *pugio* which is suspended from his *cingulum militare* (military belt). A baldric has also been fitted to the scabbard of the *gladius*, allowing the sword to be worn separately from the *cingulum*.

By the mid-first century AD the *scutum* had evolved to become a much shorter shield as the curved top and bottom had now been 'chopped' from the design. However, it still retained the iron boss and metal edging of the older types. The example shown here is sheathed in a *tegimen* (goatskin cover) to prevent the shield from becoming waterlogged in bad weather and could be slung off the shoulder on a leather harness while on the march.

As well as two *pila* (javelins), the legionary is also carrying his *impedimenta* (marching pack). This consisted of a *furca* (carrying frame), from which could be suspended a *loculus* (leather satchel) which contained smaller personal effects and mess kit. A separate string bag contained three days' grain rations and this legionary also has a blanket and bronze cooking pot attached, along with a *dolabra* (an entrenching pick). Other items which the legionary could be expected to carry were a pair of *pilum muralis* (wooden defensive pickets) and a grid iron for use with cooking fires. In poor weather conditions the legionary would have also have worn a *paenula* (hooded cloak). (Author's illustration)

Plate 18

Rather than using an invasion fleet which was comprised solely of sleek warships, such as *Liburnians* and *Triremes*, the fleets used by both Caesar and Claudius to carry their armies to Britain would have been comprised in the main of variants of the *Corbita* type of vessel, a 'coaster' variant of that which is shown here. Although far removed from the more glamorous image of the classical warship, the *Corbita* was a true workhorse of the seas of the ancient world and came in a variety of sizes which all largely conformed to the same broad beamed, sturdy design. This allowed it to carry a variety of cargo from troops to livestock, wine and oil, bulk foodstuffs such as grain, cargo container foods such as olives and building materials such as timber and stone.

The example shown here is a medium-sized coaster which is a speculative composite created by the author and derived from both the Blackfriars ship and the Comacchio Wreck, both of which are excellent examples of well-preserved archaeological finds. The boat shown has two large open holds and the tiled roof at the stern of the vessel covers a small galley area which allowed the crew to prepare hot food.

Ships of this design were built in the carvel style of construction, which means that the hull planking was butted together and nailed to the frame before being sealed with tree bark and resin, or caulking cord and pitch or tar, providing a water-resistant filling for the gaps between the planks. Typically, these vessels did not have a single-piece keel but were built upwards from separate keel boards with prow and stern posts attached to each end. The outer planking was then added to separately attached ribs, most typically by using iron nails, although there are examples known of boards being sewn together with cord.

As well as being powered by sail, the vessel was also capable of being rowed and, typical of vessels of its time, it was fitted with a pair of steering boards. The broad and shallow draft of the vessel afforded it excellent stability in rough conditions and also assisted when the ship needed to get close in shore or required to be beached. More information on *Corbitas* and other Roman vessels can be found at the Navis 1 Project website (http://www2.rgzm.de/Navis/Home/Frames.htm) which is a database of ancient shipping. (Author's illustration)

Plate 19

The plate shows the author's reconstruction of what the original Claudian defence line at Richborough may have looked like. The outside of the defences are west facing and archaeological study of the defence line has traced the ditches running for a total length of 640m. The double-ditch system comprised of an outer ditch of around 2.13m wide and 1.2m deep, while the inner ditch was a more difficult obstacle to negotiate with an average width of around 3m and a depth of around 1.8m. Both ditches have a V-shaped section, typical of Roman ditches of this type.

The spoil from the ditches was used to make a defensive earth rampart, which is likely to have been around 12–15ft in height and topped off with a timber palisade running along its entire length. This structure was no doubt accessed at intervals by steps rising from the inner compound, which would have allowed the occupying troops to quickly man the defences in the event of attack. Along the length of the defences, archaeologists have found only one gateway, around 3.3m wide and deep. The reconstruction shows an elevated watch platform above the gate, similar in design to those portrayed on Trajan's Column and the modern reconstruction at the Lunt Roman Fort near Coventry in the West Midlands. It is entirely possible that, in line with known Roman army practices, this structure was prefabricated in Gaul and shipped over for instant use, cutting down construction times and avoiding the need to source and fabricate timbers locally in a potentially hostile environment.

Behind the defences can be seen leather tents for accommodating the defending troops, and in the distance the masts of supply ships anchored in the Wantsum Channel. It is believed that the early Claudian defences were dismantled around AD 45 when the first phase of the permanent fort and supply base at Richborough were constructed. (Author's illustration)

Plate 20

An aerial perspective of the Wantsum Channel during the Roman period, as viewed from the south. The landscape view is based on the conjectural coastline suggested by Moody. The top left-hand corner of the image shows the northern mouth of the Wantsum Channel, close to Reculver, as it opens out into the Thames Estuary. The major river discharging into the Wantsum just below this point is the Stour, which leads back to modern Canterbury. The network of rivers around this part of Kent is clearly visible as they flow towards the west shore of the Wantsum.

The bottom right-hand corner of the picture shows the southern mouth of the Wantsum flowing into Pegwell Bay via Stonar Beach, which is the thin, sandy coloured spit of land projecting south from the Isle of Thanet. Directly opposite this is a small creek and Richborough is located on the northern side of this, while the modern town of Sandwich now occupies the land on the southern side.

A more precise orientation of the location of modern towns of north-east Kent and Thanet can be seen on the map at Fig. 6.

BIBLIOGRAPHY

Allen, D.F., 'Did Adminius Strike Coins?', *Britannia*,Vol. 7
(Society for the Promotion of Roman Studies, 1976), pp. 96–100.
Barrett, A.A., 'The Career of Tiberius Claudius Cogidubnus', *Britannia*,Vol. 10
(Society for the Promotion of Roman Studies, 1979).
————, 'Chronological Errors in Dio's Account of the Claudian Invasion',
Britannia,Vol. II (Society for the Promotion of Roman Studies, 1980).
Birley, A.R., *The Roman Government of Britain* (Oxford University Press, 2005).
Black, E.W., 'Sentius Saturninus and the Roman Invasion of Britain',
Britannia,Vol. 31 (Society for the Promotion of Roman Studies, 2000).
Bogaers, J.E., 'King Cogidubnus in Chichester: Another Reading of RIB 91',
Britannia,Vol. 10 (Society for the Promotion of Roman Studies, 1979).
Boyce, A.A., The Origin of Ornamenta Triumphalia, *Classical Philology*,Vol. 37, No. 2
(April 1942).
Collingwood, R.G & Myres, N.G.L., *Roman Britain & English Settlements*
(Oxford University Press, 1937).
Corpus Inscriptionum Latinarum (CIL),Vol.VI.
Cunliffe, B., *Iron Age Communities in Britain* (Routledge & Kegan Paul PLC D., 1974).
Frere, S. & Fulford, M., 'The Roman Invasion of AD 43', *Britannia*,Vol. 32
(Society for the Promotion of Roman Studies, 2001).
Gilliver, C.M., *The Roman Art of War* (Tempus, 1999).
Green, M.J., (Ed.), *The Celtic World* (Routledge, 1995).
Hassall, M.W.C., 'Batavians and the Roman Conquest of Britain', *Britannia*,Vol. 1
(Society for the Promotion of Roman Studies, 1970).
Hazel, J., *Who's Who in the Roman World* (Routledge, 2001).
Hind, J.G.F., 'The Invasion of Britain in AD 43 – An Alternative Strategy for Aulus
Plautius', *Britannia*,Vol. 20 (Society for the Promotion of Roman Studies, 1989).
Keppie, L., *The Making of the Roman Army from Republic to Empire* (Batsford, 1984).
Lanciani, R., *Pagan & Christian Rome* (Houghton, Mifflin & Co, 1892).
Manley, J., *AD 43, the Roman Invasion of Britain, a Reassessment* (Tempus, 2002).
Moody, G., *The Isle of Thanet, from Prehistory to the Norman Conquest* (Tempus, 2008).
Olson, W., Doescher, R.L., Beicker, K.N. & Gregory, A.F., 'Moon and Tides at Caesar's
Invasion of Britain in 55 BC', *Sky & Telescope*, ★116★ (No. 2), 18 (August 2008).
Ordnance Survey, *Roman Britain, Historical Map & Guide* (5th Edition).
Peddie, J., *Conquest, the Roman Invasion of Britain* (John Sutton Publishing, 1987).
Potter, D., *Emperors of Rome – The Story of Imperial Rome, from Julius Caesar to the Last
Emperor* (Quercus, 2007).
Roman Inscriptions of Britain – Volume I, Inscriptions on Stone (Alan Sutton Publishing, 1995).

Bibliography

Roman Inscriptions of Britain – Volume II, Instrumentum Domesticum (Alan Sutton Publishing, 1995).

Salway, P., *Roman History – The Oxford History of England* (Oxford University Press, 1981).

Sauer, E.W., 'Inscriptions from Alchester: Vespasian's Base of the Second Augustan Legion (?)', *Britannia*, Vol. 36 (Society for the Promotion of Roman Studies, 2005).

Scarre, C., *Chronicle of the Roman Emperors – the Reign by Reign Record of the Rulers of Imperial Rome* (Thames & Hudson, 1995).

————, *The Penguin Historical Atlas of Ancient Rome* (Viking and Penguin Books, 1995).

Smith, W., *Dictionary of Greek & Roman Antiquities* (University of Michigan, 1870).

Stallibrass, S. & Thomas, R., (Eds), *Feeding the Roman Army – the Archaeology of Production and Supply in New Europe* (Oxbow Books, 2008).

Thornhill, P., 'A Lower Thames Ford and the Campaigns of 54 BC and AD 43', *Archaeologia Cantiana*, Vol. 92 (1976).

Victoria County History of Kent – Romano British Kent, Vol. 3 (1932).

Webster, G., *The Roman Invasion of Britain* (Batsford, 1980) (Routledge, 1993 revised edition).

CLASSICAL REFERENCES

Augustus, *Res Gestae Divi Augusti*
Caesar, Julius, *The Gallic Wars*
Dio, Cassius, *Roman Histories*
Eutropius, *Braeviarium Historiae Romanae*
Josephus, *The Jewish Wars*
Paterculus, Velleius, *The Roman History*
Pliny the Elder, *Natural History*
Polybius, *The Histories*
Pseudo-Hyginus, *De Munitionibus Castrorum*
———, *De Metatione Castrorum*
Strabo, *Geography*
Suetonius, *The Twelve Caesars*
Tacitus, *The Agricola*
———, *The Germania*
———, *The Histories*

INDEX

Other titles published by The History Press

Cartimandua: Queen of the Brigantes
NICKI HOWARTH

This is the first major study of Cartimandua, a contemporary of Boudica, whose story is one of rebellion, intrigue, betrayal and scandal. This is a unique look at a fascinating yet often overlooked figure of British history, at her world and at the influences that shaped the turbulent events in her life.

978-0-7524-4705-6

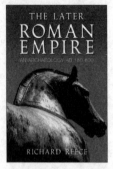

The Later Roman Empire: An Archaeology AD 150–600
RICHARD REECE

This analysis of the changes that occurred between AD 150 and 600, which led into the medieval world, has been widely hailed as a masterpiece: 'Books by Richard Reece are typically individual, opinionated and insightful; and this is no exception.' – British Archaeology, 'Richard Reece's writing is always stimulating; this book will appeal to both specialists and enthusiasts.' – Oxbow Book News

978-0-7524-4205-1

UnRoman Britain: Exposing the Great Myth of Britannia
MILES RUSSELL & STUART LAYCOCK

Roman Britain is usually thought of as a land full of togas, towns and baths with Britons happily going about their Roman lives under the benign gaze of Rome – but this is a myth. This book explores how many Britons failed to acknowledge the Roman lifestyle at all, while others were only outwardly Romanised, clinging to their own identities under the occupation.

978-0-7524-6285-1

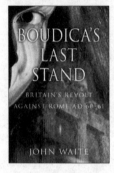

Boudica's Last Stand: Britain's Revolt against Rome AD 60–61
JOHN WAITE

In AD 61, Roman rule in Britain was threatened by a bloody revolt led by one of the most iconic figures in British history. However, the debate about the revolt has developed little. This work therefore offers fresh proposals about why it started, how it spread and where Boudica fought her last battle against an overstretched and outnumbered Roman army.

978-0-7524-5909-7

Visit our website and discover thousands of other History Press books.

www.thehistorypress.co.uk